Little Apocalypses

Praise for *Little Apocalypses*

"*Little Apocalypses* is a beautifully wrought excavation of the love and fear that define a parents' relationship to their children and how that love and fear inform the particularity of a parent's grief and terror concerning the future of the planet. This is not a book about wistful hope, so much as it is an urgent call to be courageous enough to hope, and then steadfast enough to turn that hope into collective movement forward."

—Sara Petersen, author of *Momfluenced*

"Reading *Little Apocalypses* feels like taking a nourishing walk with a brilliant, compassionate, relentlessly curious friend. Kaitlyn Teer is a graceful guide through questions of care work and the climate crisis; subjects that, in her hands, transform into sites of hope for our collective future. Brimming with clear-eyed optimism and a palpable love of the land, *Little Apocalypses* refreshed my sense of wonder."

—Tajja Isen, author of *Some of My Best Friends*

"Kaitlyn Teer writes with the rare ability to hold contradiction without flinching. *Little Apocalypses* is at once a tender reckoning with early motherhood and a sharp interrogation of the doomsday rhetoric that shapes how we think about our warming world, offering not answers but something better: new questions and the courage to sit with them. A beautiful balm for the soul. A must-read."

—Chelsea Bieker, author of *Madwoman* and *Godshot*

"Whether you have a racing heart, a muddled mind, or firmly covered ears when it comes to climate change, Kaitlyn Teer's beautiful, lyrical, exquisitely researched book is a balm. She tackles what's actually happening with muscular hope and so much love for her family and the natural world. Just as daily life and existential threats are woven together, the essays move from her sudsy kitchen sink and family bicycle, to wildfires and hurricanes, then back for bean soup and bedtime stories. Powerful insights from philosophers, scientists, activists, and her own small children make this book feel as layered and rich as oceans and forests themselves; yet somehow her guidance feels collective and energizing, never overwhelming. *Little Apocalypses* feels like a hand slipping into yours as we look together toward the future."

—Joanna Goddard, founder of *Cup of Jo*

Little Apocalypses

Essays on Motherhood, Climate Change,
and Hope at the End of the World

Kaitlyn Teer

NEW YORK • LONDON • TORONTO • SYDNEY • NEW DELHI • AUCKLAND

HARPER ● PERENNIAL

Without limiting the exclusive rights of any author, contributor or the publisher of this publication, any unauthorized use of this publication to train generative artificial intelligence (AI) technologies is expressly prohibited. HarperCollins also exercise their rights under Article 4(3) of the Digital Single Market Directive 2019/790 and expressly reserve this publication from the text and data mining exception.

LITTLE APOCALYPSES. Copyright © 2026 by Kaitlyn Teer. All rights reserved. No part of this book may be used or reproduced in any manner whatsoever without written permission except in the case of brief quotations embodied in critical articles and reviews. For information, address HarperCollins Publishers, 195 Broadway, New York, NY 10007. In Europe, HarperCollins Publishers, Macken House, 39/40 Mayor Street Upper, Dublin 1, D01 C9W8, Ireland.

HarperCollins books may be purchased for educational, business, or sales promotional use. For information, please email the Special Markets Department at SPsales@harpercollins.com.

hc.com

FIRST EDITION

Designed by Jen Overstreet

Library of Congress Cataloging-in-Publication Data has been applied for.

ISBN 978-0-06-344022-7 (pbk.)

Printed in the United States of America

$PrintCode

For my children.

It could happen any time, tornado,
earthquake, Armageddon. It could happen.
Or sunshine, love, salvation.
—WILLIAM STAFFORD, "YES"

Contents

Preface xiii

Drawing a Disappearing World 1
If Birds Can't Survive 18
World Without End 36
Watching the Clock 56
Little Things 68
On Mother Trees 88
Predictive Text 104
What to Expect 125
The Looking Glass 141
Little Apocalypses 154
Mother Nature 172
Mother of All Messes 195
Because I Said So 213
Saving Seeds 231

Acknowledgments 251
Notes 255

Preface

I began writing this book when my children were five and two. Over the course of working on it, my daughter has learned to swim and tie her shoes and has lost four teeth. My son has learned to count and ride a balance bike and no longer sleeps in a crib. I can see from the pencil markings on the door frame just how many inches they both have grown. Now, my daughter can read over my shoulder while I'm working and ask what it all means.

I, too, have changed while writing this book, learning through my research and conversations with other parents, as well as through encountering previous versions of myself in the essay drafts and journal entries I wrote in the earliest months of parenthood. In researching, I have often felt like a forager, gathering insights from fields as rich and varied as geology, anthropology, theology, and psychology. In writing, I have been guided by the idea that the climate crisis is a storytelling crisis, and that every story is a climate story.

My thinking about motherhood and climate change has been shaped as much by my own children as by the Salish Sea, which is why it's important to state that I write from the traditional and unceded ancestral homelands of the Coast Salish peoples. Acknowledging the historical and ongoing impacts of colonization is a crucial step toward climate justice. I honor how our Indigenous neighbors, the Lummi Nation and the Nooksack Tribe, have cared for these lands and waterways since time immemorial and are leading the way forward into a just and sustainable future.

What follows is a record of my evolving attempts to understand where I live—to locate myself in place but also in stories and in relationships. To *assay* means to try or attempt, as I often told my writing students, and while the writing of these essays is over, I have every reason to believe that my attempts to understand and to reimagine the stories that have shaped me will continue, that my storytelling will continue to shift and sharpen.

I have attempted to say something about what becoming a mother in this place and at this time has meant to me, and in doing so, have represented only my own experiences of motherhood and family life. While I often use the word *mother*, especially when writing about the stories we tell about motherhood, I also use the phrases *pregnant people* and *birthing people* because they are most accurate and include the experiences of trans and non-binary parents. In *Revolutionary Mothering*, Alexis Pauline Gumbs uses mothering as a verb, calling it "the practice of creating, nurturing, affirming, and supporting life." This perspective has shaped my belief that mothering is an act anyone can do.

While writing this book, the world has changed and is continuing to change in ways that many of us are still trying to understand. As I write this, it has been 100 days since the second Trump presidency began, sowing chaos and confusion and attacking the abortion rights and environmental protections that are essential to reproductive justice and climate justice.

The morning after the election, my children asked me to read them a picture book about starlings. My kids cuddled up next to me, hair still ruffled from sleep, and I turned the pages to see a stunning murmuration of starlings lifting and falling, shapeshifting through the sky.

"We find strength and safety in numbers." I read. "We all guide each other. I veer. My allies veer. Their allies veer. We all change course."

The book was about murmurations, the mesmerizing shapes that flocks of birds make as they move through the sky, but as I read aloud, I realized that I was also reading to my children about collective action.

In her book *What If We Get It Right?*, climate expert Ayana Elizabeth Johnson calls for us to "move from 'I' to 'we.'" In doing so, she writes, "We will expand our sense of interdependence. We will rein in our sense of individualism. We will ask, 'What should we do, together?' Survival is collective, our fates are intertwined."

In my attempts to move toward interdependence, I have tried to be thoughtful about my use of the word *we*. I have written this book primarily for parents who, like me, are raising children in the Global North and are among those who most need to change to meet the moment. I have sometimes reached for the first-person plural, even when I know it to be imperfect, using it aspirationally, as in the *we* that I hope we become.

May we, like the starlings, find strength and safety together.

May our movements create magic and beauty that fills the skies.

May we all change course.

Little
Apocalypses

Drawing a Disappearing World

"Draw a baby."

I was newly pregnant and sitting at the kitchen table with my two-year-old on my lap. We were drawing together on a small, gray absorbent pad with a water pen. I was sketching with water as quickly as I could, and just as quickly, the figures kept evaporating.

My daughter asked me to draw a baby, so I began with the round circle of a baby's head. I made two curved lines for closed eyes, then a tiny curl of hair. By the time I sketched the simple folds of a swaddle blanket—foregoing the time-consuming details of a body in favor of producing a quick, round little bundle—the baby's head had disappeared.

She asked me to draw a fish, to draw the moon, to draw our family.

I was up against the clock as I dashed out three stick figures—a toddler and two adults, one with stick arms encircling the looping scribble of a pregnant belly. The first time I watched our family vanish, even as I was drawing it, it felt like a curse, a cruel magic trick.

"All gone," I said, pressing my face into her hair.

I'd ordered the drawing pad from a list of mess-free toddler activities, but when it arrived, I saw that it wasn't a child's toy at all but rather intended as a tool for practicing mindfulness—something that caring for my daughter was already teaching me.

So much of parenting, I'm realizing, is learning to live with impermanence, to draw with water and watch it all fade.

Once, my daughter took the water pen and smashed its small, wet brush against the drawing pad until its bristles frayed. She swirled a leaky puddle so damp and dark I thought it might never disappear. But it, too, is gone.

My children are now just six and three, and already, so much has disappeared.

Just before my daughter's first birthday, I came face to face with the disappearing frogs.

I was wheeling her stroller through the corridors of the Vancouver Aquarium when we reached the *Frogs Forever?* exhibit, and I got stuck on the question mark looming over it all.

At the time, I was teaching college writing classes, and I'd just finished reading dozens of final papers about apocalyptic narratives—literature like Octavia Butler's novel *Parable of the Sower*, but also film and television, even video games, like *The Last of Us*. I'd asked my students to consider why humans across time and space have told stories about the end of the world and to analyze such texts for what these imagined futures might reveal about our present. I hoped they would come to see the value of storytelling in response to climate change and other contemporary threats. In times of crisis, I argued, we need the meaning-making work of the humanities—philosophers and historians, artists and poets.

I was energized by my students' projects, but after submitting final grades, I was also tired—tired from waking to my baby's cries in the early morning hours, then nursing her back to sleep before shuffling into the kitchen to make coffee and grade papers, tired from an academic term spent contemplating the end of human flourishing.

I hoped the sharpness of my fears for the planet might be dulled by a trip to the aquarium, with its mellow radiance, its darting fish and rippling light.

All I wanted was to name the coastal marine life for my baby, holding her as she squirmed out of my arms with excitement and pressed her dimpled palms against the thick glass. I wanted to stand in the otherworldly glow of a tank lit with rising and falling jellyfish, mesmerized by the ruffled tentacles of Pacific sea nettles. I wanted to gaze up toward the water's surface as a white sturgeon swam overhead, casting its enormous, ancient shadow over us.

I wanted a break from thinking about final things, about grand and global destruction, but there I was, pushing our stroller back and forth under a sign that warned of the world's imperiled frogs: NOW YOU SEE THEM, SOON YOU WON'T.

I went to the aquarium in search of wonder, and there I found it alongside despair.

We were looking at a handful of Panamanian golden frogs, a species now extinct in the wild.

"There's a frog plague," stated the exhibit's signage in bold print, followed by a grim explanation of the highly infectious and deadly chytrid fungus, which endangers amphibians worldwide by causing suffocation and cardiac arrest. The worst known infectious killer of wildlife, this pathogen has wiped out at least ninety species and contributed to the decline of nearly five hundred more. Remnant populations of the Panamanian golden frog—which, I later came to find out, is technically a toad—were now confined to living out their lives in captivity. Outside of a global network of zoos and aquariums with biosecure habitats and active breeding programs, the golden frogs had all but vanished.

According to the display, the thing about the disappearing frogs was this: "Naked skin makes frogs very vulnerable to chemicals and other changes in their environment—they are exposed to everything in water, as well as on land. This makes the health of frogs in the wild a good indicator of our world's health."

As indicator species, amphibians have been called the "canaries in the coal mine" of mass extinction, although declines among birds, insects, and other plants and animals tell their own stories of ecosystems unraveling.

What the frogs' vanishing act indicates about the world's health—I thought, feeling grateful that my daughter wasn't yet old enough to read the signs for herself—can't possibly be good.

I was halfway through my first pregnancy, in 2018, when I started keeping a list of apocalypses, great and small. That year, headlines announced the decline of nearly everything, it seemed, from democracy to higher education. Even fashion houses picked up on the anxious mood, sending menswear models down runways styled in the face masks and rescue vests of doomsday preppers and extremist militias. Closer to home, evidence of the changing climate fell in the form of ash from burning wildfires. Seattle-area scientists warned that summers of wildfire smoke were becoming the region's "new normal" and public health officials issued recommendations for adapting to fire season. I felt a sort of whiplash, turning from these news stories to my library copy of *What to Expect When You're Expecting*. Was I supposed to be packing a go-bag or a hospital bag, preparing for the end or the beginning?

On my phone, a pregnancy app pinged with daily updates on fetal development, and just as often, news alerts brought fresh signs of impending climate disaster. In my third trimester, the UN released the 2018 Intergovernmental Panel on Climate Change (IPCC) special report on the consequences of 1.5 degrees Celsius of global warming—what came to be known as the "Doomsday Report." It called on governments to make "rapid, far-reaching and unprecedented changes in all aspects of society" in efforts to drastically reduce global carbon emissions and avert the worst climate outcomes. Meanwhile, I was reading everything I could to prepare for the far-reaching changes a baby would bring to our lives. *How would a changing climate change parenting?* I wondered. Newspapers announced that the "planet has only until 2030 to stem catastrophic climate change"—at which point, I realized, counting on my fingers, the child I was carrying would be twelve.

Soon after, my husband and I attended a birthing class for pregnant people and their partners. As we inhaled and exhaled through different yoga stretches and supportive postures, my thoughts kept returning to the IPCC report. Until that point, my womb was the only world our child had ever known. I knew that bringing a child into the world—this world with its changing climate, this world which was speeding toward catastrophe—would force me to confront my fears in ways that would surely change me.

Though I composted and bussed to work, brought my cloth tote bags to the food co-op, and like most people, tried in small ways to do what I could for the environment, I didn't anticipate how the pressures of early motherhood would intensify my commitment to climate justice, as well as my experience of difficult climate emotions. I couldn't see coming the pandemic that would reveal the unsustainability of contemporary parenting, nor the year of climate disasters that would follow as the Pacific Northwest weathered a once-in-a-millennia heat dome followed by once-in-a-century flooding, nor the back-to-back years that would go down as the hottest in recorded history.

But as I sat on my mat, breathing and preparing for giving birth, I could feel myself braced for change.

Near the end of the class, the instructor lowered the lights and invited us to sit across from our partners for a silent meditation. I faced my husband, he smiled, and I smiled back. And then, to my dismay, instead of settling into a moment of profound connection, I began to laugh. The kind of frantic, red-faced, stifled laughter that you have to seal your lips to hold in. It struck me all at once, the absurdity of our efforts to plan for an increasingly uncertain future.

At first, my husband looked concerned, but then his shoulders started shaking, too. We were trying to suppress our laughter, trying not to distract from what was meant to be a meaningful, contemplative ritual for all the other soon-to-be parents, who were like us, I think, swimming in fear but also deliriously happy. We sweated out the remaining minutes in silent fits, avoiding the instructor's disapproving gaze, until we could make a mad scramble for our things and walk out into the cool, dark air, arm in arm, feeling chastened but infinitely lighter. Something inside of me was shifting as I began to accept how little I could control about childbirth and all that would come after.

I was trying to keep my expectations in check, trying to hold my hopes and fears with an open hand, but this proved difficult when it came to my hopes for the child I was carrying. As I opened gifts at my baby shower, I said to the guests gathered around me in a friend's living room, "I've been thinking a lot about hope." Only, I couldn't finish whatever it was I'd wanted to say, and instead, thanked my friends and family for their support. In that moment, I realized that, of all the things I could give or be given, hope was what I most wanted for our child.

I wasn't even clear what I meant, exactly, by hope and felt embarrassed, selfish even, for wanting it so desperately when there was so much evidence to the contrary. I hadn't resolved anything about hope, or my desire for it, by the time my water broke suddenly in the early morning hours of a long December night.

When, finally, I emerged from the birth center beside my husband, who was carrying our newborn in her infant car seat, I felt like the last surviving dinosaur in the Italo Calvino short story, who takes a look around and says: "The world had changed: I couldn't recognize the mountains any more, or the rivers, or the trees."

Only, what rendered the world changed, to me, wasn't the absence of my species, but the presence of my child.

In our first moments together, I was overcome by how fragile my daughter seemed, how fragile all of life seemed. It was a revelation, an awakening, like I could see mortality clearly for the first time, how we are always on the cusp of catastrophe, always just about to lose everything we love.

I can still feel the slippery weight of her newborn body as I held my daughter against my chest, the way the skin-to-skin contact in the seconds after delivery had stilled us, how there had been something vaguely amphibious about her at first—her scrunched up legs, the slimy vernix that clung to the creases of her skin.

Like a creature washed ashore, exposed to the elements and gasping at the shock of it, the aquatic phase of her development had come to an end, and her life on land was only just beginning.

Babies are born without a sense of object permanence—the understanding that what vanishes from sight continues to exist. Once developed, object permanence offers infants the security that comes from knowing when their parent or caregiver leaves their sight, they haven't actually disappeared. This belief in our ongoingness develops gradually, including through games like peekaboo. So, when our daughter was a baby, my husband and I covered our faces with our hands and entertained her with our ability to conceal and reveal. Three years later, when our son was several months old, we recruited our daughter to play these disappearing games with us.

"Peekaboo," she'd say to her giggling baby brother. "I see you!" Of the plastic dinosaur she hid under a blanket, she'd shout, "All gone!" Then, squeal as she uncovered it, making child's play of de-extinction.

Paradoxically, object permanence is what makes it possible for children to experience separation anxiety. Once our children know that, when we leave, we continue to exist elsewhere, it can make for tearful good-byes. When she started preschool, I felt pangs of guilt when our daughter quoted Daniel Tiger at drop-off, cheerfully reassuring herself and the other children that "grown-ups come back."

In these words, I could hear the unspoken promise: *always*. And the heartbeat of my own fears: *what if, what if?*

Out of sight, out of mind—like peekaboo—this is the game adults try to play with their fears. The trouble is that these days the worst impacts of the climate crisis are increasingly visible, with more people in more places experiencing climate shocks more frequently.

My children now feel confident that what is out of sight continues to exist, yet as the planet warms, I think of all that is so rapidly disappearing—about the glaciers, the pollinators, the coral reefs, the forests, and the frogs; about the people, homes, and communities lost to climate-driven weather disasters—and fear that, when it comes to object permanence, I've oversold the concept.

In the years to come, as my children mature, I know that I will face the far more difficult task of helping them face the impermanence of a damaged planet, to risk loving a world that is vanishing—only I don't know how to make a game of change and loss.

"F is for frog," is what I've said hundreds, perhaps even thousands, of times while teaching my children the alphabet. And just as often, the question mark in the *Frogs Forever?* exhibit flashed before me, prompting another F-word to come to mind. *Would mass extinction soon make our ABC board book outdated?* I wondered, a question that underscored how so much of what I was teaching my children about the world was subject to revision.

The disappearing frogs came to represent one of the many seemingly intractable, interconnected, complex problems, collectively known as the polycrisis—the confluence of environmental catastrophes, public health emergencies, global conflicts, political instability, economic inequality, and systemic injustices—that I felt powerless to solve, yet could not put out of mind. Things were falling apart, including the health of the planetary systems that make life possible, and at a scale I struggled to fathom.

We are now living through a mass extinction event as devastating as the one that wiped out the dinosaurs. Herpetologists first reported vanishing frog populations in the 1980s. Estimates suggest that since the 1970s, about 200 species have gone extinct. On average, one amphibian species should disappear about every thousand years, but today, the extinction rate for amphibians is forty-five thousand times higher than expected—a statistic made all the more tragic given that amphibians boast an impressive record of survival, having both predated and outlived dinosaurs.

Although amphibians face the steepest losses, other groups are significantly at risk, due to habitat loss, invasive species, overhunting, pollution, and the climate crisis. Across species, researchers estimate that the extinction rate is one thousand times higher than it was pre-humans, and future rates could be as much as 10,000 times higher. In her book *The Sixth Extinction*, Elizabeth Kolbert writes, "It is estimated that one-third of all reef-building corals, a third of all freshwater mollusks, a third of sharks and rays, a quarter of all mammals, a fifth of all reptiles, and a sixth of all birds are headed toward oblivion."

Such extinction events are extremely rare, having occurred just five times in about 500 million years. As one study put it, entire branches on the tree of life are not just dying, but being mutilated, and these losses are "destroying the conditions that make human life possible."

Commenting on the scope and significance of human-caused

mass extinction, Kolbert observes, "[T]hose of us alive today not only are witnessing one of the rarest events in life's history, we are also causing it."

And, what will become of our own species in a time of mass extinction remains an open question.

That day at the aquarium, I'd read the exhibit's signage that warned of the dire consequences of amphibian extinction and felt frozen with dread, while everywhere around me children bubbled with excitement, dashing from tank to tank.

I feared the human impacts of biodiversity loss, but I was also dismayed by how the exhibit explicitly appealed to the value of frogs in terms of their benefits to humans—that they eat disease-carrying and crop-destroying insects and produce valuable chemical compounds used in medicine. Though I understood its purpose was to persuade people to support conservation efforts, in terms that even young children could understand, I didn't like what this messaging implied about our collective ability to care about the more-than-human world. Did we need a reason to save frogs beyond the miraculous fact of their existence?

Standing there, I did not want to see the Panamanian golden frogs—just out of reach in their glass terrariums—as a natural resource, or to reduce frogs to "hopping drugstores." Instead, I wanted to grieve what we are losing, what is not ours to destroy: a thriving planet with abundant plant and animal life.

The grief I felt when I thought of the disappearing world became part of my parenting. I was so often caught between hope and despair. What hope—I had to know—could I truthfully offer my children?

When it comes to facing the realities of the climate crisis, Buddhist philosopher of ecology Joanna Macy urges us to take a clear-eyed look at the ecological problems of our time, even if it's difficult. "If we fear that the mess we're in is too awful to look at or that we won't be able to cope with the distress it brings up," she writes, "we need to find a way through that fear." Drawing on mindfulness practices, she encourages people struggling with difficult climate emotions to cultivate what she calls "active hope"—hope that is grounded in reality and action.

Because of its association with toxic positivity, spiritual bypassing, and American optimism, nearly everyone who speaks of hope within the context of contemporary crises seems to do so with reluctance, attaching an adjective to it or redefining it.

Marine biologist Ayana Elizabeth Johnson admits that hope makes her cringe but puts forward a vision of "catalytic hope." Journalist Krista Tippett calls it "muscular hope." Writer Rebecca Solnit calls it "hope in the dark," likening it to an emergency ax used to break open doors in a fire, and writing, "Hope, like love, means taking risks and being vulnerable to the effects of loss. It means recognizing the uncertainty of the future and making a commitment to try to participate in shaping it."

Activist Greta Thunberg argues that hope must be earned. As does moral philosopher Elizabeth Cripps, who writes, "To earn hope, we must first face reality."

Especially within climate discourse, there doesn't seem to be a consensus on hope. A more recent trend is denouncing the need for hope altogether, as if the time for hope has passed, and what's left now is to brace ourselves for the work that needs doing.

All this tough talk about hope makes sense to me, especially when it is directed, as I believe it is, toward adults. I agree that we shouldn't wait to take meaningful climate action until we feel hopeful about the future, confident that efforts to decarbonize will be successful. And, I would never, could never, judge anyone for feeling hopeless; there are just so many reasons to lose hope.

It's hard to speak carefully of hope and despair since *we* can mean so many different things, and our social locations mean we experience the effects of the climate crisis unequally. Writing in response to this age of apocalyptic fears, Buddhist teacher and activist Lama Rod Owens observes, "I have often noticed that those who are loudest about how we are doomed are those who have never had to struggle in collective survival." I am conscious of how my identity, as a white, middle-class parent raising kids in the Global North, complicates any predisposition I might have toward hope, but I am just as suspicious of my predisposition to despair.

Perhaps the worst hope I could give my children is false hope. But when we make a habit of denying hope, I worry about the impact on young people, who are developmentally tasked with creating their futures. As a parent, I have come to think of hope much as I did as an educator. Just as it is important to be honest with young people about the state of the world, so too, do I believe it is imperative to hold out hope—not hope as a feeling to be performed, not hope as empty promises of progress, but hope as a practice.

By hope, I mean the insistence that it is yet possible for young people to shape lives of meaning, that they can still anticipate and enjoy moments of beauty and awe, that they can contribute to their communities with creativity and courage, and that no matter what happens in the future, they will not face it alone.

By hope, I mean holding onto whatever it is that remains true about this experience of being human, what even a changing climate cannot change.

The revolutionary education philosopher Paulo Freire argued that, in addition to unveiling difficult truths about the world, it is the role of progressive educators to also "unveil opportunities for hope." For Freire, who wrote in exile from Brazil, hope is not a feeling but a practice of struggle, hope is an "ontological need," and hope is an ineluctable part of movements for social change. Hope both generates and is generated by action.

"When it becomes a program, hopelessness paralyzes us, immobilizes us," he writes in *Pedagogy of Hope*, "We succumb to fatalism, and then it becomes impossible to muster the strength we absolutely need for a fierce struggle that will re-create the world."

Freire calls this "critical hope," and notes that it is born of rage and love.

Whatever you call it, one litmus test I have come to hold for hope is this: hope is not hope if it does not include all of us.

Conservation biologist Michael Soulé says, "People save what they love." I don't mean to offer love as an easy solution to the crises we face (although, really, what has ever been easy about love?) but I do take it seriously as a force for change.

The so-called Amphibian Ark keeping endangered frogs afloat is now twenty years into its venture, and the hope for a return to the wild—as well as the financial support that funds it—is getting harder to maintain, yet a global network of caring, committed people persist.

In a video about the Panamanian golden frogs, I watch as conservationists describe their efforts. Sometimes it sounds like the stuff of science fiction, like cryopreserving cell lines to ensure population diversity, genetic material that, if efforts to save the species someday fail, will likely end up alongside the remains of other extinct species in one of several "frozen zoos."

But mostly, it sounds like caregiving: feeding, bathing, sanitation. As one cultural anthropologist observed, "Within Amphibian Ark facilities I found people committed to the practical work of care whose imaginations were constantly probing future horizons."

This finding struck me immediately as one of the best descriptions of parenting I'd ever read. It calls to mind the many times I have brought my hands to a task—cleaning my children's sticky faces with a warm washcloth or scrubbing stubborn vegetables from a sheet pan at the kitchen sink while contemplating their futures.

This kind of thinking is something that conservationists and parents hold in common. Writing of multispecies care, theorist Donna Haraway notes, "To care is wet, emotional, messy, and demanding of the best thinking one has ever done."

When my family and I returned to the Vancouver Aquarium—our first visit following the reopening of the U.S.-Canadian border after its pandemic closure—I saw that we'd missed the *Water Babies* exhibit. Its Parenting 101 placards offered advice based on the parenting practices of frogs, humorous tips like stick baby on a plant or leave babies in a puddle or keep them moist by peeing on them (this unexpected scatological joke the surest sign the aquarium understands its audience).

The exhibit was meant to engender a kind of multispecies solidarity among parents, and I suppose it did. But what I most wanted to know about parenting, the frogs couldn't tell me: How to raise babies in a time of mass extinction? How to, as the signs advised, release them into the wild? How to mind the disappearing world, while I am also minding my children?

Before returning to the aquarium, I was consumed with thinking about care ethics and proximity. Because of our social location, I know that my family and I are nearly always closer to the causes of the climate crisis than to its effects; we are among those who most need to change. I was trying to locate myself in my relationship not just to the disappearing frogs, but also to the frontline communities already experiencing impossible climate realities, including the Coast Salish peoples who, for millennia, have lived in and cared for the place I now call home.

I was also conflicted about the artificial proximity afforded by the aquarium, even if it offered opportunities for children to learn about marine life they might not otherwise encounter. I was not naïve about aquariums, and while this one seemed reformed in its commitment to conservation and sustainability, I felt uneasy about staring at a species on life support.

What I remember most about the philosophy I encountered in graduate school is Emmanuel Levinas's writing on the significance of face-to-face encounters. Such an encounter involves recognizing our infinite ethical responsibility to an Other, which is as overwhelming as it sounds.

"To ask to whom, or to what, does one come face-to-face is to ask to whom or to what am I responsible?" writes anthropologist Deborah Bird Rose, in her attempt to extend Levinas's thinking to nonhuman Others, "This is the question of our time."

But what was my responsibility to the disappearing frogs? When I ticked my way through the list of helpful actions on the Save the Frogs website, I saw that many weren't relevant—I don't eat frog legs, keep pet amphibians, stock fish ponds, or spray pesticides—and the rest were reminders of environmental basics—reduce, reuse, recycle—that seemed too broad to make a difference in bringing a species back from the brink. I was left with the usual options: donate money, raise awareness, contact policymakers. And there was something else I could do: to refuse to look away from the frogs in their distress and to learn to see myself in the systems that harm them.

When we reached the *Frogs Forever?* exhibit, I was as prepared as I could be to face the disappearing frogs, but I did not count on facing my children's disappearance. I turned from the exhibit of Panamanian golden frogs to look for my children but could not find them. Before panic could set in fully, I spotted their jeans and sneakers peeking out from beneath an exhibit table and watched as my children's heads appeared within the pop-up dome of a terrarium. Within this bubble, their eyes were wide, their hair rose with static, and their fingers left smudges on the glass where they were pointing to tadpoles.

"Look, mama!" they were saying to me, though their voices were muffled—and, of course, I was already looking at them—only it was completely disorienting, to see them, now embedded in the frog exhibit as if they were two young volunteers welcomed to the stage for the vanishing act.

To face the frogs, from this vantage point, was to face my children.

If before giving birth, I was occupied with matters of hope, what I really should have been worrying about was how to bear the overwhelming crush of love.

During her preschool's marine life unit, my daughter learned about the oceanic zones. She carried home art projects about many of the animals we saw at the aquarium and just as many surprising facts about the creatures who dwell in the ocean's coldest, darkest depths, beyond the reach of sunlight.

One night before bed, I told her for the thousandth time how I love her to the moon and back. And she replied, no surprise, that she loves me to the sun and back. We were finding increasingly silly ways to profess the bounds of our love for each other, when she finally said to me, "I love you to the Mariana Trench and back."

The deepest point of the ocean, she told me. And when I looked it up, later, I saw that the pressures there in the deep-sea trench, much like the one from which all of life may have first emerged, are bone-crushing.

I believe my daughter when she says that love lives there.

It's true that since becoming a parent my fears have intensified, but what has intensified all the more is the ferocity of my love. Parenthood has shown me that love is capacious enough to hold both hope and despair, that love makes its own light in the abyss.

These days, when we walk the shoreline at the beach near our home, my son likes to pick up a large stick and drag it in the sand while he walks along, leaving a thick squiggle in the wake of his footprints. My daughter likes to use a stick to write her name. I take up a stick, too, and draw beside my children on the beach, where impermanence is commonplace, the push and pull of change, a constant.

We point our sticks in the sand and spin until we are dizzy, making compasses of ourselves, inscribing overlapping circles in the wet sand.

When we leave, we know that the tide will rise, and the sea will wash away our marks.

If Birds Can't Survive

I was running late to the "Baby and Me" class I signed up for after reading the first line of the course description: "The early months of parenting are filled with extremes—from sheer joy to incredible sleep deprivation." While it didn't advertise relief from these extremes, the course offered, at least, a supportive peer group and answers to common parenting questions, and I was eager for both.

Though the class was the only commitment on our calendar, since I was on summer break, I'd spent the morning preoccupied with how to time my six-month-old daughter's first nap so that we might arrive rested and fed. While other parents seemed comfortable feeding and napping their babies on the go, I hadn't yet figured out how to pull it off with ease. Before leaving, I attempted to nurse my daughter one last time, followed by a diaper change, just in case, which made us late, and I had the thought, as I often did, that it would be easier to just stay home.

It was a warm, sunny day that otherwise would have been clear, but wildfire smoke had turned the sky hazy. By the time I'd hurried with our stroller to the church nursery where the technical college held parenting classes, I smelled faintly of sweat and milk.

I parked my stroller alongside several others in the hallway and took a seat in the circle the other mothers had formed on the primary-colored floor mats surrounded by nursing pillows and diaper bags. The class was open to all parents of six- to nine-month-old babies but, unsurprisingly, given the lack of a federal family leave policy, consisted only of mothers who had flexible, part-time work or who didn't work outside the home. Missing from our group were parents with full-time jobs, including fathers who also need support and guidance, which reinforced the all-too-common dynamic in which mothers are the primary gatherers of parenting information, reporting it back to their partners.

While our babies crawled and played with teethers and sensory toys in the circle's center, we practiced baby sign language and performed hand motions to nursery rhymes. We sang revised lyrics to lullabies, versions in which babies don't fall from trees and mothers don't coax their babies to sleep with promises of consumer goods. I was grateful for the softness and the singing. My daughter played happily while I clapped along and pretended my fears weren't existential.

Each week, we focused on a different aspect of parenting, like language development or introducing solids, while carefully avoiding the minefield of topics, like sleep training, that have sparked so-called "mommy wars." Mostly, we spent each session asking our instructor questions. With so much conflicting information available online, it was a relief to turn from a search engine to a living, breathing person who could tell us what to do.

One mother asked how to safely unload groceries from the car, given her home's steep driveway, its location on a busy street, and her early-walking daughter's propensity for toddling downhill. Our instructor suggested a leashed backpack, her voice bright with the confidence that our problems could be solved.

Another mother asked how to persuade skeptical family members to accommodate her baby's food allergies, so she guided us through a role-playing exercise in which we practiced setting boundaries with judgmental relatives.

Another asked how to administer the infant Heimlich maneuver. Our instructor balanced a baby doll prone on her forearm and dispensed five swift back blows.

I got the sense that our instructor, an unflappable retired pediatric nurse who could boast of two happy, healthy grown children and who greeted us always with a bouncing gray bob and boundless cheer, had firsthand experience with every sort of early childhood emergency.

She warned about threats that lurked in the purses and backpacks houseguests may set on the floor, where a crawling baby might find cigarettes or prescription medications. She railed against the risks that latex balloons posed to small airways. A broken balloon, she said, if inhaled by a surprised infant, can stretch and mold to the throat, where it's too slippery to remove by finger.

We discussed how to childproof window shade cords while we crafted noisemaker toys from disposable water bottles—which I'd bought specifically for this project and gulped down on the way to class—filling them with grains of rice and brightly colored beads. We applied hot glue to the bottle lids and screwed them back on tightly to prevent our babies from choking, but the babies, for their part, were mostly uninterested in what we were rattling their way.

At the end of class, we nibbled crackers and baby carrots and attempted to make plans that, in the end, most of us wouldn't keep.

I wondered if the other parents were also looking out at the wildfire smoke with concern, were also worried about raising their children in a changing climate, but I feared that I'd spoil our fledgling camaraderie by bringing up what might be an overwhelming or polarizing topic.

Though most of our questions were about preventing avoidable tragedies, it never felt like the right time to ask about parenting in the climate crisis. When we discussed fire safety, our instructor urged us to buy an escape ladder in case we needed to evacuate the second floor of a house that is burning. I imagined a window opening to the night sky, a plume of smoke, a rope ladder unfurling.

In grade school, after a fire drill, I became preoccupied by fears of a house fire. I used to lay in bed and rehearse crawling through my smoke-filled bedroom, checking the temperature of the door with the back of my hand, worrying over which beloved stuffed animal I'd attempt to save and whether I'd shiver with cold out on the street in my pajamas while watching our home burn. Now, I had a child and no escape ladder from a burning planet.

"But how will we hold onto our baby," one mother asked, "if we are also holding onto the rope?" The instructor told us she once asked a firefighter this very question, and he recommended placing your baby in a pillowcase so you can shoulder it on the way down.

That fall, my daughter clapped her hands together for the first time while watching bushtits foraging in the bamboo that grew along our backyard fence. She stood on our sunroom's faded sofa and looked out through the wall of windows, absorbed in the action of birds flying across the yard, flitting between the bamboo and butterfly bush.

Bushtit, chickadee, creeper, nuthatch—I named these backyard birds for my daughter as best as I could, consulting my field guide, while practicing baby sign language, placing my thumb and finger beside my mouth and making the gesture of a beak opening and closing.

"Bird," I said, slowly and clearly. She clapped. I pointed out the window, "Bird."

My daughter liked to pull from the shelf a board book called *Colors of the Pacific Northwest*, so I read to her again and again of the green Douglas fir, the silver coho salmon, and the white-headed bald eagles.

My collection of field guides and parenting books shared a shelf on our bookcase, and, in early motherhood, I reached for them frequently, painfully aware of myself as an amateur birder and an amateur parent. I so often felt bewildered, and what I longed for most was a field guide that could help me identify what I was experiencing as a mother in the climate crisis.

Because my daughter liked to watch the birds, the stuffed animal she picked out at the toy store was a northern flicker. When she squeezed it with her chubby hands, it played a recording of the woodpecker's ringing and drumming. We hid her bird beneath the sofa cushions, and she found it by listening for its call, and when she was cutting teeth, she'd chew on the flicker's beak and tail feathers.

There was a merlin that occasionally perched on our backyard fence. We knew the merlin was coming when the backyard birds disappeared into the bamboo. The merlin perched; the birds went still and silent. During one visit, I pointed out the merlin to my daughter.

"Look," I said excitedly. "Look at the bird!" I signed the word as my daughter clapped.

From the sofa in the sunroom, we watched as the merlin dove into the bamboo. For several seconds the branches thrashed. My daughter and I were both quite still. I could hear her breathing. It happened so quickly, it didn't occur to me to offer a distraction before the merlin flew away with a sparrow in its talons.

At nightfall, the dark windows of our sunroom became like mirrors. My daughter would pull herself up in front of the glass, which no longer revealed birds, but instead, to her amusement and ours, reflected herself and her family.

We began birding, as a family, in a nearby coastal river valley. I wore my daughter in our baby carrier while we walked through muddy fields and down shoreline trails together, observing bald eagles, short-eared owls, and snow geese. Our friends, who are experienced birders and were expecting their first child, were our guides.

Birding was an activity that soothed my anxiety, allowing me to shift from sitting at home, trying to do everything right and fretting about all I was doing wrong, to immersing myself in the present moment, focusing my senses on what I was seeing and hearing in the world around me. It both grounded me and opened me to wonder.

On one birding excursion, we walked along a bay view trail bordered by tidal mudflats and marshes, hoping to observe American pipits. As we walked, we listened for the songbird's call.

"Listen," I said to my daughter, repeating what I'd been told, "For the peep-peep."

I was holding my binoculars just above her head, which I'd covered with a knitted hat and the hood of her windbreaker since it was early autumn and there was a chill blowing in over the bay. My walking lulled her to sleep, so she did not see when my friend pointed out the northern harrier, a hawk floating easily above the rippling marsh grass.

The next morning, we attended a church service as part of our city's climate action week. The call to worship praised the beauty of the earth and the beauty of the skies, and in the next breath, confessed the mined earth and poisoned skies.

With my daughter on my hip and the bulletin in my other hand, I joined my voice with all those standing in the sanctuary, who read along, asking, "Will we rise if birds can't survive; will we, ourselves, go extinct?" It was the first time I'd voiced such a question aloud, and it was a comfort that I did not have to voice it alone.

Later that week, a push notification on my phone alerted me to a newly published wildlife study, which found that in the United States and Canada, bird populations have decreased by nearly 30 percent since 1970—all told, a loss of about three billion birds, a number too large to comprehend. I thought of the harrier hawk rising above the marsh and the bald eagles nesting high in the trees along the slough, but also the brown creepers and our neighborly bushtits, and I was stunned. "Declines in your common sparrow or other little brown bird may not receive the same attention as historic losses of bald eagles or sandhill cranes, but they are going to have much more of an impact," said one conservation biologist in response to the news.

According to the directors of two major research institutes behind the study, these losses suggested "the very fabric of North America's ecosystem is unraveling." And all I could think was, I don't know how to make a home on a planet that's unraveling, how to childproof for a world on fire. I thought of all the parents I knew, near and far, and all those I didn't know but with whom I felt a sense of solidarity, who were doing everything they could to keep their children safe despite so many unanswerable questions.

In the earliest fitful nights after giving birth, I woke from a nightmare to the sound of my daughter crying in her bassinet and found that I was tangled in sheets soaked with sweat. In my dream, I had been shouting for help because someone had attached an explosive device to my newborn. I was yelling, "This baby is a bomb!" And still, as the timer ticked down, I refused to let go, gripping my daughter to my chest, holding together my love and my fear.

"What will we do with our fear?" writes Eula Biss in *On Immunity*. "This strikes me as a central question of both citizenship and motherhood. As mothers, we must somehow square our power with our powerlessness. We can protect our children to some extent. But we cannot make them invulnerable any more than we can make ourselves invulnerable."

Biss was writing about the importance of routine childhood vaccinations for public health, rather than the climate crisis, but it made me think of my environmental concerns, which I also understood to be public health concerns. I felt newly confronted with my power and powerlessness, the responsibility I felt to protect my daughter and my inability to, ultimately, keep her safe.

What I had now was a firsthand understanding of maternal fear.

In her book *Ordinary Insanity*, about the prevalence of fear and anxiety in early motherhood, Sarah Menkedick makes the astonishing claim that motherhood's "salient contemporary emotion is no longer love, but fear." She demonstrates how maternal anxiety—both clinical and subclinical—has become a normalized and culturally sanctioned condition of mothering. I recognize something of my own experiences in Menkedick's descriptions of the hypervigilant risk assessment that comes with pregnancy, as well as the decision fatigue and overwhelm that can mimic "care and love and intelligence" in early motherhood.

Of maternal anxiety's utility, she writes, "Anxiety is a handy device with which to keep oneself in line with a grueling and ever-changing regimen of coded behavior: a thousand minuscule decisions, from the proper tone of voice to take with a screaming child to the proper daily serving of protein, each freighted with importance and societal judgment."

In early motherhood, I spent much of each day in indecision. When I read that a survey found new parents make, on average, 1,750 challenging decisions in their baby's first year, I laughed. It seemed to me a gross underestimation. For guidance, I tried turning to friends and family as well as seeking expert advice, but this usually meant parsing contradictory viewpoints and approaches that ultimately left me more confused.

Sustainability was one of the many standards by which I evaluated my parenting decisions, and one I, so often, didn't meet. When we failed to switch to cloth diapering, as planned, once my daughter outgrew newborn disposables, I felt incompetent and ashamed. Right when we would have made the change, I was overwhelmed with breastfeeding issues. Feedings were painful and I had an oversupply of milk, which led to blocked milk ducts and recurrent mastitis, flu-like infections that left me wracked with fever and fatigue. I was worried that my daughter, who was eventually diagnosed with a tongue tie, wasn't receiving enough nutrition.

I can see, now, why I chose to put off the diaper question, but I'm still haunted by the fact that it takes 500 years for single-use diapers to decompose in landfills.

This interplay of maternal anxiety and climate anxiety exacerbated how I scrutinized the thousands of decisions I was newly responsible for each day, especially the big decisions that, taken together, seemed like they communicated something essential about my identity as a climate-aware parent.

In her book *Matrescence*, science journalist Lucy Jones describes how she turned to existential philosophy to make sense of her transition to motherhood. She suggests that the existential crisis of matrescence involves both a mother's reckoning with mortality and with what philosopher Jean-Paul Sartre called the "burden of responsibility." Writes Jones, "Keeping a baby alive, making decisions for another person, is surely the ultimate fraught pinnacle of responsibility."

Researchers who study matrescence—which, like adolescence, describes a life stage in which intense physiological and psychosocial developmental changes occur—have identified the transition to motherhood as a period in which a person may "awaken to ecological concerns and question their ethical relationship to nature."

Though the term matrescence was first used in the 1970s by medical anthropologist Dana Raphael to describe what happens when a person adopts a child or experiences pregnancy, childbirth, and caregiving, it has in recent years been revived and popularized by reproductive psychologist Aurélie Athan.

"It's a holistic change in multiple domains of your life," said Athan, in an NPR interview. "You're going to feel it perhaps bodily, psychologically. You're going to feel it with your peer groups. You're going to feel it at your job. You're going to feel it in terms of the big philosophical questions."

In my own matrescence, the philosophical questions I felt pulled toward were existential in nature. I was grappling with the uncertainty and sense of loss that Joanna Macy gives voice to in her description of environmental despair. "[U]ntil the late twentieth century, every generation throughout history lived with the tacit certainty that there would be generations to follow," she writes. "Each assumed, without questioning, that its children and children's children would walk the same Earth, under the same sky . . . That certainty is now lost to us, whatever our politics. That loss, unmeasured and immeasurable, is the pivotal psychological reality of our time."

As I pushed our stroller along neighborhood sidewalks or hiked through muddy fields while birding, I realized, I was already walking with my child beneath changed skies—skies which filled with smoke each summer, skies increasingly emptied of birds.

It's a realization many people come to terms with in their matrescence. Athan, along with ecotherapist Allison C. Davis, has coined the term "maternal ecodistress" to describe how becoming a mother can intensify environmental concerns. "[M]aternal ecodistress represents both a deeply personal concern and an ethical shift, prompting mothers to reflect on the world they are nurturing for their children," writes Davis. "This concept of maternal ecodistress reflects an emotional and cognitive response not just to individual anxieties but to the shared, existential challenges of climate change."

As Athan and Davis indicate, it is overall a positive development for new mothers to move from an anthropocentric to an ecocentric worldview, but it also poses mental health risks, especially if they don't receive enough support from family and friends or if their attempts to make sustainable lifestyle changes are limited by gendered inequities in caregiving.

Athan and Davis identify three primary conflicts mothers face as they attempt to navigate this shift in worldview: isolation, perfectionism, and self-sacrifice. If climate concerns aren't shared or discussed by their others, it can worsen the sense of isolation that is all too common in early motherhood. Mothers can also exhaust themselves in efforts to become perfect environmentalists and sacrifice their well-being and relationships in pursuit of performing the ideal of green motherhood.

One response to these conflicts is to participate in what's been called the "greenwashing of motherhood," by acting primarily as a hypervigilant consumer who only buys the right products. As an alternative, Athan and Davis suggest that mothers experiencing ecodistress can cultivate "deeper and warmer" ways of relating to the Earth by learning to see themselves within a wider web of relations and to recognize their niche role in the ecosystem.

As I grappled with these conflicts, I felt maternal anxiety merge with climate anxiety, mom guilt with climate guilt, but I also felt more a part of our ecosystem, felt my circle of care widening more than ever before to include both the human and the more-than-human world.

"I have hope like an ocean in my soul."

I couldn't speak these words, though I tried to, during the church service that lamented the birds—my hope felt more like whatever it is that is the ocean's opposite.

But, holding my daughter a week later during the student-led 2019 Global Climate Strike, I marched and participated fully in the call and response.

"What do we want?"

Our voices lifted, "Climate justice!"

"When do we want it?"

"Now!"

I wore my daughter in the front-facing carrier because it was easier than navigating the bus with a stroller, but also because at the protest, I wanted her to be able to see what was taking place before her. Carrying her, I felt the weight of the future on my shoulders.

We'd joined the crowd rallying at city hall. I was there to protest in solidarity with the millions of people, inspired by Greta Thunberg and other young activists, who had gathered in cities worldwide to demand climate action.

In the pauses between speakers, a teenager who climbed a tree urged us to shout louder. To shout, he said, quoting Thunberg, like "our house is on fire."

Children wearing green T-shirts took turns at the podium naming their fears and calling for change while I blinked back tears. Later, I read in our local paper a quote from a twelve-year-old who said, "The future doesn't look promising. . . . It's not fair to the kids if the adults don't leave us a fair world to live in."

When it was time to march, I listened, once more, to a child shouting out directions. He told us to fall in line behind Coast Salish elders, an affirmation of Indigenous leadership in the climate movement. To me, it was also a reminder that some of my neighbors were already living in a post-apocalyptic world. In a country built on stolen land by stolen labor, generations of mothers have raised their children without the promises of fairness or safety. Black, Indigenous, and immigrant mothers continue to do so, making climate justice just one of the many existential threats their families face.

It also illustrated that climate justice is not just future focused, but also deeply tied to colonization, to the past and the present. As intersectional climate activist Tori Tsui writes in her book about climate anxiety, *It's Not Just You*, "Climate justice tells us that the Eurocentric obsession about the future is not only harmful and negligent of frontline communities, but it is also damaging in rectifying the root causes of climate change. Roots often gather strength from years and years of growth, and in the context of climate justice, we need to make sure that we understand the importance of how history has become the bedrock of much suffering in the present."

Back at home, I held my daughter in our rocking chair and looked out at the wind swaying the bamboo and thought, it has, historically, never been a fair world. Some of us have always known that, some of us are still learning, and some of us are in denial.

I knew then that my daughter would not remember this protest, but someday I wanted to be able to tell her about marching together. About how it felt to shout, the back of her head resting against my sternum, my ribcage expanding and vibrating as I chanted with the crowd.

I'd understood from the moment our midwife administered the heel prick test on our newborn daughter—as I watched the tiny drops of blood form on the surface of her skin, then stain the test paper red— that I was contending with mortality.

But I hadn't realized, then, that a primary emotion of my matrescence was grief. Underneath all the anxiety and guilt, the rage and love, was grief. Grief not just for how my children, and all children, would be tasked with making their lives on a damaged planet, but also grief for all that we have already lost to a changing climate, and grief, too, for the harm I've caused.

As climate grief researcher Britt Wray observes in her book *Generation Dread*, "The principal emotion that can help us build a better world is love, and so it is also grief."

Taking action began to feel more urgent than ever—a feeling that was heightened by the noticeable and alarming rise in extreme weather and climate headlines—yet, at the same time, as a new parent, I had less time and energy to effect change, both personally and collectively. I didn't yet have a vision for how my mothering could become a form of climate action.

Increasingly there are more spaces for climate-aware parents to seek support. When my children were five and two, I joined such a group through the Good Grief Network. I felt compelled to sign up after a mother I befriended through my daughter's outdoor summer camp told me about her transformative experiences as a participant and facilitator. Finally, I could ask the questions that troubled me most about parenting in the climate crisis, questions I struggled to voice at my "Baby and Me" class.

For 10 weeks, I committed to a weekly two-hour Zoom session with a dozen other people as we worked our way through the 10-step program outlined in the book *How to Live in a Chaotic Climate*, written by the Good Grief Network's founders. Meetings are loosely based on addiction recovery programs—in this case, the addiction to the dominant paradigm of business-as-usual—and each began with a grounding exercise, poem, or journaling prompt that prepared us for a discussion of the week's chapter. Then we spent the rest of the time listening to each other.

I was surprised at how the simple act of listening could open me up to change. It reminded me of what care work expert and labor organizer Ai-jen Poo said in an interview on fostering solidarity among caregivers: "Listening is an act of solidarity; it's also an act of love."

The program's final step was to "reinvest in meaningful climate action," and I was surprised to see parenting included on the list of possible actions. As I read along, I underlined these words:

> We can teach younger generations to look for openings and to be absolutely present in the current moment. To do this, we must learn how to feel our feelings and not project our fears and anxieties onto our children. As parents, we can model a life with increased emotional intelligence, a willingness to question our questions, an ability to be with each other without rushing to fix, and a commitment to bringing more meaning, joy, and connection into our lives.

Climate psychologists call this effort to integrate difficult climate emotions "inner activism," and suggest that engaging in this work is essential to sustaining external, or conventional, activism. They warn that if external action is taken as a shortcut through feelings of fear and grief, it can lead to burnout.

When the 10-step program concluded, I reached out to our group's lead facilitator Kristan Childs, who is a parenting educator and also the mother of three young adults, because I wanted to hear more about parenting as climate action.

Kristan told me that when her children were old enough to understand the reality of the climate crisis, activism became something they did as a family, but when her children were young, she focused on teaching them how to self-regulate. Young children have a well-deserved reputation for expressing their big feelings, often behaving as if the world is ending over minor disappointments, like the wrong color cup or an apple cut in the wrong shape; meanwhile, parents who are keenly aware that the world may possibly be ending, are tasked with helping their children learn to cope. "If our goal for kids is to be resilient, then we have to help them expand their capacity to be with what is and to not get dysregulated so easily," Kristan told me. "We can't access our empathy and creativity and flexibility when we're upset because our prefrontal cortex is off limits. What we want, for the future, is for our kids to be able to access all that good thinking. I think that's climate work."

Kristan's efforts laid the groundwork for assisting her children through difficult moments, like when they had to evacuate their family home in northern California during fire season. Kristan said, "Making your kids pack their evacuation bags—helping them figure out what they should put in and why they need it—is one of the more poignant and terrible and tender things I remember doing as a parent."

But, she adds, they were fortunate to stay with extended family who tried hard to make the evacuation as comfortable as possible for her kids. Looking back on the experience, she said, "Yes, we can grieve and say that we're scared, but also we can play board games and be silly."

As one Good Grief participant and parent interviewed in the book put it: "For kids to thrive, they're going to need. . . . To become experts at metabolizing grief while acknowledging and managing loss. To celebrate beauty in the midst of collapse."

These are tasks we, as parents, need to become skilled at, too, as much for our children's sake as for our own.

And there is still so much beauty to celebrate, even in the changed skies.

Migratory waterfowl were once in severe decline—threatened by habitat loss and poisoned by lead shot—but international conservation efforts have been successful in restoring their populations. On a recent drive home through the valley where we go birding, we happened upon the sudden wonder of thousands of snow geese swarming the skies above us in a thunderous cloud of white wings.

After our second child was born, our friends who taught us to bird loaned us the cloth diapering system they'd used for their daughter. My friend came over and demonstrated how to fasten the soft cotton liners and waterproof covers and how to launder them at home. We used these cloth diapers for nine months, until I returned to work, and I came to appreciate how, while drying them on the line, sunlight can bleach even the most stubborn stains. When I returned them, my friend shared the cloth diapers with several other families before using them to diaper her second child.

Rather than participating in the "greenwashing of motherhood," I felt this sustainable choice to be part of something deeper, warmer, and wider, an outgrowth of the inner work I was doing to connect my actions to my values and my community.

Though I continue to wrestle with the existential questions provoked by the climate crisis, and suspect I always will, I feel less alone in the face of it.

Last summer, we went to the beach with our friends. I was watching my toddler son wade in a tide pool while the older kids scrambled over wind-pocked sandstone formations, when we noticed a bird flying toward the nest she'd built into the rock.

"Look," my friend said, of the bird, "A violet-green swallow."

I stood where my husband and I were sitting on our beach blanket and walked over to where the children had gathered beneath the nest. I was urging them to give the bird space, when I saw that her nest was filled with hatchlings.

"She's trying to feed her babies," I said. And to the swallow, I whispered, "Good job, mama."

Behind me, I heard my daughter reply, unprompted, "What a good mama, just like you."

It's what I want to say to all the parents who are working so hard to make a home, to make a family, to make dinner while making change.

World Without End

One morning, in late fall, my daughter and I were in the garage buckling our bike helmets when she asked if we could drive instead.

"But we bike to preschool," I said, lifting her onto the back of our cargo e-bike.

Looking up at me, she asked, "Or else the planet will die?"

I stalled, pulling on my winter gloves as I considered my response. That sort of apocalyptic language wasn't in the picture books about the environment we read together or the way I spoke about it at home—at least, I hoped she hadn't overheard it from me. Yet, here were my own fears, voiced by my four-year-old.

I wanted her to connect our family's actions to our values, but I also didn't want to scare her. To discuss the stakes of the climate crisis was too fraught, too ill-timed for the moments before preschool drop-off. So I looked at her, bright eyes framed by the contours of her bike helmet, and lied a little bit.

"It's just more fun to bike!" I said, which is technically true, but certainly not the whole truth. Then, we coasted down the driveway and out into the street.

"Whee!" I called out in an attempt to demonstrate my stated commitment to fun.

But as I pedaled us into the bike lane, my mind was spinning over the shock of my daughter's question and my disappointment over how I'd handled it. I blinked against the cool wind blowing in off the bay and tightened my grip on the handlebars, feeling once more the grief and rage that comes with raising children on a warming planet.

What, I wondered, could the end of the world even mean to a four-year-old?

I tried to recall, from my own childhood, what I had learned, and when, about the planet. The first story I remember hearing about the natural world was of its creation, the second, its destruction. In my illustrated children's Bible, I'd barely turned the page on the Garden of Eden before reading of the great flood and the boat Noah built to save his family and fellow creatures from extinction.

I hadn't planned to introduce these stories to my two-year-old, but while out on a walk, she picked out a retelling of Noah's Ark from a neighbor's free pile because she liked the illustrations of animals bounding across the page. I was pregnant with my son then, and after her bath, we sat in the nursery's rocking chair and read bedtime stories, both of us shifting around my pregnant belly to get comfortable, her wet hair dampening the sleeve of my shirt.

I read this book to her reluctantly that night, worried about what lessons she might learn from a religious story I associated with judgment and annihilation. I left out the part about God being so disappointed in humanity's wickedness that he sought to destroy everything—except for Noah's family and the animals they'd gathered into the ark—so that he might begin again, in a kind of cosmic do-over. I skipped it so deftly it was as if those two pages were glued together, and my daughter was none the wiser.

After reading the story to my daughter one night, I returned to the kitchen to finish the dishes and turned on a podcast interview with poet Ocean Vuong. I could see my reflection in the rain-splattered window above the sink, my arms elbow-deep in hot, soapy water as Vuong spoke of how, in childhood, he'd imprinted on the story of Noah's Ark. His thinking about it helped me see new possibilities in the story. It's a story whose central question he believes is this: "[w]hen the apocalypse comes, what will you put into the vessel for the future?"

Soon after, I removed the book from my daughter's bookshelf, but ever since, I've wondered what early stories might shape the questions my own children carry forward.

Climate activist Bill McKibben recommends against telling very young children about climate change. "It isn't their fault, and it's too big for them to entirely comprehend," he writes. "Instead, our job is to make our children fall in love with the natural world—and very few people fall in love with the terminally ill. So: hikes, and bikes, and trips to the park, and watching the weather, and keeping animals, and all the stuff that continues to make me happy late into life."

The trouble with this advice, much as my husband and I have tried to follow it, is that kids are endlessly curious and profoundly perceptive. We are all mortal—a fact my daughter noticed at age three, when she began asking questions about death: hers, mine, and everyone else's—and still, all the time, we are falling in love.

Plus, these days, the simple act of watching the weather can quickly turn unsettling as climate change causes so many unprecedented extremes. When we experience wildfire smoke, as we often do in the West in late summer and as much of the United States did in 2023, my children have questions, and true to their years, those questions lead to more questions—questions that I do my best to answer with reassurance and simple, but honest answers.

At five, my daughter asks why it's bad to breathe wildfire smoke, which I know to be more harmful to children's respiratory health than regular air pollution, especially since their lungs are still developing and they breathe faster than adults. She stands at the window beside her brother and asks, "When can we go outside?" She wants to know how the fires started, and why it's so hard for firefighters to put them out. She wants to know if people's houses will burn and whether trees and forest animals will die.

My toddler son responds to my every answer with: "But why?"

I wish my children didn't have to ask these questions; I wish I didn't have to answer them. But I'm convinced that children deserve factual, age-appropriate information about their bodies and their world, so I share enough to satisfy their curiosity and to earn their trust.

In our home, we read books and talk frequently about topics like gender, race and racism, consent and bodily autonomy. These aren't talks we have just once, instead they are open-ended and evolving conversations. Similarly, I'm learning how to discuss climate change with my children in ways that inform but do not overwhelm—even if my own climate anxiety sometimes keeps me up at night.

When I spoke to climate scientist Heather Price, she shared that it can be helpful to approach talking with children about the climate as we would a family member's illness. "If grandma is sick, you wouldn't talk about her illness with a four-year-old in the same way you would with a fourteen-year-old or a twenty-four-year-old," she says. With a child, you might explain that grandma isn't feeling well and needs extra help, but with a teenager, you might share details of her diagnosis and updates on test results. A young adult may even wish to accompany their grandmother to a doctor's appointment. "Similarly, with climate," Heather says. "It's important to let kids lead the way with their questions, which can help us gauge what they are ready to learn."

But it can be difficult, as parents, to know how and when to introduce children to the existential threat of climate change without overburdening them with guilt or fear. Climate-aware psychotherapist Jo McAndrews succinctly summarizes the goal of this approach as "truth without trauma."

I was ten when I first learned how the world would end. At a Bible study for fourth- and fifth-grade girls, I sat on a faded blue sofa with ruffles and little embroidered flowers and listened as a pastor's wife led a discussion about the "end times." It was the height of the *Left Behind* franchise's popularity and the Y2K panic, and my family had recently started attending an evangelical church. When I admitted to the other girls that I'd never heard of the Rapture—the foretold second coming of Christ, the moment when believers will be swept up into heaven, leaving behind everyone else to face a series of trials and tribulations before the final Judgment Day—they eagerly told me everything they knew. They leaned forward confidentially and spoke in hushed, excited tones, as if they were exchanging gossip instead of recounting strange and alarming prophecies.

When I left evangelicalism in college, I thought I'd left behind any real concerns about the end of the world, but the apocalypse is referenced constantly in popular discourse, including in serious, responsible reporting about the climate. The possibility of our planet's ultimate destruction looms large in the popular imagination.

Many religions look to apocalyptic narratives to make meaning in times of crisis. Some take a cyclical approach to time, while evangelicals take a linear view, believing that the end times represent a literal end to the world. Historian Matthew Avery Sutton argues that apocalyptic thinking is central to understanding the evangelical movement and its historical and contemporary impact on U.S. culture and politics. In his 2014 book *American Apocalypse,* Sutton writes, "The urgency, the absolute morals, the passion to right the world's wrongs, and the refusal to compromise, negotiate, or mediate, now defines much of American evangelicalism and a significant part of right-wing politics. We now live in a world shaped by evangelicals' apocalyptic hopes, dreams, and nightmares." Now, more than a decade later, Sutton's observation rings truer than ever as evangelicalism is becoming synonymous with the Republican Party. That's not to say that every evangelical identifies with these political beliefs. Evangelical climate scientist and *Saving Us* author Katherine Hayhoe resists this politicization of faith and makes the case for climate action in terms of her Christian beliefs, citing "the biblical mandate for stewardship and care for creation." And, within Protestantism more broadly, there is support for environmental stewardship. Environmentalist Heather McTeer Toney, for example, affirms the growing embrace of green theology among Black Christians in her book *Before the Streetlights Come On*. She writes, "The spread of Green Theology—the teaching of biblical tenants of faith as the Christian's responsibility to protect and preserve the environment, is becoming widely accepted in the Black church."

Nonetheless, research indicates that even for highly religious people, positions on climate change may be driven more by political affiliation than by theology. For example, while many evangelicals affirm connections between their religious beliefs and care for the environment, according to a 2022 Pew Research Center survey, they are also more likely to express concerns about environmental regulations that curtail individual freedoms or that negatively impact the economy—opinions that reflect political partisanship. Writes senior researcher Becka A. Alper, "[w]ithin each of the major Christian traditions, as well as among Americans who do not identify with a religion, Republicans are consistently much less likely than Democrats in the same religious group to say the Earth's warming is mostly caused by humans."

The survey also reports that some four in ten American adults believe that we are living in the end times, including more than 60 percent of evangelicals, and finds that end-times believers express the lowest levels of concern about climate change.

In her work with apocalyptic texts, ecotheologian Catherine Keller warns that the "long Western imagination of The End" often serves as a self-fulfilling prophecy and a justification for suffering and violence. She writes, "[T]he dangerous hope for a final, one-off destruction and salvation persists—largely but not exclusively on the right. It feeds the presumption that history and nature move down linear tracks to the Last Stop."

If end-times theology is disempowering and leads to self-fulfilling prophecies, so might secular arguments for climate action that draw upon apocalyptic rhetoric to stoke urgency. Put another way, if I'm concerned about the impact of telling my young children that it's the end of the world, perhaps it's also worth questioning the impact of this rhetoric more broadly. What would happen, I wonder, if we were to reach for alternatives to apocalypticism, alternatives that shape imaginations for change by describing not just the end of fossil fuels, but also the beginning of a more just world, one that is worth hoping for and working toward?

That night at Bible study was my introduction to evangelical eschatology. We ate popcorn while my new friends described what I later learned were traumatic but fairly typical rites of passage: one girl spoke of the nightmares she had after watching *A Thief in the Night*, the 1972 low-budget Rapture-themed thriller intended to scare viewers into getting born again before it's too late; another shared about the time she'd panicked when she walked downstairs into an empty kitchen because she thought her family had been raptured—swiftly and suddenly disappeared to heaven—and she'd been left behind. Before that evening, I had simply counted on the world to go on existing. I sat very still and picked at the sofa's tiny pink flowers while listening to the other girls speak cautiously of their plans for the future, how they worried that before they had a chance to go to college, to get a job, to start a family—to do any of the things they hoped to do—the world might end.

I don't want my own children or their peers to feel the confusion and distress that comes from believing that just as their lives are beginning, the world is ending. Yet, emerging research suggests that many adolescents and young adults struggle with difficult climate emotions. A 2023 survey of 16,000 people ages 16–25 in the United States found that about 40 percent of respondents said their feelings about the climate crisis negatively affect their daily life. Nearly 60 percent indicated that climate change has led them to question whether the work they are putting into their education or career will matter. And an international poll conducted in 2021 found that three-quarters of young people fear the future and more than half believe "humanity is doomed."

As parents, how should we respond to these existential fears, especially when we ourselves are afraid? Our children are among the first generation that will experience, from the moments of their birth, the effects of an irreparably changed climate, which means that we are among the first generation of parents tasked with raising children in such conditions—a responsibility for which there is little available guidance. And yet, it's up to us to help them understand their changing world.

If the future looks grim for the next generation, it may be especially bleak for children for whom the present is already rife with existential threats. A UNICEF report called "The Climate-Changed Child" reveals how the world's children are already suffering from climate impacts, calling it a "child rights crisis." In recent years, for example, there have been an average of 20,000 children displaced by weather-related disasters every single day, and in 2024, at least 242 million students living in 85 countries faced schooling disruptions due to extreme climate events.

In addition, the report finds that nearly every child on earth is exposed to at least one climate hazard, including heatwaves, flooding, cyclones, air pollution, and water scarcity, and one third are exposed to four or more of these stresses. But the world's children do not bear these risks equally. One billion, or nearly half, of the world's children are at extremely high risk of climate impacts, and global inequality means that the 10 countries estimated to face the most extreme climate risks are responsible for emitting less than 0.5 percent of global carbon emissions.

Children have not caused the climate crisis, but as the report indicates, because of their still developing brains, lungs, and immune systems and their smaller bodies, they are uniquely vulnerable to its effects. Yet, for the most part, according to UNICEF, climate discourse ignores their needs and rights, with projects supporting child-responsive activities receiving less than 2.4 percent of climate funding.

Catherine Russell, UNICEF's executive director, argues that children must be placed at the center of the global response to climate change. "Children and young people themselves have consistently made urgent calls for their voices to be heard but they have almost no formal role in climate policy and decisions," she writes. "They are rarely considered in climate adaptation, mitigation or finance plans and actions. But they have not lost hope."

Taken together, this means that parents of young children are now tasked with figuring out how to support their children's physical, mental, and emotional well-being as they grow up both experiencing and witnessing intersecting crises—all while advocating for their children's rights to a livable planet.

The climate crisis is an intergenerational injustice. Even though climate science was settled by the 1980s and could have been effectively addressed in the earliest years of my own childhood, it is now the crisis that shapes my children's everyday life. Scientists estimate that children born in 2020 will experience a two- to seven-fold increase in extreme weather events, compared with people born in 1960, including floods, heat waves, droughts, and wildfires. In the six years since I've had my daughter, my community has experienced some form of all of these.

For strategies on talking with children about the climate risks they face, I reached out to Leslie Davenport, a psychology educator who is at the forefront of practicing climate-aware therapy and the author of two children's books about climate change.

When I spoke with Leslie, she told me that one of the most important things parents can do to support their children is to establish ongoing opportunities for conversation. Leslie says, "I try to have it be very child-led—especially for younger kids—in terms of their curiosity, their interests, their worries. What do they want to know more about? What have they heard? What are their feelings?"

Through visiting classrooms and interviewing children and their parents, Leslie came to realize that kids' exposure to accurate information varies widely. Reflecting on her conversations with fifth graders, Leslie says, "Some students knew more than their parents and could explain about carbon in the atmosphere and why it's warming and why that was a problem. While another might say something like, 'I think the sun broke.'"

Many indicated they were turning to Google to research climate change, meaning they weren't visiting websites designed with age-appropriate information specifically for children. Their parents were often surprised by what their children knew and how they had learned it.

Fortunately, children are increasingly gaining access to climate science education in public schools, including in states like Washington, which introduced a climate literacy curriculum in 2018. This K–12 curriculum is rooted in the understanding that "every student has the right to learn about the impacts of climate change and the effective adaptation and mitigation strategies necessary to address these challenges."

Leslie says that she hears from teachers who include social-emotional learning in their climate science units based on the open-ended journal prompts and other exercises from her books, which include activities like making a "what-if worry chart" or writing out a personal climate story.

I asked Leslie how parents can respond, truthfully, to children who, upon becoming aware of the seriousness of the problem, seek reassurance that everything will be okay. First, Leslie encourages parents to make sure they have their own emotional support for processing difficult climate emotions. "You want to empathize with your children, not process with them," says Leslie. She adds that parents can participate in free or low-cost resources like climate cafes and climate circles—which meet in person or online and are either therapist-led or peer-led—especially since not everyone wants to go to therapy or has the means or availability to do so.

The challenge for both children and adults, says Leslie, is this: "How do you get real information? And then, how do you cope with what you learn—for your emotions, your nervous system, and your thoughts?"

When children express their anger, fear, and grief, Leslie suggests that parents begin by validating their children's feelings. "For a parent to be able to hold those feelings, with love and care and without freaking out, it takes some skill and some practice. You can say something like, 'It *is* scary,' and validate whatever it is your kids are saying.'"

Parents can validate feelings while also holding open possibilities for the future. Leslie says parents can do this by saying something like, "It *is* so big and so complex that there are a lot of unknowns, and while the unknowns are scary, it's also where change can happen."

In our home, our conversations about climate change are, for the most part, driven by my children's observations. We listen and respond to my daughter's questions about the weather and our family's choices, about what she's learning at school and from picture books and cartoons.

One of my children's favorite animated shows is the *Octonauts*, about a team of animals who live and work on an undersea research station built to resemble an octopus. Together, they save their fellow creatures from ecological disasters. Each episode presents a problem that can be solved in roughly ten minutes, at which time Captain Barnacle puts the Octonauts "at ease, until their next adventure."

It's a show that is teaching my children to think ecologically, to notice the interdependent relationships that exist among species, and to appreciate biodiversity, especially through the educational "creature reports" that conclude each episode.

"I want to be Peso," says my daughter, of the penguin who is the resident medic. "Because he's scared of everything but also can heal animals."

"I choose Kwazii," says my son, between bites of an apple slice, expressing his admiration for the eye-patch wearing pirate cat who performs daring feats of watercraft navigation.

Lately, while we watch, my thoughts keep drifting back to *Captain Planet and the Planeteers*, a cartoon I watched during my own childhood in the '90s, about a team of five young people who combine their powers to summon Captain Planet in order to fight villains with names like Looten Plunder and Hoggish Greedly. It's been several decades since I last watched an episode, but the first few lines of the cartoon's theme song come easily to mind: "Captain Planet, he's our hero. Gonna take pollution down to zero."

Both shows underscore the importance of working cooperatively on behalf of the environment, but I can't help noticing that in the *Octonauts*, there are no real villains and humans are conspicuously absent. Instead, animals heroically save other animals from problems that just sort of happen, like when the introduction of an invasive species threatens a coral reef.

I was surprised when my daughter came home from preschool talking about "goodies and baddies." It was language I immediately objected to, so it took some gentle questioning to tease out that some of her friends had become interested in superheroes and villains. I know that superhero play is a developmentally appropriate phase—it allows children to imagine they have the power to solve problems and to act morally—but I'm wary of binary framings, like good and bad, hero and villain.

I wish I had a simpler narrative to share with my children, a tidy story with heroes and villains, but reality is more complicated than a cartoon, and when it comes to the climate crisis, many of us are, to varying degrees, complicit and responsible for taking action, and the scale of the problem means that it will require governments and corporations to work cooperatively and urgently to solve it.

When we bought an electric vehicle, a used hatchback, my daughter was excited and we talked about how we would now plug in our car to charge it instead of filling up at the gas station, but I was careful to avoid framing our choice in terms of good and bad. We were making a sustainable choice that fit with our budget and our lifestyle, but I didn't want my children to shame people who make different choices in different circumstances.

When she was in kindergarten, I was driving my daughter to

swimming lessons one evening, when she said, matter-of-factly, "The Earth is getting warmer and the weather is changing."

"That's true. It is," I said, making eye contact in the rearview mirror. "Did you talk about that at school today?"

"Yeah," she said. I asked for her thoughts about what she'd heard and offered to answer questions, but she simply moved on to telling me about who she sat with at lunch, as if we really were just talking about the weather.

I was in high school when I learned that the word "apocalypse," which comes from the Greek *apokalypsis*, can properly be understood to mean "revelation." At the time, I took this to mean that, in the end, the Truth, as I'd underlined and highlighted it in my student Bible, would be revealed.

It's fitting that Sutton begins his book on evangelical apocalypticism with the sinking of the *Titanic*, one of many disasters that American evangelicals have interpreted through their end-times theology. He quotes an evangelist who was aboard the *Carpathia*, the ship that changed course to rescue those fortunate enough to secure seats on lifeboats, and who attributed the disaster to the "hand of God" and believed that it was "an epitome, a miniature, of the great shipwreck that is coming in the fast-approaching day when the Lord shall rise to shake terribly the earth."

As a teenager, salvation was presented to me as if the world itself was something I needed to be saved from, as if salvation were a lifeboat and if I believed the right things and was good enough then I could be counted among the spared. I was haunted by the idea of a god who would save some while damning others, but still I was terrified of being left behind.

I didn't know it then but I was practicing a coping strategy that climate psychoanalyst Sally Weintrobe calls "arkism," which describes escapist and entitled responses to existential threats. Writes Weintrobe, "Arkism is bailing out the self and the group at the expense of the other, but it also entails thinking like an exception: 'I am entitled to be saved and entitled to have the world as I want it saved for me.'" It's the sort of thinking that allows the precious few lifeboats to be distributed by social class, that leads to crisis responses that replicate existing hierarchies and systems of oppression rather than dismantling them and building something better. It's the sort of thinking that leads people to believe that the future of the planet doesn't matter if you'll be in heaven by the time it burns, or that purchasing a well-stocked bunker or acreage in New Zealand will be enough to shield you and yours from the worst impacts of the climate crisis. The former is a kind of climate denial, the latter a form of climate doomism, but they are two sides of the same coin.

In her book *Hope in the Dark*, Rebecca Solnit responds to the kind of climate doomism that produces inaction. As a counter-analogy, she points to the response of boat-owners in the aftermath of Hurricane Katrina, those who did not flee disaster but rushed toward it when the levees broke. She writes, "None of them said, *I can't rescue everyone, therefore it's futile; therefore my efforts are flawed and worthless.* . . . All of them said, *I can rescue someone, and that's work so meaningful and important I will risk my life and defy the authorities to do it.*" In other words, these were ordinary people who were more interested in saving each other than in being good.

In college, my perspective on apocalyptic prophecies shifted as I embraced more progressive forms of faith. Before ultimately leaving the church, I came to associate apocalyptic revelation with the consciousness raising of social justice movements. I encountered ways of reading the prophets which emphasized their role as cultural critics—not so much soothsayers but truth-tellers who boldly rebuked the powerful, sided with the oppressed, and called for justice.

Writing of the apocalypse as revelation, Lama Rod Owens, in his book *The New Saints*, argues that it's not the end of the world, but the end of the lies we've told ourselves. He writes, "[W]e are confronting truth—truth about ourselves and our relationship to death and dying, to systems and institutions of violence, to transhistorical trauma, to the health of our planet, to capitalism, and ultimately, to the fact that we can no longer continue living like we have in the past."

Owens argues that "[t]he apocalypse has been happening for a long time" and traces its origins through histories of violence and oppression. Likewise, Keller writes: "Worlds, in that sense, have ended over and over—in conquest and in enslavement, in human genocide, and nonhuman extinctions, but also in radical change."

There's a terrible irony to this—apocalyptic rhetoric and fears of a future world-ending event persist in shaping our cultural imagination, even as history reveals a past and present marked by genocidal violence and catastrophic suffering. That the apocalypse is an old, old story suggests that there may be nothing new about all this. Parents, especially those in marginalized communities, have always raised children in dire circumstances, like the families presently suffering in Gaza and Sudan, while also preparing them for the threats they face. Worlds have always been ending, and people have always acted courageously in the face of that fact.

The picture books my children and I read together about the environment don't invoke apocalyptic rhetoric or mention a dying planet. This seems to be a reflection of the choices made by illustrators and publishers as much as it reflects the preferences of parents. And few picture books explicitly connect environmental degradation to human activity and the burning of fossil fuels. One of these is *The Water Protectors*, about an Ojibwe girl who tells the story of her people's fight against the fossil fuel industry—and her participation in protests against the Dakota Access Pipeline—a book that places its hopes not in superheroes but in collective action. Instead, what usually happens is this: a child learns about environmentalism, then sets out to make their home more sustainable and overdoes it to the irritation of their parents and siblings.

At the end of the picture book *Arthur Turns Green*, Arthur says that he wants to "save the planet." Perhaps my daughter, upon subsequent readings, has noticed that the planet needs saving. Perhaps she has asked herself the questions the book does not answer: Why does the planet need to be saved? And from whom does it need saving?

Because Arthur wants to "make the planet a better place to live," he goes green by switching out light bulbs, setting the table with cloth napkins, and unplugging electronics that are still in use. Similarly enthusiastic, Fancy Nancy wants to make every day Earth Day, and she chides her parents to be more eco-friendly with sayings that rhyme, sayings my daughter has at times repeated to me, helpful reminders like, "Less than a mile? Bike in style."

I have been Arthur, I have been Fancy Nancy. I have also been their chastened, inconvenienced parents. And yet, I wonder what my daughter is learning from these stories in which children who, upon realizing the importance of environmental action, become well-meaning but annoying scolds. I suspect that this can result in a misplaced emphasis on individual action over collective action.

As McKibben notes, "at a certain point, kids are going to find out that things are not as they should be, at which point it's necessary to give them things to do." While changing light bulbs might be doable, he points out, it won't solve the crisis. Instead, he writes, "What will solve it is activism and engagement, and no one is too young to be part of that."

Heather, the climate scientist I spoke to, also mentioned the importance of emphasizing collective action when discussing climate change with kids. "When we help kids understand that climate change is not so much about our individual choices, but that it's the system that's the problem, I think that helps with the shame and blame," she says. "In my opinion, one of the best ways we can protect our kids in terms of climate anxiety is to show them that it's systemic."

Still, I understand why my first response to the climate crisis is to focus on individual action. I can use what power I have to reduce my family's carbon footprint and to influence those closest to me. Too, these small-scale changes—like commuting by bike or bus, installing solar panels, driving an electric vehicle, and eating a more plant-based diet—help me manage the cognitive dissonance of going about my everyday life in the midst of a global emergency. It makes me feel like I'm doing something, anything, even if that's simply being a slightly more conscious consumer.

Collective action feels like a more overwhelming ask. Even though we march together, call and email our representatives, and vote for climate policies, it feels more manageable to plan a week of meatless meals than to figure out how to meaningfully support the passage of a Green New Deal. Reflecting on this challenge, climate journalist Naomi Klein writes, "The vast, complex planetary crisis requires coordinated, collective effort on an international scale. That may be theoretically possible, but it sure is daunting. Far easier to master our self."

Yet, I know myself to be an unruly subject. Despite my efforts, I often fail to live in alignment with my values and my shortcomings at living sustainably are a glaring disappointment. Obsessing over personal purity and pointing out the shamefulness of hypocrisy, though, are hallmarks of the kind of black-and-white thinking encouraged by evangelical theology—it's also a tactic used by people opposed to climate action to discredit those who advocate for change. Even now, decades later, like Fancy Nancy, I'm prone to making inflexible rules that govern my personal conduct—rules that, as a therapist once suggested to me, can veer toward scrupulosity.

I don't want to pass along this kind of sanctimonious thinking to my children, so I'm deliberate about letting them see my compromises and contradictions while welcoming their questions and feedback. And I turn to children's media as a shared reference point for having conversations about the importance of making sustainable choices while advocating for structural change.

I know that choosing to bike to preschool will not keep the planet from dying, but my hope is that it's one small change among many that help my children to see that we have the power to make different choices, to give them a glimpse at what alternative ways of moving through the world might look like.

For all the efforts we've made to shrink our family's carbon footprint (and the many ways we've failed to do so), for all our hikes and bike rides and trips to the park and all the ways we're teaching our children to love the world, still I sometimes lay awake at night questioning whether, in the face of so much loss, the force of my love, as a parent, might ever be enough—strong enough to create social change, soft enough to sustain my children in the world they will someday inhabit without me.

Alone at my desk, I take up the copy of Noah's Ark that I removed from my daughter's bedroom and notice for the first time the missing rainbow. The rain stops, the dove returns, and life begins again on earth. But in this retelling, there is no rainbow—the symbol of God's promise to never again destroy the earth by flood. I flip through the pages of the book once more, in case I've somehow missed it, and wonder about the omission. How strange that a children's book would describe the punishment of wicked people but not include the story's final promise, the promise of a livable planet.

When I think again about the ark and what I'd preserve for the future. My answer now comes easily: all of us. I don't want an ark or a lifeboat, I want a planet.

One night in the bathtub, my daughter asked, "Do we start over again?"

The sleeves of my sweatshirt were rolled up to my elbows and I was cupping my hand over my son's brow to keep the soap from his eyes.

"Do we what?" I asked, only half listening.

"Start over again," she said. "When we die, does life start over?"

"I'm not sure," I answered honestly. "Some people think so."

I want to believe that when we die we go to be with those we love, we go to be with Love itself, but I don't know what happens after death or whether the planet is dying, and so often, I feel ill-equipped to answer my daughter's existential questions.

But once, after a storm, there was a double rainbow so brilliant it drew us out of our home, and we witnessed the collective astonishment of our neighbors on balconies, on porches, someone even perched on a rooftop, all of us looking up.

Maybe we can start over.

Maybe the end doesn't have to be The End.

Maybe life begins again.

I want to raise my children to know the hope that comes from taking collective action and the resolve that comes from believing that *anything is possible*, and to preserve, for as long as I can, their ability to hear in that uncertainty not just a threat, but a promise.

Watching the Clock

My three-year-old was learning to tell time. She stood in front of the oven, hopping on one foot, looking up at the blue digits on the stovetop clock. She could read off the numbers, but couldn't yet name the minutes greater than twenty. "It's six-five-eight," she'd say. "Is it bedtime?"

In the morning, the ring around the face of her okay-to-wake clock glowed yellow as six a.m. approached, then turned green to let her know when she could start her day. I wake early to write, and some mornings I'd hear her door creak open and watch her shadow descend the stairs. Other mornings, I'd hear her still in bed, calling for me, "Can you come wake me up?"

When negotiating more screen time, she'd plead her case: "Just five more minutes." In the kitchen before supper, she'd shout "Freeze!" And my husband and I would hold very still in exaggerated poses until she reversed her spell by yelling, "Unfreeze!" From her car seat, she'd make eye contact with me in the rearview mirror on the way to swim lessons. "Are we going to be late?" For months, every memory my daughter recounted happened "yesterday." Now, she speaks of the past in terms of last week, last month, last year. And what she has already intuited about the future is that time runs out. Sometimes when tucking her into bed, she'd turn to me, her face searching mine in the dim glow of the night light, and ask, in a voice that cut through the shushing of the white noise machine: "Mama, when will you die?"

According to the Climate Clock, just as time was entering my daughter's consciousness, there were six years, three hundred and thirteen days, two hours, twenty-eight minutes, and three seconds left to limit global warming to 1.5 degrees Celsius—an important target under the Paris Agreement and the point at which many of the worst impacts of climate change become reality.

As heat waves, fires, and floods crowd the headlines worldwide, the clock keeps ticking. If it feels like the extreme weather has been relentless lately, it's because it has been. The makers of the Climate Clock argue that its fifteen digits are the most important numbers in the world. "Earth has a deadline," they announced when they reprogrammed the Metronome, a sixty-two-foot digital clock in New York City's Union Square, to display a countdown until the moment when the worst effects of global warming become irreversible.

I can watch the seconds tick by on a bright red banner at the top of the project's official website. I can hear my daughter reading off the clock's numbers: "six-three-one-three-two . . ." Like the busy people walking in Union Square, I can feel the clock's red glare looming overhead as I go about my day. While caring for my children or answering emails or making dinner, I am watching the clock, marking my own countdown. When the Climate Clock's time runs out, my children will be ten and seven.

"Where do rocks come from?" Another of my daughter's bedtime questions, one that tested the limits of what I remember learning about geology in school. I kept a rock collection as a child, filling several shoeboxes, but now I can offer only a rough overview of the rock cycle.

"Let's learn about rocks together," I said the next morning. Seated at the kitchen table in front of my laptop, I pulled up our public library's catalog to request several picture books about fossils and rocks, and, for me, geologist Marcia Bjornerud's *Timefulness*, in which she argues that the field of geology holds wisdom for addressing the climate crisis. I hoped the book might offer perspective for reframing my climate grief, or at the very least, help me nurture my daughter's curiosity about the natural world.

Rock by rock, Bjornerud says, geologists mapped time. In doing so, these geochronologists plotted the story of Earth's earliest days, a record of how it transformed over billions of years. I tried to contemplate deep time, but I kept getting interrupted. Geologists may speak of epochs, yet parenting has so contracted the timescales by which I measure life that I speak of it in much smaller increments. It's hard to hold in mind the immensity of planetary history when the demands of the present feel so immediate and overwhelming, and thinking about the uncertain future my children face is almost more than I can bear.

Among the problems Bjornerud identifies with Western conceptions of time is the pervasiveness of time denial, or chronophobia. There's pressure from the beauty and wellness industries to avoid the appearance of aging. There's the influence of evangelicals who preach Young Earth creationism and prophesy that the end is imminent. There's capitalism's refusal to take the long view, insisting instead on ever-increasing levels of productivity and consumption in the name of short-term gains. This cultural ignorance of the planet's past combines with a reluctance to seriously contemplate its future, complicating efforts to address climate change.

In response, Bjornerud advocates for what she calls a "polytemporal worldview," one that holds together the various rates of change that take place on our planet—some fast, some slow. While it's true that geologic changes are the result of unimaginably slow processes, the pace of the climate system is quickening. Take, for example, the mindbogglingly fast rate at which coastal Louisiana is losing land: one acre per hour.

Even if I can't fathom deep time, motherhood, at least, has prepared me for this polytemporal worldview; my children are always changing and the passage of time feels paradoxical, fast and slow. This approach, Bjornerud says, may help with another kind of chronophobia: the fear of death, a fear that is newly present in my daughter's consciousness, a fear that I've experienced anew through her questions.

Reading Bjornerud, I practice thinking about time like a geologist, but, mostly, I can manage only to think about it like a mother.

Motherhood has fundamentally altered my perception of time, giving me the opportunity to witness a human lifetime from the beginning. From birth, I counted my children's ages in days, then weeks, then months. It wasn't until my daughter's second birthday that I started referring to years.

When she turned three, my daughter's preschool invited us to participate in her birthday celebration. During circle time, my daughter's classmates sat, cross-legged and squirming on carpet squares, while she stood with her arms around a stuffed globe. Holding the planet to her heart, she orbited a small Sun at the circle's center. As she walked, her teacher read a version of my daughter's life story, one I'd written in my own handwriting, filling in the blanks of the worksheet from her take-home folder. I could feel time's passage in my body as I watched her, each year a revolution completed in a matter of seconds. For a moment, I felt seized by chronophobia, and I tried not to flash forward to her at ten years old, when the time remaining on the Climate Clock will expire. Then, just as suddenly, I was swept up in the chaos of toddlers clamoring for small party favors, the temporary tattoos my daughter had picked out for her classmates.

I know that if our lives proceed as hoped for, at some point, my children will go on without me. It's a fact I feel with greater urgency after my grandmother passed away, an event that prompted my daughter to ask more questions about death.

"Did the dinosaurs die and turn into dirt?" she asked from the back seat.

"Some did," I said, "and some turned into fossils."

Then she asked, "When I die, will I turn back into dirt?"

"We all will," I heard my husband say, as my mind reeled in the silence.

"And then no one will ever see us again?" she asked—a question that felt hard and heavy as a rock. Then, quieter, she said, "I don't like dying."

I don't like it, either. My attempts to provide age-appropriate explanations about what happens when we die and reassurances about how much time we have left, feel false at worst and inadequate at best. In moments like these, reminded of our mortality, I wish I had more power over time. I feel the childish urge to freeze it, as if we could remain together forever in a state of suspended animation.

Whether I am watching the clock as it ticks down to bedtime or I am so immersed in playing with my children that I've forgotten to mind it; whether I desire more time with my children or more time for myself; whether I feel time's passage as too fast or too slow, I never have enough of it. Time runs out.

The makers of the Climate Clock were inspired by the Doomsday Clock, a clock which has been ticking my whole life. For decades, it was the cover art for the *Bulletin of the Atomic Scientists*, and it has since become a universally recognized symbol for assessing the risk of global catastrophe.

The Doomsday Clock was the work of Martyl Langsdorf, a landscape artist who was married to one of the Manhattan Project physicists who organized the *Bulletin*'s nuclear nonproliferation efforts and petitioned President Truman not to use the atomic bomb. She created the clock in 1947 and, in order to convey the urgency of the moment, set the time to seven minutes to midnight. Its bold, modern design is simple but iconic. Black and white. A quarter-circle. Two lines for hands. Four dots in place of numbers.

I was born with three minutes left on the Doomsday Clock. That was before the grassroots Nuclear Freeze Movement, before the fall of the Iron Curtain, before the signing of the Strategic Arms Reduction Treaty, before the dissolution of the Soviet Union—events which turned back the clock to seventeen minutes to midnight.

My daughter was born with two minutes on the clock, owing not just to nuclear armament, but also to the interconnected threats of bioterrorism and global warming.

On the day I gave birth to my son, the *Bulletin*'s president announced that the clock was set at 100 seconds to midnight. The official statement read: "[T]he Clock remains the closest it has ever been to civilization-ending apocalypse because the world remains stuck in an extremely dangerous moment."

A question and answer on the FAQ page of the *Bulletin*'s website: "Which is the greater threat: nuclear weapons or climate change? At the end of the day, trying to answer the question is like standing around in a burning house arguing about whether it is better to die of smoke inhalation or from a falling timber."

I keep meeting my children in these midnight hours. If the Earth is a house that's burning, I can hear the smoke detectors blaring as I try to rock my babies back to sleep, patting their backs in the age-old rhythm of reassurance.

Each summer, now, I notice a meme circulating during heat waves. In it, a child whines, "This is the hottest summer of my life." In response, a parent warns, "This is the coldest summer of the rest of your life." This dialogue is often superimposed on an image of Bart and Homer Simpson. Aesthetics aside, the meme is a sobering reminder of what's at stake when it comes to global warming, and yet, it promotes a kind of climate nihilism that I'm trying to resist.

Summers of extreme heat and catastrophic natural disasters are a hard-to-ignore example of the present climate reckoning. I remember sitting poolside, in 2023, at my daughter's swim lesson when I opened a push alert with an alarming headline. The Earth had just recorded its hottest day yet (in what was the hottest week yet). The spike in global temperatures, due to both human-caused climate change and the return of El Niño, astonished even climate scientists.

Like the other parents at the pool, I was relaxing on a sun-faded chaise lounge, phone in hand. I wasn't braced for such shockingly bad news. I thought about a phrase I first encountered in a book about climate anxiety: *brokenrecordrecordbreaking*. It's that "recurring feeling of déjà vu, quiet terror, and slow shock, which is both acute and familiar, that occurs when opening a newspaper, radio program, or website and reading a headline that that year (month, season, day) has broken the record for the hottest on record."

I keep feeling that I should be used to this by now, the too-familiar experience of absorbing the news that something terrible has happened while also carrying on with the everyday tasks of parenting. In the moments after the headline flashed across my phone screen, I handed my son his reusable water bottle, then watched as my daughter approached the lowest diving board. Swallowing against the anxiety I felt rising in my chest, I gave her a smile and a thumbs up and clicked out of the news app to take her picture.

My thoughts about the "hottest summer of your life" meme are connected to another parenting meme that circulates each summer, one I've come to resent for what it implies about keeping time. Of its many iterations, nearly always there is a sunlit child playing near water, the camera at their backs. The text reads something like: "We only have eighteen summers together." Not unlike the Climate Clock or the Doomsday Clock, the eighteen-summers meme is a kind of countdown that puts pressure on parents, especially mothers. A good mother knows to make every moment count, an imperative that haunts me.

These memes illustrate what is, for me, one of the most frustrating parts of parenting: I am always on the clock. I have come to associate the clock with guilt—mom guilt and climate guilt. I feel guilty for the time I spend working instead of with my children; guilty when I resent how mothering keeps me from my work; guilty when I choose extractive, time-saving conveniences instead of more sustainable, albeit slower, methods of managing care work. I live in a perpetual state of time scarcity, one that's heightened by the existential threat of the climate crisis.

Biographer Julie Phillips calls this time scarcity "maternal time" in her examination of how twentieth-century artists, writers, and activists held together the demands of mothering and creative work. Maternal time is at odds with Western constructs of time. Some forms of labor simply take time; they cannot be optimized for profit and may not produce results for decades, if ever. Like making art or engaging in activism, the work of caregiving is inefficient and undervalued. It's a conflict exacerbated by the same oppressive forces that threaten the planet.

Phillips writes, "The work of care alters time, linking humans to the past and future, tying us to the present, insisting on simultaneity, allowing moments of selfhood, committing us to nostalgia and futurity."

When my daughter was a newborn and I was recovering from giving birth, I rocked her to sleep in my arms, and while she slept, I read

Braiding Sweetgrass, a collection of essays by Indigenous botanist Robin Wall Kimmerer. I wanted to read something tender, and the book promised stories of healing, of restoring relationships with the land. I did not expect so much of it to be about time and mothering.

When Kimmerer's daughters were young, she moved with them to a farmhouse by an old pond. In "A Mother's Work," she writes of her yearslong efforts to restore that pond, of weekends spent raking mats of algae. "Making my pond swimmable would be an exercise in turning back time. That's just what I wanted, to turn back time," she reflects. "My daughters were growing up too fast, my time as a mother slipping away, and my promise of a swimming pond yet to be fulfilled."

As her last summer with a child at home comes to an end, the pond is not yet swimmable. Kimmerer finds comfort in imagining that, if not her own children, someday her grandchildren may swim in the pond.

She concludes that caregiving is circular and finds that as she ages, her circle of care grows beyond her family, to encompass her community, and even planetary systems.

Later in the book, she writes of circular time. She holds that origin stories are both history and prophecy. In her view, time does not run out: "Time is not a river," she says, "running inexorably to the sea, but the sea itself—its tides that appear and disappear, the fog that rises to become rain in a different river." Rooted in a sense of abundance rather than scarcity, her perspective on time offers a corrective to my chronophobia.

I am trying to see time as circular, like water; something that can change states, turn from liquid to ice and back again, that can cycle through the landscape endlessly, a renewable resource.

I feel its circularity when my mother tells me that my grandmother, from her hospice bed, cried out for comfort from her own mother, whose death had preceded hers by decades. I think of my grandmother now, her calls for her mother echoing like ripples in a dark pond, when my daughter calls for me in the middle of the night.

While writing this, I was interrupted by the sound of my daughter's bedroom door creaking open. It wasn't yet late, but it was past her bedtime. By the time she called down for me, I was already at the stairs. She jumped into my arms as I approached the top step and wrapped herself around me as I carried her back to bed.

She asked for another story.

Earlier, we'd watched the beginning of *Frozen*, a film we hadn't yet finished because of the wolf chase scene, which frightened my daughter so much she would stop watching. When this happened, I tried to soothe her fears. I tried to explain to her that this is how many stories work, that things fall apart and get scary, but that usually everything works out well in the end. But she wasn't comforted by my promises of a happily ever after. So, the kingdom remained frozen, the film paused on screen. Neither of us knew what would happen next, which is another way of saying anything could happen.

We lay on my daughter's bed, face to face, our hands touching. "Tell me a *Frozen* story," she said. So I did. "The end," I said, when it was over. "It's time for sleep now." But she protested. She wanted to linger in the world of story, she didn't want me to leave.

"But Mama," she said, "It isn't the end, yet."

How we tell time and the stories we tell about it matter. When it comes to climate action, there is a productive tension between metaphors that remind us that time is running out and those that remind us that there is still time in which to act.

Bjornerud cautions against watching the clock for midnight. It is a mistake to think of planetary processes as moving only very slowly, when in fact some shifts can happen quite rapidly. "[I]f the 4.5 billion-year story of the Earth is scaled to a 24-hour day, all of human history would transpire in the last fraction of a second before midnight," she writes. "But this is a wrongheaded, and even irresponsible way to understand our place in Time." Not only is this metaphor disempowering, it also minimizes the impact that humanity can make in a relatively short amount of time. Worse still, it makes the end seem inevitable. After all, she asks, "[W]hat happens after midnight?"

This question reminds me of the climate anthology, *Not Too Late*, which offers an explicit appeal to making the most of the remaining time and includes the work of writers and activists who insist on the radical power of imagination, of envisioning a future of global flourishing after midnight.

"It takes my breath away to write these words, but we did it," writes climate strategist Mary Anne Hitt in her love letter from the clean energy future. "Rooted in our deep love for this planet and one another, we stepped back from the cliff of irreversible climate change." Celebrating policy solutions, she writes, "We needed to build so much clean energy infrastructure to avoid a climate apocalypse, and we didn't just build it; we built it with family-sustaining jobs and with an eye toward restitution and reparations."

The letter might be speculative, written from a place in the imagined future, but I keep reminding myself that we *could* do it, we could build a clean energy future, that when it comes to the Climate Clock or the Doomsday Clock, it's possible to turn back time.

I learned to tell time by moving the red hands of a Judy Clock. Seated at a table in my first-grade classroom, I spun the minute hand and watched the clock's red and green gears turn as the hours advanced around its cheerful yellow face. I could spin the hands counterclockwise, too, and watch the gears of time reverse.

Now that I'm teaching my children to tell time, I'm realizing that there's more to it than just reading off numbers from the clock. Someday my children will be able to read the Climate Clock's countdown and determine for themselves what it means. Soon I'll listen to them tell their own stories about time.

Summer is over now, perhaps the hottest-coldest summer of my daughter's life. It was the summer of temporary tattoos, hours spent snipping out colorful cartoons with her child-sized scissors and applying them to her skin and mine. Hundreds of little things that have marked us, then worn off. A thermometer, a red heart, a clock.

In the backyard, she cut out another tattoo for me. Words written backwards so that they would be legible once applied. She placed it on the inside of my wrist, covering it with a wet cloth, which she held tenderly as she counted to twenty, skipping only the number sixteen.

She removed her hand to reveal the message on my skin: *carpe diem*.

Hours later, I looked down at my wrist, and already it was fading.

Little Things

"What's what?" I asked, gripping a creeping thistle and pulling until it gave way with a spray of loose dirt. I tossed it onto the pile of weeds on the sidewalk and looked back at my five-year-old, who was holding out her bug catcher.

"Mama, what's this?" she asked, repeating herself.

My son was standing beside her in his rain boots and 2T shorts, muddy from playing in a pile of mulch, scooting down it as if it were a slide. Eyes wide, he strained to get a better look at the long, black beetle wriggling within the bug catcher's magnified viewfinder.

My husband was several yards away, removing old landscaping cloth along the slope between our fence and the sidewalk, while I followed behind, weeding. The cloth hadn't worked to control weeds, and as I'd learned while researching alternatives, wasn't even cloth in the traditional sense but instead was made from synthetic fibers that shed harmful microplastics. So, we were replacing it with mulch and planting native plants, like bearberry, beach strawberries, checkerbloom, and bear grass.

I peeled off my gardening gloves and knelt to see the bug that my daughter had found. I didn't recognize the beetle, which was much larger than our usual backyard specimens—the roly-poly bugs and ants, ladybugs and earwigs, my children catch and release while playing. Though I tried not to let my face betray me, I didn't like the look of the beetle's armored abdomen and pincer-like jaws nor the way it reared back, like a scorpion about to strike.

I opened an app on my phone to photograph and identify it. We watched as it sorted through taxa, confirming order, family, and genus, until it homed in on a positive identification.

"It's a devil's coach horse beetle," I said. The kids crowded the screen while I scrolled through facts about the species. A beetle native to Europe, I saw that in Ireland it's called the coffin cutter, since it's attracted to carrion and one of the first insects to arrive to a dead body.

"Why's it called a horse devil?" my daughter asked.

"A devil's coach horse beetle," I said more slowly, brushing some dirt from my knee and standing. "I'm not sure, but we should let it go."

"Carefully," I added, "way over there."

I picked up my son and we walked over to a corner of the yard, far from where we were working. My daughter gently placed the bug catcher on the ground at the base of a lilac bush and pressed the button to open its sliding trap door. She stepped back and the beetle scurried away into the shadows.

As a new parent, I was ostensibly tasked with introducing my children to language, but I often felt like I was the one who was learning to speak. "Gentle hands" is a parenting phrase I adopted early in motherhood after hearing it somewhere, or more accurately, everywhere. It's hard to say whether I found it, or it found me. Along with phrases like "big feelings," it is ubiquitous in contemporary parenting discourse. I say, "gentle hands, please," in moments when previous generations of parents might have just said, "Be careful!" Like when a curious toddler first reaches for a friend's giggling baby or a dog's soft fur.

Now that my kids are older and do more hands-on exploring while out and about, I've continued to remind them to use "gentle hands" with the creatures they find, simply because it often works. As it turns out, even very young children are capable of great gentleness.

While gardening, I've witnessed my son pause to move a dangling, squirming earthworm from harm's way, shouting "It's so huge, Mama!" before taking up his shovel to resume digging. I've watched my daughter place her cupped hand in the path of a daddy longlegs, letting it crawl cautiously from one hand to the other, before returning it to the cool, dark shade of the kale leaves. I've watched both kids screech to a halt on the sidewalk mid-ride—my daughter on her pedal bike, my son on his balance bike—to avoid squishing the snails and slugs that emerge during spring rains, shepherding them carefully into the grass and out of danger.

Though sometimes their best efforts are a bit clumsy, wherever they go, whether in the backyard or at the park, in the woods or at the beach, my children are always on the lookout for much smaller lives, eager to observe them with curiosity and care.

Grown-ups generally don't read books about bugs for fun, unless they're in the company of small children, or, at least, I hadn't since childhood. But the picture books I now read to my kids are filled with facts about the natural world that adults, like me, would do well to contemplate.

"Vertebrates look big and powerful in comparison to invertebrates," I read aloud, moving my finger across the page of our bug book demonstratively, helping my oldest, who was learning to read, follow the line of text. "But the truth is that without bugs and their close relatives, most vertebrates would become extinct." My children loved hearing about this power reversal, how the big and strong are dependent on the small and powerless. Perhaps unsurprisingly, given the power dynamics that structure their own lives, kids often have an affinity for small creatures and are quick to defend them.

Most children's books about bugs will tell you that insects play an outsized role in maintaining ecosystems by pollinating plants, maintaining soil health, decomposing waste, recycling nutrients, controlling pests, and forming the base of food webs. About two-thirds of all known animal species are insects, and this doesn't include the other centipedes, spiders, and ticks that we informally call bugs, nor does it account for the fact that scientists suspect there may be four million insect species yet to be documented.

Despite their relative diversity and abundance, 40 percent of insect species are in danger of going extinct, and populations are already in sharp decline. Naturally, while reading our bug books, I did not pause to warn my children about what scientists call the "insect apocalypse," though I wondered how long I could keep it from them.

In a 1987 paper on the importance of conserving invertebrates, entomologist and champion of biodiversity E. O. Wilson famously called insects "the little things that run the world." Sketching out a dystopian vision of what would happen if invertebrates were to disappear, he concludes, "I doubt that the human species could last more than a few months."

Thirty years later, a landmark study sparked headlines when it found that insects gathered in German nature reserves had decreased over that same time span by as much as 75 percent. One researcher, reflecting on this propensity of humans to live alongside diminishing species for decades, noticing only when it's nearly too late, remarked, "Humans seem innately better able to detect the complete loss of an environmental feature than its progressive change."

But spending time with small children may be a corrective. It sharpens our perception of the natural world, including our ability to notice incremental losses. Citizen-scientists—many of them parents troubled by the absence of bugs they recall from their own childhoods—have played key roles in collecting data about the insect world. Perhaps this is an inescapable part of parenting, we can't help but compare our childhoods to our own children's experiences, and therefore are more inclined to notice what's changed.

It's not just insects, birds, and other species disappearing from the natural world, but also our language for them. "Once upon a time, words began to vanish from the language of children. They disappeared so quietly that at first almost no one noticed—fading away like water on stone. The words were those that children used to name the natural world," writes Robert MacFarlane in the introduction to the picture book *The Lost Words: A Spell Book*.

The book's title glitters in gold leaf, and its sumptuous watercolor illustrations are shot through with golden letters that gleam like honey and spell out the names of plants and animals to form acrostic poems that describe these creatures. Insists MacFarlane, "We do not care for what we do not know, and on the whole we do not know what we cannot name."

The book emerged as the result of an open letter signed by prominent British writers and naturalists in 2015 to protest the removal of some 40 words for nature from the *Oxford Junior Dictionary*, which replaced entries for *acorn*, *kingfisher*, and *magpie* with the likes of *voicemail*, *blog*, and *broadband*. Words that are, decidedly, less enchanting, but were thought to be more useful to elementary students.

Though the changes to the dictionary were first made in 2007, they went largely unnoticed until a mother of four living in Northern Ireland was helping her son with his homework and caught the absence of *moss* and *fern*. It does not surprise me that it took a parent to pick up on these missing words. Alarmed, she went looking for other struck entries, tracking changes across six editions of the dictionary before bringing her findings to the public.

The resulting open letter advocates for the right of all children to connect with nature and protests falling rates of outdoor play. According to the letter, the missing words are symptomatic of a broken relationship with nature and indicative of a move toward childhoods that are increasingly taking place indoors, isolated, in front of screens. The letter's signatories call on the dictionary to exercise its cultural authority and reinstate the lost words as a symbolic step toward restoring children's relationship to the natural world.

I am sympathetic to the letter's aims, and cherish our copy of *The Lost Words*, and yet, it's clear to me that the open letter struck a nerve, in part, because of the way it fuses unprecedented concern for the environment with entirely precedented generational handwringing over the language and technology usage of young people. People have always worried about how younger generations talk, interact with technology and media, and spend their free time. Plus, previous changes to dictionaries have inspired similar debates about language, which are usually debates about power, because languages are always evolving.

I ordered *The Lost Words* in hopes my children would come to know and care about the plants and animals that surround them, but when it arrived, I began to suspect it was a book made more for adults than young children, finding that it was too big to fit on the nursery bookshelf and perhaps too gilded for little hands still learning to be gentle. So, the book remains, for now, high on a shelf, out of reach. But, when I take it down and we read it together, the book promises my children power: "You hold in your hands a spell book for conjuring back these lost words."

Leafing through its pages in search of magic words that might reverse the loss of insects, it strikes me that even in a book that so nobly seeks to harness the power of language to help children connect to the environment, insects are conspicuously absent.

So, my children and I have learned to look for and identify bugs in our backyard and farther afield—using technology. I am intent on naming the world for them, even when I don't know the words myself. When I open my identification app to review our list of observed species, I can scroll through photos like the one of the false black widow spider in our garage or the mason bee buzzing about the lavender in my kitchen garden or the western tiger swallowtail on the laurel hedge at the playground. A delight, too, to discover together how many things are named for other things: a bird's nest fern, a horse chestnut, a leopard slug, a crab spider.

Once, when I went to take a photo of my daughter, the app was still open. Registering the thick, blonde bangs she cut for herself, it said she was a gilled mushroom.

As a toddler, for months, my daughter persisted in calling every insect—every ladybug, every ant, every spider, every little thing that flew or creeped or crawled across our path or the pages of our books—*bee*.

Each year during our preschool's field trip to the farm, we heard more about bees than any other farm animal. "Most of the produce we eat depends on honey bees," the farmer explained one year to the preschoolers assembled before her on rough-hewn benches. "But the cold, wet spring," she said with a sigh, as she gestured toward the orchard beyond the barn walls, "made it hard for the bees to do their job. And that hurt our apples."

In 2022, a late season cold snap had hampered pollinator activity and damaged apple crops across the state, and the spring's weird weather had persisted into fall. It was such an unseasonably warm October that the strawberry plants in our backyard were still yielding handfuls of ripe fruit, which had stained our fingertips pink before we set out for the field trip to the pumpkin patch.

"Who do you think is the hardest worker on the farm?" the farmer asked, prompting the children to wag their hands above their heads and shout out guesses. "Me," she answered, laughing. "But actually," she clarified, pulling on a honeybee hand puppet, a black glove with tiny, yellow balls of pollen that clung to her fingers, "bees are the hardest workers on the farm."

The honey bees used in commercial agriculture are as intensively managed as any other livestock and trucked around the country to pollinate a wide range of crops, as much as one third of U.S. diets. Because of their importance to our food supply, the movement to save the honey bees took off in the aughts when hives began dying en masse.

Beginning in 2006, commercial beekeepers reported staggering annual losses—about a million colonies, or a third of the U.S.'s hives. Worker bees simply up and vanished, leaving their queen and her brood to perish. There wasn't a name for this uncharacteristic abandonment of their posts, and it didn't resemble any known threat, so at first it was called disappearing disease, then, finally, colony collapse disorder, or CCD.

By 2007, the mysterious beekeeping crisis, and the scientific community's search for answers, was major news and covered in books like *A Fruitless Fall* and *A Spring Without Bees*—titles which seem determined to call to mind Rachel Carson's 1962 *Silent Spring*, her groundbreaking book on the devastating ecological effects of DDT, the first modern synthetic insecticide. DDT was banned a decade after Carson's book was published, but a newer class of pesticides called neonicotinoids—a chemical form of nicotine that is systemically applied to the leaves and seeds of crops like corn and soybeans—emerged as the suspected culprit for CCD.

Like many people, I heard about CCD and developed a newfound appreciation for honey bees. I liked the idea of social insects that work cooperatively for the greater good. I liked that the product of their labor, honey, is a substance as brightly beautiful as it is superfluously sweet. I liked that honey bees organize themselves into matriarchal societies, like elephants and orcas. I liked how the golden jars of wildflower honey I buy at our food co-op shine in the afternoon light. What I'm saying is, how could I not like honey bees?

But in my concern for their well-being, I committed a kind of conceptual flattening by extrapolating what I knew about honey bees to all pollinators. The European honey bee, *Apis mellifera*, isn't native to the United States and most native pollinators have little in common with them—many are solitary creatures who don't produce honey. Though agricultural beekeeping operations continue to experience losses, it's actually native bees that are at the greatest risk of extinction, and in fact these pollinators may be harmed by the widespread efforts of backyard beekeepers to save the honey bees, which compete for food sources.

One such native bee is the endangered rusty-patched bumblebee—whose numbers have plummeted by 87 percent over the last twenty years—not to be confused with the hairy-footed flower bee or the hairy-banded mining bee or the orange-tipped wood-digger bee or the horn-faced mason bee or the brown-belted bumblebee or the red-belted bumblebee or the lemon cuckoo bumblebee or the perplexing bumblebee or any other native bee so charmingly named.

In northwest Illinois, not far from where I grew up, a pair of rusty-patched bumblebees were sighted in Bell Bowl Prairie, a 15-acre strip of undisturbed 8,000-year-old prairie that is owned by Chicago Rockford International Airport. The presence of these endangered native bees was almost enough to save the ancient prairie from being paved over. In the end, the airport bulldozed much of it—leaving just six acres in a state where less than one-hundredth of one percent of its native prairies remain—but the fight to save this ecologically priceless habitat underscores the importance of preserving even small places.

I was familiar with the term "nature deficit disorder" to describe the negative impacts when humans, especially young children, spend less time outdoors and miss the connection to nature they need to thrive. But this term has also been used to describe the general decline in available natural forage for honey bees and native pollinators.

"Sprawl, monocrops, flawless lawns, weedless gardens, and a general decline in pastureland have made it hard for bees to find a suitable diversity of nectar and pollen sources," writes journalist Hannah Nordhaus. To save the bees, native pollinators included, one solution, she says, quoting apiarist Dennis vanEnglesdorp, is to "make meadows, not lawns." This movement seems to be catching on. In the young reader's edition of his book *Nature's Best Hope*, entomologist Douglas W. Tallamy calls for the reclamation of lawns, writing, "What if half of every lawn in the United States was covered with native plants instead of grass—plants that the animals who live there can actually eat? If we did that, we'd create twenty million new acres of land that would be a functioning part of the natural world." To do so, would benefit the entire ecosystem, providing habitat for pollinators but also for the caterpillars that birds and other animals depend on for food. As Tallamy points out, twenty million acres is larger than a dozen national parks combined. And, crucially, these reclaimed lawns would serve as biological corridors, connecting other state parks and nature reserves.

It's an example of a phenomenon activist adrienne maree brown calls emergence. "The crisis is everywhere, massive massive massive.

And we are small," writes brown in their book *Emergent Strategy*, "But emergence notices the way small actions and connections create complex systems, patterns that become ecosystems and societies."

I'm learning to think of our home as a habitat, not just for wildlife, but also for my children. Like insects, children are, in a very real sense, the little things that run the world, and they are similarly underappreciated, considered by many to be pests, more a source of annoyance than wonder, and sought to be brought under control by whatever means possible.

In the epigraph to her book about children's rights, *It's Not Fair*, sociologist Eloise Rickman quotes Eleanor Roosevelt who said, in a 1958 speech commemorating the adoption of the Universal Declaration of Human Rights, "Where, after all, do universal human rights begin? In small places, close to home—so close and so small that they cannot be seen on any maps of the world." Rickman lays out a vision for understanding children's rights and argues that parenting can be a radical act, part of challenging the adultism so pervasive in society. As Rickman defines the term, adultism is "the structural discrimination and oppression children face from adults, and society's bias toward adults." Recognizing the agency and full personhood of children, while acknowledging their vulnerability and need for special protections, Rickman says, would change everything, from ending child poverty to addressing the climate crisis. Rickman's argument for children's liberation goes beyond the right to be safe from corporal punishment and other forms of violence and connects child-rearing practices to social justice issues more broadly. "The roots of much of the violence we see in society can be traced back to the domination, humiliation, and powerlessness so many of us experience as children," she argues.

Adultism takes a deficit-based view of childhood, emphasizing what children lack and framing them as "immature, irrational, and somehow incomplete" subjects who are inferior to adults. And this way of thinking about childhood, influenced by the Christian doctrine of original sin as well as colonialism, has been extended in the United States to justify its oppression of groups deemed inferior and subjected to measures of control. Rickman continues, "Adultism is the first injustice we experience, and it paves the way for all the rest."

When it comes to concrete actions parents can take to combat adultism, Rickman declines to offer prescriptive parenting advice, instead she outlines ten guiding principles, among them: trusting and respecting children, listening to children, accepting that children belong to themselves, welcoming dissent, and apologizing often. These principles run counter to the authoritarian parenting style, which the American Psychological Association (APA) characterizes as a high-control approach that emphasizes obedience, discourages collaboration, restricts child autonomy, and employs harsh punishments. In an age of authoritarianism, choosing to parent in ways that are respectful of children's rights may indeed be a radical act.

All this sounds a lot like gentle parenting, and for her part, Rickman is enthusiastic about the gentle parenting movement and its possibilities for parenting for children's liberation. Despite the extent to which my own parenting practices have been shaped by gentle parenting, I hesitate to suggest that just one parenting philosophy, especially one that is largely associated with white, middle-class, and highly educated parents, offers the way forward into a more just world for children. Plus, as one study found, "Gentle parenting can be really hard on new parents." Instead, I find myself appreciating the perspective of journalist Jessica Grose, who categorizes the two main styles of prescriptive parenting advice as either seeking to control the child or seeking to control the parent—both, it strikes me, are rooted in a deficit model.

As a new parent, I came to feel that the one thing most parenting experts seemed to have in common was that they were keen on monitoring what mothers say to their children. And by adopting the scripts so many experts were imposing onto my parenting, I felt myself begin to lose touch with my own words. Grose offers a much-needed corrective: "The broadest agreement among experts is that what works best is authoritative parenting, described by the APA as parenting that is 'nurturing, responsive and supportive' yet at the same time sets firm limits and boundaries. But there are probably a million ways to authoritatively parent that can be inclusive of and borrow from many styles or methods or none at all."

When I find myself getting too in the weeds with prescriptive parenting advice, I return to one of my favorite parenting books, which argues that parenting books are a terrible invention. In *The Gardener and the Carpenter*, developmental psychologist Alison Gopnik observes that adhering to prescriptive parenting advice doesn't produce measurable outcomes. You just can't find reliable, empirical evidence for causal relationships between the kinds of decisions parents obsess over and the attributes of their adult children. Instead of seeking to parent with precision and control, Gopnik advises parents to, instead, think about their task as that of a gardener making a meadow. Writes Gopnik:

> In England, that land of gardeners, they use the term "hothousing" to refer to the kind of anxious middle-class parenting that Americans call helicoptering. But consider creating a meadow or a hedgerow or a cottage garden. The glory of a meadow is its messiness. . . . [A] good garden is constantly changing, as it adapts to the changing circumstances of the weather and the seasons. And in the long run, that kind of varied, flexible, complex, dynamic system

will be more robust and adaptable than the most carefully tended hothouse bloom.

I am drawn to this alternative to control—one that seems to offer liberation to both children and parents. I read this as an invitation to step outside the borders of rigidly defined parenting philosophies and embrace instead the messiness and adaptability needed to provide an environment in which my children can thrive.

These days, in parenting as in gardening, I am aiming to make meadows, not lawns.

Last summer, while my oldest attended an outdoor day camp about "incredible insects," I spent the week rereading Rachel Carson's *Silent Spring*, a book that issued a clarion call for a ceasefire in what she called "man's war against nature." I already knew to brace myself for the apocalyptic vision unveiled in its first chapter, "A Fable for Tomorrow." But what I hadn't noticed previously was Carson's invocation of magic to suggest the severity of DDT's impact on the environment. The opening scene tells of an idyllic small town with its checkerboard of prosperous farms. But its harmony and beauty is soon marred by a strange blight that creeps across the landscape.

"Some evil spell had settled on the community," Carson writes, before describing the missing birds and bees, the fruitless apple trees, the chickens and pigs unable to bear young, and the lost laughter of children at play—the latter as much a part of the natural world as any other animal sound. Ultimately, she concludes, "No witchcraft, no enemy action has silenced the rebirth of new life in this stricken world. The people had done it themselves."

This fictional town was based on Carson's factual reporting of real-life disasters caused by the widespread, indiscriminate use of chlorinated hydrocarbon insecticides. It's a paradox that our food supply and public health depends so much on preserving some insects, while controlling others. But, Carson concludes her book with alternatives to the broad application of chemical controls she likens to a "crude weapon" that we've "hurled at the fabric of life."

Many credit Carson's writing with launching the contemporary environmental movement in the United States and leading to the creation of the Environmental Protection Agency and its decades of progress in improving air and water quality. But perhaps her most paradigm-shifting contribution has been in contributing to our understanding of the relationship between humans and the environment. "*Silent Spring* proved that our bodies are not boundaries. Chemical corruption of the globe affects us from conception to death," writes Carson biographer Linda Lear.

When it comes to ecological interdependence, our bodies are not boundaries, nor are our backyards or fences or borders. In my family, we are learning to share our home with the more-than-human world, to live as part of it instead of seeking to control it or master it. Carson's preferred metaphor for this ecological view of the world was to speak of the "web of life."

Carson died of breast cancer shortly after the publication of *Silent Spring*. At the time of her death, she was working on a book—inspired by her relationship with her nephew, Roger, whom she adopted when he was orphaned at age five—based on an essay called "Help Your Child to Wonder." In it, she tells stories of taking Roger to the beach and on walks through the woods near her home in Maine. But she clarifies that she didn't interfere with his exploring by lecturing him about the natural world and identifying each plant and animal they encountered. Rather, she prioritized his experience of the natural world over developing his expertise.

Her point rings true today that parents needn't be naturalists to have these kinds of transformative encounters with their own children. Even if we cannot name what we see, we can be moved by wonder to care about it. Wonder comes first through our senses, she seems to say, through being present with our children and experiencing nature together.

Still, researchers have observed that young children have extensive animal vocabularies, which isn't necessarily what you'd expect, since most children aren't surrounded by animals in their home environments, nor are these words simple to say or used often in everyday speech. Instead, they believe it has to do with how frequently and how reverently adults call children's attention to the natural world. One study on language acquisition and biophilia—Wilson's term for humans' love for the natural world—analyzed transcripts of parents speaking with their children. It found that when adults say "look," nearly half the time they are directing the child's attention to an animal.

Psycholinguist Jean Burko Gleason, the study's author, argues that language acquisition is a joint activity between parents and children, having as much to do with what is innate within children as what is innate within their nurturing adults. "The point is that we have an enormous connection to the rest of the living world and that we love the living world," she says, of young children's animal lexicons. "We love animals and we love plants. And this is reflected in what we are doing with children."

For many parents, that love is often tinged with grief, as we remember the fireflies of our own childhoods and look up to find them missing from our children's summer skies. Carson believed that wonder was a force powerful enough to break the evil spell of humanity's determination to control nature, destroying it, and ourselves, in the process.

"It seems reasonable to believe that the more clearly we can focus our attention on the wonders and realities of the universe about us, the less taste we shall have for the destruction of our race," she said in a 1952 speech. "Wonder and humility are wholesome emotions, and they do not exist side by side with a lust for destruction."

Near the end of *Silent Spring*, Carson quotes the Dutch biologist C. J. Briejèr, who said, "The insect world is nature's most astonishing phenomenon. Nothing is impossible to it; the most improbable things commonly occur there. One who penetrates deeply into its mysteries is continually breathless with wonder. He knows that anything can happen, and that the completely impossible often does."

Perhaps nowhere is this truth about the power of little things—small creatures, small places, small actions—to make a massive impact more evident than in the insect world.

In the weeks following bug camp, my daughter and I began reading E. B. White's *Charlotte's Web* at bedtime. I chose this classic because I remembered the pleasant company of the farm animals and my fondness for the little girl, Fern, and the spider, Charlotte, who work together to save Wilbur, a pig who is the runt of his litter. Because like Charlotte, I am so often searching for the right words to save what I love.

I did not remember the novel's startling first line: "Where's Papa going with that ax?" And, for the sake of bedtime, I confess that I sometimes attempted to soften the subject of Wilbur's fate whenever it was discussed violently and insensitively, especially by the ornery old sheep, but I trust that someday my daughter will read this novel for herself without my interference as editor. Even so, my daughter understood the threat of that ax and expressed her empathy for Wilbur as clearly as her willingness to believe in the talking animals who populate so many of her books. When asked to theorize about the insect and rodent protagonists in children's books like *Charlotte's Web*, author Kate DiCamillo replied, "It's because that's how we treat kids . . . you're in the way, you're small, you're powerless, and it feels very familiar to a kid."

In the novel, language is a tool wielded skillfully by the small and the powerless. The words Charlotte weaves into her web are a protective spell that leads the farmer and his family to preserve Wilbur's life, they are an incantation and an invitation to awe. Townspeople gather around the web, taking it to be a miracle, and the local preacher admonishes his congregants to "always be on the watch for the coming of wonders."

For a time, my daughter and I lived in the aftermath of the miracle, watching for wonder—we hadn't yet reached the novel's end. Though Wilbur's life was preserved, my daughter did not anticipate Charlotte's death, nor that her many children would balloon away from the farm, carrying something of her magic with them into the air. I did not keep the novel's grief from her, because grief is as much a part of the web of life as wonder. This tension is one of life's hardest truths and one of the book's most stunning accomplishments. DiCamillo calls this balancing act the "sacred task of telling stories for the young."

After dinner one night, I sat on our living room floor beside my children, reading aloud the novel's final chapters while they constructed tiny worlds with Playmobil. At first, they were caught up in their play, chattering and interrupting to ask questions, but eventually they fell under the novel's spell. I had to pause to clear my throat when I read Wilbur's final good-bye to Charlotte, and again, when Charlotte's children set out their draglines to drift off into the world where they would make their own webs.

By the time, we reached the last page, which memorializes Charlotte and the miracle of her web, my children had settled into my lap, my daughter with tears in her eyes. "Are you sad, Mama," she asked. I nodded.

"But I'm happy, too," I said.

We hugged, the three of us, and then, my children scampered off to wrestle on the couch before bathtime.

The question for all of us is, says DiCamillo, is: "How do we tell the truth and make that truth bearable?" I think the answer may have something to do with connection, with the gentleness with which we hold each other's hands in the face of it.

It was a fall morning, several years ago, when my daughter paused at the back door and took in the thick fog that had rolled in off the coast to blanket our yard. For a moment, fear flickered across her face. She was afraid to step off the deck and out into the fog. It was as if she'd woken to find our house had magically been swept up into the clouds.

"Come on, it's alright," I said, offering my hand, and down the steps she hopped, rainboots on the wrong feet.

We stepped into the fog together, and she said, "I want to touch the ground."

"Well, you should touch it," I said.

And then, looking at the low-slung clouds stretching out in front of her, she said, "I want to touch the sky."

"You should," I said, only quieter this time, watching as she reached out a hand to the air.

We set off down the sidewalk—walking beside the fence where native plants would someday bloom—and I noticed a spider web stretching between the window of a parked car and its sideview mirror, each strand magnificently pronounced by the fog, weighty and glistening. I picked her up so she could see it.

The web did not spell out *terrific* or *radiant* or even *humble* but, all the same, we were entranced, under its spell.

"I want to touch it," she said.

"I know, but let's leave it. That's the spider's home," I explained, thinking about how, like our words, our hands can harm or heal, about the power of small creatures, small places.

And together, we walked on in the fog, feeling ourselves to be quite little in a big world.

On Mother Trees

Years ago, I sent a copy of *The Giving Tree* to a pregnant family member. Though I hadn't read the picture book since childhood, I recognized the cheerful green of its cover and vaguely remembered it being about a boy who loved a tree. A classic with an environmental message, I thought, as I typed in the shipping address along with a short congratulatory note.

It wasn't until I became a parent years later that I read the book again, a gift for my own firstborn. On the cover was a little boy in red overalls looking up at a tree. A leafy branch reached down to offer a round red apple. The boy held out his hands, wanting.

I turned to the first page. "Once there was a tree . . ." By the book's end, there was a stump. I brought my fingertip to the page, following the circles of its rings. The little boy had grown into a man who took and took and took from the tree he claimed to love. Horrified that I had ever sent this gift to a new parent, I closed the book and tucked it away in the back of a closet, where I knew my daughter would not find it. But as I went about my day, its final line returned to me: "And the tree was happy."

This was not the relationship to the natural world I wanted for myself or my children. And, in early motherhood, when so much was being asked of me, I feared what would happen if I too gave of myself until not much remained. Had I once believed that this is what it meant to love?

Where I live, in winter, maples, cottonwoods, and cedars shrug over the shingled rooftops of bungalows and craftsmen, holding up the low, gray rain clouds. Shortly after my first child was born, it was these neighborhood trees that helped me to recognize how motherhood had begun to change me.

My daughter was about a week old when we took our first walk. The winter air felt cold and wet after days spent indoors with the thermostat set higher than usual because I worried about keeping her warm enough. I wanted to do something normal, a walk around the neighborhood. I was too exhausted, too anxious to attempt baby-wearing, so I left the long, cumbersome cloth wrap wadded up on the sofa and instead slowly buckled my daughter into her infant car seat, then struggled to connect the car seat to the stroller attachments, eventually ceding the task to my husband. Before setting off, I tied a knit cap under her chin and bundled her up with a blanket.

The walk was more for me than for my daughter, since she was still unable to take in the sights of our neighborhood. When they are newborns, babies are nearsighted; they can only see as far as the face of the person holding them. Every two hours I would bring my daughter to my chest to feed her, and we'd meet each other's gaze. I spent much of my time, day and night, bending my head toward her, guiding her as she latched, assessing the position of her chin and lips, searching for signs of swallowing.

Out on the slushy sidewalk, it took time for my eyes to adjust to daylight and distance. When I looked up, it was the overwhelming sight of treetops—a sight I can still see if I close my eyes, the clarity of dark branches against a milky sky—that made me realize my own nearsightedness, born of love. Since the night of my daughter's birth, I had only been looking down at what I was holding closest.

By spring, I blinked and I could sense the myopia of early motherhood clearing. I began to crave the expansiveness of the sea, the sight of a distant horizon.

We took our daughter with us on short hikes through coastal forests, walking together beneath Douglas fir and western red cedar.

That fall, I held my daughter and listened as an activist warned of the threat that droughts and heat waves pose to the trees I've come to love, a die-off that climate scientists refer to as Firmageddon.

Six months into the pandemic, my daughter was approaching her second birthday, and I was preparing for the start of a new academic term by reading about a tree I thought of as the Giving Tree's opposite.

I'd assigned my place-based literature students Jenny Odell's account of a beloved tree called Old Survivor, found in the introduction to *How to Do Nothing*. Her book isn't actually an argument for doing nothing, but instead a critique of technocapitalism and its relentlessly extractive monopolization of our time, attention, and labor. Odell points to Old Survivor, a coastal redwood and the last old-growth tree of its kind in San Francisco's East Bay hills as an example of refusing the terms of productivity, of "surviving usefulness." Evidently Old Survivor's unruly shape and its location on a rocky slope made it undesirable to loggers, who deemed it unusable. Its apparent uselessness is what allowed it to survive. For Odell, Old Survivor is a model for what she calls "resisting in place," which she defines as making "oneself into a shape that cannot so easily be appropriated by a capitalist value system."

Rather than giving ourselves over to apps and algorithms, Odell makes an argument not for dropping out of modern society altogether, as in the back-to-the-land movement of the 1960s, but instead for dropping *into* local networks of people, things, and places. For an alternative to the attention economy, she points to bioregionalism, an environmental philosophy that emphasizes strengthening relationships between people and places in ways that are just, democratic, and importantly, sustainable for all life-forms within a bioregion. In other words, she calls for us to disconnect in order to reconnect. Throughout her book, Odell urges readers to put down our screens, if only temporarily, in order to move outward and downward, to cultivate an attentiveness to place, to discover a rootedness through which we might "resist in place."

In doing so, Odell suggests, we might reclaim activities that aren't valued by the metrics of productivity—activities that maintain and sustain life despite their unprofitability, like cooking and cleaning and caregiving, but also like making art and tending to community gardens and public spaces. To do so is to resist a "capitalist perception of time, place, self, and community." Ultimately, Odell argues, the effect might be restorative, one with the potential to ripple outward, in that it may "restore individuals who can then help restore communities, human and beyond."

The first time I read Odell's book, I found myself thinking about how capitalism devalues the labor of caregiving and how patriarchy insists that women should perform this care work without fair compensation or community support, and wondered if bioregionalism might offer alternatives for resisting other extractive systems. During the pandemic, additional questions came to the fore. Like, what lessons might Old Survivor's "resisting in place" hold for those of us who were now sheltering in place?

Though I was enthusiastic about reading Odell's book with my students, part of me came to subtly resent its title. I'd assigned it at a time when my husband and I were both working full-time from home without childcare, a time when the attention economy felt inescapable as we turned to our screens for nearly everything, a time when I felt more cut off from our community than ever before, when so much of the world had ground to a halt, but doing nothing was the one thing I could not afford to do.

I knew that I had it good in so many ways—we hadn't lost our jobs, we could isolate safely at home, my husband was a capable partner and co-parent who joined me in cooking, cleaning, and caring for our daughter, and, as the pandemic stretched on, a friend we'd formed a bubble with eventually began to watch my daughter a few hours a week while I logged onto Zoom and taught university classes. And still, working full-time without childcare, managing all this amid unfolding, intersecting crises left me exhausted and wondering how other people, especially those in much more challenging circumstances, were doing it.

The pandemic disrupted our careful efforts to split household tasks equitably. Suddenly, my husband and I were trying to coordinate our workdays without the handful of college students we had previously relied on to babysit. Since my work as an adjunct was flexible and low-paying, I took to working whenever our daughter slept, working during nap times, working in the hours after she went to bed—hoping she'd sleep through the night—and working again in the hours before she woke. My work schedule felt unpredictable, determined entirely by my parenting responsibilities. I had to adjust whenever my daughter was teething or going through a sleep regression or simply in need of additional cuddles and reassurances—all the totally normal variabilities that come with toddlerhood.

One afternoon, in an attempt at self-care, I found a short yoga video on YouTube, rolled out my mat in our sunroom, and went through the motions while my daughter crawled and played around me. I tried to follow the sequence of poses, to settle into the flow of it, but I had to keep pausing the video to hand her a toy from the shelf, to reply to her chatter, to soothe her. At the end of the video,

I stood on one foot in tree pose, arms raised above my head, trying to balance, trying to find equanimity, while my daughter wrapped herself around my leg.

I loved my family, I loved my work, I loved my students. And yet I was tired of being useful, of giving until my resources were depleted. I was tired of trying to coax my daughter to sleep so that her naps would coincide with Zoom meetings, tired of sending emails assuring everyone that, of course, I was happy to help.

I was helpful, but unlike the giving tree, I was not entirely happy.

My daughter and I walked nearly every day during the first year of the pandemic. It was a way to safely leave the house, to pass the long and sometimes lonely hours, to see beyond the confines of our house and backyard fence. Together, we marked the changing seasons by the neighborhood trees.

We walked by playgrounds that were closed off with caution tape, we walked to bring flowers to friends' doorsteps, we walked to a Black Lives Matter vigil. Sometimes we walked multiple times a day. Sometimes a neighbor saw us coming and crossed the street to avoid close contact. Sometimes I pushed our stroller down the sidewalk, weeping silently, out of my daughter's sight. Sometimes I held my daughter's hand and we progressed at a toddler's pace, stopping to notice every little thing.

At the same time, I was noticing even more about our neighborhood by reading a weekly email bulletin compiled by a neighbor who had spent twenty years facilitating exchanges about lost items, garage sales, and neighborhood events, as well as information about voting, emergency preparedness, and community service. I'd subscribed to her emails since moving to the neighborhood, but during the pandemic they became a vital source of information that kept me feeling grounded and connected to the people around me even as we practiced social distancing. This was not a coincidence. Once, when I asked what motivated her volunteer efforts, she told me that she worried less about disasters and emergencies because she knew her neighbors by name and knew how to reach them. She had the foresight to build a small-scale, free social network that her neighborhood could rely on in crisis.

It was exactly the kind of unprofitable alternative to the attention economy I understood Odell to be describing in her book. Even though I was reading my neighbor's emails on my phone and laptop, they invited me to pause from my scrolling and connect to something else, something that was still engaged with all that mattered to me, but in a way that felt more actionable, more embodied, more ecological.

Through my neighbor's postings, I joined the so-called soup brigade, which worked with mutual aid groups to distribute regular meals to a large encampment of people who were unhoused and occupying the grounds in front of city hall to protest the housing crisis. Once a week, I made several large pots of soup and delivered it for lunch the next day. Sometimes while I worked, my husband made the soup, sometimes my daughter helped us, pouring cans of beans and broth into the pot, stirring it with a wooden spoon.

While it wasn't exactly restful and didn't look like self-care, volunteering was restorative in its own way, allowing me to put my energies toward moving outward and more deeply into my community. I couldn't control what was happening in our nation's capital, but I could help feed the people gathered at our city hall, and that was something.

While lesson planning, I underlined a line in Odell's book, "A simple refusal motivates my argument: refusal to believe that the present time and place, and the people who are here with us, are somehow not enough."

Without realizing it, the walks I'd begun taking in desperation had changed me. Somehow, even in a time of isolation, I was forming deeper connections to my local community—to people and places—just by leaving our house and moving through our neighborhood. What I was paying attention to was changing.

By walking, I was doing the kind of meaningful nothing Odell extolls when she writes, "I propose that rerouting and deepening one's attention to place will likely lead to awareness of one's participation in history and in a more-than-human community."

My daughter and I continued to walk together. One day the sidewalks were covered in chalk art, a socially distant DIY art festival. One day the branches of a small magnolia tree were laden with handmade cloth masks, free for the taking. One day we noticed a new mural installed on the side of a musical instrument shop; it featured messages about climate change from local schoolchildren: *Habitat loss makes me furious. Heartbroken. Disgusted. Scared.*

My daughter and I walked together until it was early autumn and wildfire smoke forced us indoors for weeks, our walks on hold while distant forests smoldered. I felt confined and on edge. Even though the fires were at a distance, my body judged the smoke a threat. Just as my students and I were reading about Old Survivor, the air-quality index spiked to hazardous levels—which kept us indoors, moving our air purifier with us from room to room. The smoke was one of the many problems about which it felt like I could do very little, maybe even nothing, as I pondered what it means to resist in place.

Once the rain returned to the Pacific Northwest and the wildfire smoke cleared, we resumed our daily walks. One winter morning, I pushed the stroller through a fine mist while listening to a podcast about the work of Suzanne Simard. Working in the old-growth forests of nearby British Columbia, Simard was among the first researchers to use Western science to demonstrate that trees communicate with one another through a mycorrhizal network that mirrors our own neural networks. Her findings, nicknamed the "wood wide web," suggest that a forest may act as a single organism, connected for interspecies cooperation rather than competition.

Simard calls the oldest trees in a forest "mother trees," named for the way they nurture nearby seedlings by distributing carbon and water, alerting them to threats, and caring for them in distress. When I heard this, I reached in my coat pocket for my phone and removed a glove with my teeth, swiping the rain-splattered screen to rewind.

As I listened, I found myself thinking more deeply about our neighborhood trees, wondering what networks might be humming beneath my feet, whether their ties might be severed by the construction of neighborhoods like mine.

I also thought of my neighbor, who had worked for years to create and maintain connections with her neighbors to facilitate the exchange of information and resources. And, I thought of the people who have mothered me, among them several older friends and neighbors who walked alongside me and my stroller during the pandemic while my own mother was thousands of miles away. They could not change the difficulty of our circumstances, but I was nonetheless grateful for their care.

Around the time that the podcast about Simard's work aired, *The New York Times* launched its primal scream hotline, to record the distress of parents who were struggling to manage the responsibilities of working and caregiving. Mothers barely holding it together were planning meetups just to scream.

I did not phone in to the hotline, but I listened to their cries for help, and on several occasions I sat in my car and joined along in frustration. My mom friends and I helped each other as best we could, but each of us, in different ways, needed more support than we could give.

In an interview, Simard critiques Western approaches to forest management, saying, "When we manage ecosystems . . . it's like we manage them just to survive. We don't manage them to flourish. We push them to the brink of collapse . . . tak[ing] as much as we possibly can." But there are other approaches to forestry. In an ongoing collaborative experiment called the Mother Tree Project, Simard studies alternatives to clear-cutting in which the mother trees are preserved rather than harvested. The project emerges from partnerships with First Nations and offers possibilities for sustainable stewardship of forest ecosystems.

Hearing this, I thought of the forest ecosystems under threat as climate-exacerbated droughts and heat waves make for longer, more intense wildfire seasons.

I thought of the boy who grew up to be a man who took and took from the tree he loved.

And I thought of our society's myopic focus on the nuclear family, how mothers, in particular, are pushed to the brink of collapse by extractive structures, how difficult it is for mothers—especially single parents, women of color, and immigrants—to flourish.

I want a sustainable approach to mothering, I thought, as I pushed the stroller. I want us to organize ourselves with the wisdom of the forest.

Remarking on pandemic parenting, sociologist Jessica Calarco put it this way: "Other countries have social safety nets. The U.S. has women." Her words became a rallying cry for exhausted caregivers across the country. Throughout her book, which draws on more than 400 hours of interviews with struggling parents, Calarco argues that in order to create a society where people can "live with dignity from birth until natural death" we need to fund and build high-quality public systems of care: healthcare, childcare, education, and care for the elderly and disabled. Rather than replace how care flows through networks of families and friends, these systems would strengthen them and shore them up in times of stress.

She also calls for policies that "care for the people who care" by closing gaps that allow employers to deny contingent workers coverage and by solving for the problems that frustrated working parents face, year after year, like the challenges of finding after-school care or affordable programming for summer breaks. "This is the world we ought to be imagining," she concludes. "A world where we hold it *together* rather than pretending we can hold it together on our own."

To return to Odell, we need to value the kind of care work that our economy deems unproductive and unprofitable. Care that can't be optimized or scaled for growth, and yet is essential for maintaining and sustaining life. Care that connects us not just to our immediate family members, but to our friends, neighbors, and community, human and beyond. If we can make that world a reality, it strikes me that the kinds of cultural shifts required to solve the care crisis will necessarily address the climate crisis, because the root causes are the same—namely white supremacy, heteropatriarchy, colonialism, and capitalism—these forces which keep us from acting cooperatively and realizing our interdependence.

As the pandemic waned, the encampment at city hall was eventually forcibly swept, but the mutual aid network of people who provide meals persists and the visibility of that protest made an impact. Through a ballot measure, our county established a healthy children's fund to expand access to childcare and early childhood education, especially for children experiencing housing insecurity. Its implementation hasn't been without bureaucratic challenges, but already it has increased behavioral and mental health and disability services for vulnerable children and their families and created emergency childcare vouchers for parents in crisis.

While we imagine and work toward a society that cares for those who care, in the meantime, we can challenge ourselves to practice the kinds of creative and countercultural community care that Mia Birdsong describes in her book *How We Show Up*:

> We are living in a contradiction—we are made for interdependence, connection, and love, but part of a culture that espouses the opposite... There is a tension between existing in one world while trying to live into another one. That place in between them is full of friction. But like so many change processes, the thing we are trying to get to holds the key to getting there. Reclaiming and reinventing family, friendship, and community is a process we do *with our family, friends, and community*.

Since we've been able to return to normal socializing, I've noticed among my friends a desire to be more intentional about nurturing friendships. One friend issued a weekly standing invitation, which she thinks of as her office hours, for fellow parents and kids to drop by and visit. Another opens her backyard on Friday afternoons in the summer for kids to play on the swings and run through the sprinkler while the adults visit, and we all pitch in for dinner, taking turns making pots of mac and cheese and bringing juice boxes and carrot sticks. Especially for parents, like my husband and me, who don't have extended family in town, these connections make a difference.

These are the people we swap childcare with on snow days, with whom we exchange meals during sickness and surgeries, whose names and numbers I write down as my children's secondary emergency contacts. My hope is that as we strengthen existing networks of care and reexamine our regard for the people who perform the essential labor of care work, who tend to and keep our families and communities connected, who devote their lives to holding it all together—especially mothers, grandmothers, and childcare providers—it may also lead to shifts in how we regard the planet that nurtures us.

Sometimes loggers leave what is called a timber curtain, a scrim of trees that gives the appearance that a forest has not been clear-cut. Society has long upheld the timber curtain that obscures the realities of motherhood that lie beyond the myth. If anything, the pandemic has torn down the timber curtain to expose the conditions of mothering—how we undervalue and exploit those who perform care work—that have existed all along.

In *The Giving Tree*, the boy who loves the tree visits her every day to play and eat apples. As a child, he gathers her leaves so that he can play king of the forest. This way of relating to the natural world carries him into adulthood. As he ages, he takes the apples to sell for cash, takes the branches to build a house, takes the trunk to sail away. In the end, he returns to sit on the remaining stump.

Someday I may read the picture book to my children, perhaps when they are old enough to grieve for the tree and discuss its plight. I will close the book and ask them, "But do you think that, in the end, the tree was truly happy? Did the boy really love the tree?"

I haven't told you yet about my favorite tree. The decades-old fig tree in our front yard, the one I think of when I see the stump in the picture book.

When the fig tree was ripe, my husband and daughter would stand in the yard picking figs, handing them to me through an open window. I was pregnant with our son then, and the figs were a welcome indulgence. We had so much fruit that I struggled to keep up with the boxes softening on our kitchen counter, attracting fruit flies, and I worried they were going to waste. I canned what I could, making jam with my daughter and experiencing a strange yearning to somehow preserve something of her, too, something more tangible than photographs. And then I placed the rest of the figs on our front yard with a sign that said, FREE.

Within an hour, the remaining figs were gone.

The following spring, just one leaf unfurled on the fig tree; the rest of its branches remained bare. On a warm day, I looked out the window and the tree looked as it had in winter. Though it had stood for decades, I suspected the year of extreme weather, of once-in-a-millennia heat, once-in-a-century flooding, and record-breaking cold had been too much for it to survive.

I stayed inside, nursing my son, while my husband used a chainsaw to bring down the leafless branches. I was grateful that he could fell it for us, but I couldn't bear to witness him cutting it into pieces. We mourned our loss together, talking of the fruit trees we would someday plant in its place.

In a gesture of consolation, my neighbor, who has lived in this neighborhood for longer than I've been alive, walked across the street when his own tree ripened, delivering a box of fresh figs. By the next year, his fig tree, too, would be gone.

In her memoir, *Finding the Mother Tree*, Simard writes of a sweet spot at the dripline of a mature Douglas fir where water falls from its outermost needles. Directly below its canopy, the ground is bare. Nothing grows there. Its crown above and its roots below gather the nutrients the tree needs to survive. But at the dripline, close enough to share resources without starving the mother tree, seedlings take root.

The sweet spot is what many of us are still searching for, I think. Simard concludes that chapter reflecting on her own difficulties attempting to balance work and motherhood. It occurs to me that when it comes to mothering, the sweet spot may only be achievable when we recognize our interdependence and take efforts to "resist in place"; in other words, to grow in places and in shapes that disrupt our exploitation, to look up from our screens and pay attention to the places where we live embodied lives alongside other bodies, to nurture and value these connections while engaging in mutual aid and collective care.

At the kitchen table, I hold my son in my lap while my daughter draws a map of the neighborhood, marking out where her friends live and which trees have the sweetest apples. Last year, she found one tree in particular that produced delicious apples that no one else seemed to want, and she returned to it often. Once, when our fridge was empty of produce, she outfitted herself in her raincoat and set out on her tricycle to fill her basket with apples.

I'm reminded of what trees, and mothers, both, can teach us about the abundance and reciprocity that Robin Wall Kimmerer describes in *The Serviceberry*. Kimmerer cites feminist thinkers like Genevieve Vaughan and Miki Kashtan who have theorized the "maternal gift economy," which is rooted in the generosity of mothers. Writes Kimmerer, "The currency of this economy is the flow of gratitude, the flow of love, literally in support of life."

I do not begrudge my children what I give to them; I'm grateful for how mothering has altered my vision, how I am still learning what it means to love, to give generously to those closest to me and those at a distance. And, what's also true, is that it's my love for myself and for my children that compels me to refuse to be consumed by motherhood, that insists I work toward a home, and a society, where an equitable division of household labor is the norm, where parents and families have the structural support they need to thrive.

There are two jars of fig jam remaining in our pantry, golden and flecked with fruit flesh. For breakfast I open a jar and spread it thick on a buttered slice of toast. I know that, like the fig tree, a changing climate will take from me more of what I love, what I cannot protect. When that happens, I hope my neighbors will have fruit enough to share. Warm and sweet, I take a bite that reminds me of a tree I truly loved, of something I preserved before I knew it was gone for good.

Predictive Text

It was a five-hour drive to the coast, where we were camping at Cape Disappointment on Washington state's Long Beach Peninsula. The final hour, as my husband navigated the two-lane highway that curves in and out of dark, damp forests and through logging towns and fishing villages, I sat in the back, wedged between car seats, with a plastic bag at the ready in case my daughter's car sickness overtook her. It was early autumn and rain streaked the windows, which were cracked open to let in fresh salt air. The occasional rain drop struck my cheek as I leaned toward my daughter, stroking her face and rubbing her back.

It was still raining by the time we reached our campsite. I stood in the downpour in my boots and coat, waving directions to my husband as he parked our tent trailer—backing it into the muddy space between a boulder and a wooden picnic table covered in pine needles. He got to work popping up the camper and fitting together the supports for its canvas bunk ends, while I set off with the kids, who were then five and two, to find the restrooms.

While I stood, holding the door open, waiting for them to finish washing their hands, I scanned the announcements and fliers pinned to the bulletin board. An evacuation map caught my eye. It read: A STRONG OFFSHORE EARTHQUAKE WILL GENERATE A TSUNAMI. IF YOU FEEL THE GROUND SHAKE OR HEAR THE SIREN, GO TO HIGH GROUND IMMEDIATELY.

I put my finger to the map and traced the solid line that marked the long, winding road leading out of the state park to higher ground. A small note beside the map added an ominous warning: "You will have 15 minutes between the start of an earthquake and the arrival of a tsunami."

I snapped a picture with my phone, recognizing that in the unlikely event we needed the map, we wouldn't have time to stop and consult it. "What's that say?" my daughter asked, shaking the remaining soap and water from her hands and squinting up at the sign.

"Um, it's a map," I said, pausing as my thoughts flashed forward to bedtime, when fears of an earthquake and tsunami might keep us both awake. "With directions out of the park."

I held my son's hand on the walk back to our campsite, and my daughter skipped ahead, splashing through puddles. Looking up at the rain clouds, I noticed the tsunami siren towering over the treetops.

After we finished making our beds and setting up camp, we ate a quick lunch of sandwiches and chips and settled in for an afternoon nap to wait out the rain, which was still dripping from the shore pines onto the camper.

I closed my eyes and tried to remember what I'd read about the catastrophic megaquake and tsunami predicted, with an alarming degree of certainty, to someday devastate the Pacific Northwest. I knew that "the big one," a 9.0-magnitude earthquake, was overdue. I'd never been able to forget a particularly foreboding line from Kathryn Schulz's reporting for the *New Yorker*. She interviewed a FEMA representative who said that, when the big one strikes, "everything west of Interstate 5 will be toast." Everything west of I-5, meaning Portland, Seattle, and Vancouver, meaning the state park where we were camping, meaning home.

A decade before our camping trip, shortly after moving to Washington state and beginning graduate school, I was browsing our local bookstore when I picked up a copy of Sandi Doughton's *Full Rip 9.0*, about the geologists who uncovered the history of the region's active fault lines and the emergency planners who are now tasked with guiding communities in preparing for the unthinkable.

I remembered watching news footage, horrified, of the 9.0 magnitude quake and tsunami that struck Japan's Tōhoku region in March 2011, killing nearly twenty thousand people and triggering a nuclear power disaster. I didn't know, at the time, that I would come to live near a similar fault. I tore through the book in one sitting, trying to understand the seismic risks of my new home.

The Pacific Northwest was once thought to be seismologically quiet, despite that earthquake and flood stories are common throughout the region's Indigenous oral traditions, stories that settlers dismissed. But in the 1980s, a scientist tasked with assessing hazards for the construction of a nuclear power plant discovered evidence of a history of megaquakes along the undersea Cascadia subduction zone—a tectonic plate boundary located roughly 70 miles offshore, which extends from northern California to British Columbia. It's where the Juan de Fuca tectonic plate is sliding beneath the North American plate. The fault is stuck and has been quiet for three long centuries, and when it slips, it could unleash a megaquake that would displace huge quantities of oceanwater. A full rip, experts say, will shake the earth for five terrifying minutes. Following the quake, tsunami waves, up to 100 feet in height, maybe more, will slam the coast within minutes, inundating the landscape, flooding coastal villages, reservations, ports, and beaches, including the peninsula where we were camping.

My thoughts turned to the evacuation map. It was unlikely that the sole road out of the campground would withstand minutes of intense shaking, conditions which could cause the ground to experience soil liquefaction. Plus, scientists predict that parts of the coastline could sink by up to seven feet, leaving some areas submerged before the first waves ever arrive.

Once all that shaking stopped, we could try to run on foot, carrying our children, to higher ground, but it seemed impossible that we'd ever make it to the basalt rock cliffs that overlooked the beach, navigating an unfamiliar route over buckled roads and felled trees, possibly in the dark.

How fast and how far could we run?

I heard my son stirring from his nap. I lay still with my eyes closed, listening as my husband helped him into his rain jacket and shoes, heard the soft squeak of the camper screen door opening, then closing.

I woke, later, to the sound of knocking.

"Hey, you've got to come see this," my husband whispered through the screen door, our son in his arms.

The rain had stopped, and the sun was breaking through the clouds. I woke my daughter and we slipped on our shoes to follow my husband and son down a shaded dirt path through the forest. At the edge of the trees, there was a small rise where the path crested between swaying grasses and deposited us onto a sandy beach.

As a family, we'd spent countless hours along the inland shores of the Salish Sea, but my children had never before witnessed the open ocean. My son toddled after my daughter as she ran barefoot toward the surf, stopping just out of reach of the waves washing ashore, standing with her arms outstretched, wonderstruck by the immensity of it, the wind tangling her hair.

"It could be ten minutes from now, or it could hold off until today's toddlers are great-grandparents," writes Doughton, noting that earthquakes are the most difficult disaster to prepare for because they come with little warning and "operate on a time scale that's both inevitable and inscrutable."

Taking into account 10,000 years of geologic evidence, scientists have determined that the average recurrence of a Cascadia earthquake on the order of 8.0 magnitude is about once every 250 years. It's been 325 years since the Cascadia subduction zone's last megaquake, and the converging plates have been deadlocked ever since. Scientists put the risk of a big quake occurring within the next 50 years at one in three. The chances of a full rip within that same time frame are, by some estimates, one in seven.

I don't know what to do with these odds.

"The Cascadia situation, a calamity in its own right, is also a parable for this age of ecological reckoning, and the questions it raises are ones that we all now face," writes Schulz. "How should a society respond to a looming crisis of uncertain timing but of catastrophic proportions? How can it begin to right itself when its entire infrastructure and culture developed in a way that leaves it profoundly vulnerable to natural disaster?"

Questions such as these are enormously difficult for any society to answer, and they may be even more confounding for individuals. How should the risks posed by natural disasters and climate change shape the decisions my husband and I make, especially ones that impact our children's lives?

Where my family and I live, we are less likely to be inundated by the tsunami waves that imperil coastal communities, and those that reach our city's waterfront will take at least two hours to arrive. But the threat of a catastrophic megathrust quake, one that would cut off critical access points to our entire region, remains ever present. I've grown accustomed to the risks of living here, probably due to a kind of necessary cognitive dissonance, but whenever I drive past signs designating tsunami evacuation routes, like the ones near our favorite beach, I'm reminded of the upheaval that could happen at any moment.

In these moments, I'm left wondering, what does it mean to make a home and raise children in a place that's overdue for disaster?

"[W]e humans are bad at understanding uncertainty," is what the *New York Times* had to say about the problem of forecasting presidential elections. The postmortem was written in the wake of the 2016 election, for which the publication had placed the odds of a Donald Trump victory at 15 percent, about the same chances as a full rip. In it, the *Times* cops to its failure to communicate the meaningful difference between an 85 percent chance and a 100 percent chance. Some readers, optimistically, rounded up in favor of a Hillary Clinton victory, and many woke the next morning to the devastating blow of a country changed against the odds. The reporters summarize the problem with models, quoting statistician George Box, who said, "All models are wrong, but some are useful."

Sometimes I picture my climate anxiety like the now-infamous jittery election needle of 2016, constantly fluctuating in real time in response to the passage of climate legislation, the shattering of global temperature records, the toll of climate-exacerbated disasters, the outcome of elections. To gain a sense of how current events are shaping climate predictions, I look to the Climate Action Tracker. In an update for COP29, released in November 2024, it estimates that we are on a path to experience a rise in global average temperatures of 2.7 degrees Celsius above pre-industrial levels by 2100.

All models may contain some uncertainty, but unfortunately, climate models have proven to be stubbornly, reliably accurate. To test their accuracy, scientists use a process called hindcasting—like forecasting, but looking backwards—in which they take early climate models and compare projected temperatures with actual observed temperatures. A hindcasting study assessing the accuracy of climate models generated between 1970 and 2007 found that 14 of the 17 closely matched observed temperatures, lending confidence to the ability of these same models to accurately forecast global temperatures.

We know that the Earth is the hottest it has ever been in human history and that temperatures will keep rising. The ocean is not just warming but also becoming more acidic as it absorbs excess carbon dioxide. Glaciers are melting, sea levels are rising, heat waves, droughts, and wildfires are worsening, and storms and floods are intensifying. This is all reason enough for alarm, and yet there is still so much we can't know about what happens next, because so much depends on our actions in the years and decades to come.

Even within the wide range of possible outcomes, the future can feel nearly impossible to envision. Philosopher Timothy Morton calls forces like climate change *hyperobjects*, because the scale of the crisis is so immense it reaches across time and space in ways that humans find not just existentially terrifying but also mindboggling. Hyperobjects, writes Laura Hudson in a profile of Morton, "threaten our survival in ways that defy traditional modes of thinking about reality and humiliate our cognitive powers, a disorienting shift that sends many people reeling into superstition, polarization, and denial."

It's hard to imagine a world of unchecked warming in which one-fifth of the planet's land area is as hot as the Sahara. A world in which plants and animals migrate poleward, and one million species are driven to extinction. A world in which hundreds of millions of climate migrants are forced to abandon their homes, fleeing communities struck by drought, storms, and wildfires.

It's hard to imagine, harder yet to plan for such a future. But people *are* planning for a changed climate, or at least are attempting to, especially younger people who must make major life decisions—

where to live, what profession to pursue, whether to have children—amidst an unfolding global crisis. In her book *Climate Anxiety and the Kid Question*, Jade S. Sasser, a professor of gender and sexuality studies, reveals how climate change is impacting reproductive decision-making, focusing especially on the experiences of people of color and those in Gen Z. "Although climate change is far from the first or only existential threat human communities have faced, it poses the most comprehensive and farthest reaching challenges to the systems that sustain life on Earth," she writes. "It is a matter of scale, and the scale of this problem is not one that we as a human species have collectively faced before."

The question of whether it was ethical to have children was not something my husband and I, both of us elder millennials, seriously grappled with when we were first trying to conceive. Discussions about climate-driven reproductive anxiety hadn't yet gone mainstream. But by the time we decided to have a second child, the kid question had gained traction in the media, in part, through comments made by politicians like Alexandria Ocasio-Cortez and celebrities like Miley Cyrus.

In addition to worries about the rising costs of housing, childcare, and higher education, many people in their reproductive years are expressing concerns about the environmental impacts of having a child—as well as fears about the state of the planet their children will inherit. A 2021 survey of 10,000 people aged 16–25 in ten nations, found that 40 percent say fears about the future make them reluctant to have children. In the United States, a 2024 survey by the Pew Research Center found that 26 percent of childless adults under age 50 cite concerns about the environment as a major factor in their decision not to have children.

In many ways, the fact that my husband I were already parents made our decision to have a longed-for second child less fraught, since we'd already reorganized our lives around caring for a child and saw ourselves as committed to the fight for a livable future. Our conversations mostly circled around managing our growing family's carbon footprint—although we recognized that the concept is one that deliberately shifts responsibility from governments and corporations onto individuals.

Still, my husband and I wondered, how should we think about headlines that declared the best thing a person can do to help the environment is to have fewer children, or research that suggests raising a child in the United States could add up to 9,441 metric tons of carbon dioxide to the environment? Most of these arguments are supported by an often-cited 2009 research paper, whose conclusions some scientists have called into question. For one, the study doesn't account for changes in policies that would more strictly reduce carbon emissions and assumes that future generations will continue emitting at 2005 levels. But in the United States, for example, per capita emissions have fallen since the study was published, decreasing by 21 percent between 2005 and 2019.

As some have pointed out, we have headed off the most apocalyptic scenarios. Scientists once warned that without a change in course we risked as much as five degrees Celsius of warming, but because of steep drops in renewable energy costs and the implementation of ambitious climate policies, limiting rise to two degrees remains possible. While this would still result in vast suffering and environmental degradation, a rise of two degrees, writes David Wallace-Wells, "is a more hopeful outcome than many dared to believe less than a decade ago."

Some scientists also take issue with the concept of a carbon legacy, saying that the 2009 study holds the current generation of parents responsible for the emissions of their descendants for several hundred years into the future—raising the question, at what point does a person's child or grandchild become responsible for their own emissions—all while assuming that fossil fuel consumption rates remain constant through 2400. An alternative model relies on two assumptions: what would happen if the United States met its climate goals, and that a parent is responsible for half of the emissions of their child for only one generation. This approach puts the carbon savings of having one fewer child on par with abstaining from a couple transatlantic flights.

Some have argued that by zooming out and taking the long view of human history, by many standards, conditions for human flourishing are improving. In this view, now is perhaps the best time in human history to be born. Global child mortality rates have fallen drastically in the last two centuries—whereas 43 percent of children once died before their fifth birthday, that percentage is now 4 percent, with every single country seeing improvements within the last 50 years. There have also been substantial improvements in maternal mortality, life expectancy, food insecurity, and access to clean water and education, and both the percentage and share of people living in extreme poverty have fallen significantly. But even within this optimistic framing, there remains the great tragedy of preventable human suffering. Further, these markers of progress suggest all that we stand to lose, especially the most vulnerable, if efforts to decarbonize fail.

While these counterarguments may assuage some environmental guilt, there's still something that bothers me about seeing the choice to have one fewer child plotted on a bar graph alongside the choice to purchase an electric vehicle. On the level of individual responsibility, even for prospective parents living in high-emitting countries, bringing a child into the world isn't a lifestyle choice akin to taking an expensive vacation or driving a truck. And, on the policy level, linking population to climate change risks veering dangerously close to this country's racist legislative past.

Here, it's important to place conversations about personal reproductive anxiety in political and historical context, especially since research on reproductive anxiety has tended to ignore factors like race and LGBTQ+ identity. There's also an appalling history of population control campaigns targeting women of color and poor women. In the United States, Black women, Indigenous women, and other marginalized communities have been denied reproductive self-determination through enslavement, eugenics, and sterilization. Yet, people of color have always practiced reproductive resistance, which Sasser defines as "an active way of fighting back against the undesirable conditions shaping pregnancy, birth, and parenting." Historically, this includes the range of tactics used by Black enslaved women to prevent pregnancy, with more recent examples being the fight for access to safe contraceptives and abortion. Likewise, people of color have exercised reproductive resilience and found ways to survive and thrive amidst existential threat, such as navigating discriminatory systems in order to advocate for their children and participating in activism. Writes Sasser, "This kind of reproductive resilience may be less familiar for white parents, but as climate change worsens, parents across race and class divides will have to navigate reproductive resilience in new ways and will have to do so intentionally."

Recognizing that climate change unequally impacts vulnerable and marginalized communities, leading to adverse pregnancy and birth outcomes, Sasser advocates that reproductive justice must include climate justice, writing: "Reproductive justice comprehensively supports the ability to *have* the children you want, not have the children you *don't* want, and raise those you *do* have in safe and sustainable environments."

Whatever their reasoning, people don't owe anyone an explanation for their reproductive choices, but for the many people wrestling with the ethics of having kids, moral philosopher Elizabeth Cripps suggests that committing to collective action may offer another way to think about the decision. She writes, "The choice young people face is not this: (1) Have kids, and leave them a doomed world or (2) don't have any kids at all. There's a third option: Have kids, and cooperate with other adults to leave them a thriving, biodiverse, and socially and environmentally just future."

I share Cripps's commitment to working cooperatively toward a just future, and I worry about the combined threat that abortion bans and the climate crisis pose to reproductive freedom. "When people feel like they cannot have children because we live on a dying planet," writes Roxane Gay in an essay on reproductive justice, "their choices are as restricted by the climate as they are by misogynistic legislation."

I've come to know firsthand all the ineffable joy and meaning that raising children can bring, and I want it to remain possible for anyone who longs to bring a child into the world—including someday, perhaps, even my own children—to be able to do so in good conscience.

My husband and I are part of the generation that entered adulthood while reckoning with the severity of global warming, our children's generation, on the other hand, will only know the reality of a changed climate. In the mid-2050s, when my children will be in their early 30s and making their own decisions about where to live and whether to raise a family, by some estimates, more than 100 million Americans could regularly experience at least one 125-degree day each summer. It's difficult for me to imagine that world, difficult to anticipate how my children might think and feel about it or what solutions their generation might contribute to the many crises we face. At least, as Britt Wray points out, this next generation of children will likely be more clear-eyed about the future. She writes, "The kids coming now won't have to fight their way out of society's old delusions that we had laid on us, which is radically hopeful."

The project that lies ahead is nothing less than working together to dismantle a world built on fossil fuels so that our children have the opportunity to make a better one—a world that's abundant with clean energy, a world that's more caring and more just.

For my part, when it comes to the kid question, I can't say whether I made the right choice, only that having children was the right choice for me, and I'm grateful I was able to make it. I didn't always know, deep down, that I wanted to become a mother. After coming of age in a religious culture that overvalued my capacity to procreate and sought to restrict reproductive freedom, it took me years to sort out whether I wanted to become a parent because that was what I'd been told to want, or because that was what I truly desired. Even after I'd conceived, I felt some lingering ambivalence as my first pregnancy progressed. I read parenting memoirs but even the most starkly revealing narratives could not help me fully predict what it would feel like to have a child.

"On many days I think of the baby as a drug," writes Rivka Galchen in her book *Little Labors*. It's the sort of reflection on early motherhood I read with fascination but little understanding until I held my daughter in my arms and understood the full force of my need for her. I used to cringe, inwardly, at phrases like "baby fever." There was something embarrassing, I felt, about comparing the desire to procreate to an illness. Yet, when my husband and I were discussing whether to try for another, I knew, with a searing clarity that didn't feel entirely rational, what I wanted. My desire for a second child was all consuming.

I didn't have any difficulty conceiving our first child, but after months of failed attempts to conceive our second, I did what many people planning to become pregnant do, I took matters into my own hands. I transformed our bathroom counter into a makeshift laboratory cluttered with pregnancy tests and ovulation prediction kits. I lurked on trying-to-conceive message boards and learned enough acronyms to sift through comments for whatever information or consolation they might yield.

Gathering statistics temporarily soothed me. I could read tables with the odds of getting pregnant, by age, after one month, six months, and 12 months of trying. But no one could tell me what I really wanted to know, which was whether, in the end, I would have another child. It was another kind of uncertainty, an outcome that I felt both overwhelmingly responsible for, yet, unable to entirely control.

It's not as if my husband and I, throughout all this, sat down with climate models and attempted to calculate the chances of our child having a good life. I'm not sure that I would hazard to define such a concept, nor its inverse. I recognize that life always holds the risk of great loss and I wouldn't want to reduce the sum of my child's existence to whatever forms of suffering I might fear for them. Instead of a decision driven by facts and figures, it was one that came down to feelings. Even if I could not articulate my reasoning, my bone-deep longing for another baby was undeniable. When I finally discovered that I was expecting our second child, I was elated.

Though she herself did not choose to have children, Hannah Arendt once described the kind of love that prompts a person to bring a child into the world, saying it's the kind of love that declares, "'I want you to be,' without being able to give any particular reason for such supreme and unsurpassable affirmation."

My children are here because I wanted them to be, and now, I have no option but to live in such a way that my children don't come to resent my decision making, to set myself against the odds of leaving them a doomed world, to take seriously the question of what I owe my children, and all children, for generations to come.

From the risks of global warming to the odds of a megaquake, scientific research can offer data and models, but I confess that I rarely know how to make sense of such numbers in ways that make them relevant to how I live my everyday life. Have my husband and I doomed our children to disaster, for example, by choosing to live in a seismically dangerous region? One particularly snarky Redditor answered a similar question this way: "'Will there be any warning' you ask about an event that will happen sometime in the future. You have been warned."

Climate fiction, writes professor of literature Min Hyoung Song, "puts into narrative form what might otherwise seem a mass of unrelated events and facts." Likewise, reading about disaster has helped me conceptualize how my family and community might prepare for the coming megaquake and tsunami.

"The human mind has a tendency to wander after one too many worst-case scenarios, and earthquakes are the toughest natural disaster to wrap the brain around anyway," writes Doughton. To address this difficulty, journalists across the Pacific Northwest have turned to fiction to communicate the dangers of the Cascadia subduction zone to the public and spur on disaster preparedness efforts.

Following Schulz's viral *New Yorker* story, several publications issued speculative reporting that imagined the days and weeks following the disaster. *Vice*, for example, published "After the Big One," a five-part work of reported science fiction written by Adam Rothstein. He describes walking home from work across an earthquake-ravaged Portland. There are landslides and crumpled buildings, traffic accidents and damaged roadways, downed power lines and busted utility pipes, collapsed bridges and overpasses. Storage tanks leak petroleum into the Willamette River and it catches fire. By the time Rothstein makes it home, his neighbors have leapt into action, led by volunteers who had completed emergency preparedness training.

The role that neighbors play in disaster is a common theme in these reports, yet one of the most damaging cultural stories that persists about disaster is that it brings out the worst in people—making them selfish and violent as the fabric of society unravels. But, actually, as Rebecca Solnit demonstrates through her careful reporting on the San Francisco Earthquake, Hurricane Katrina, and other disasters in *A Paradise Built in Hell*, the most dangerous people are typically those in power. In the midst of crisis, people are often remarkably cooperative and generous. "We remain ourselves for the most part, but freed to act on, most often, not the worst but the best within," writes Solnit, "The ruts and routines of ordinary life hide more beauty than brutality."

Reading this, I longed to know how to create the conditions in which the beauty of interdependence might be revealed well before disaster strikes. Years ago, I heard about a Washington-based program called Map Your Neighborhood (MYN), which is intended to help small groups of neighbors meet to discuss emergency preparedness. I often saw information about this program in our neighborhood newsletter. Many times, I clicked on the link, feeling it was something I should do, and just as many times, I decided I had too many other obligations to commit to organizing and hosting such a meeting for my own block.

I was also put off by the prospect of approaching neighbors I didn't know well in order to invite them to my home to discuss a looming catastrophe. I didn't want to develop a reputation as the neighborhood's Cassandra. I suspect that many people have similar reservations, which likely explains why the last time I visited the program's website, I saw that the MYN workbooks were discontinued.

But this statement remains: "In a disaster, your most immediate source of help are the neighbors living around you. Take action today; go say hi!" This, I thought, I can do.

Since moving into our home four years ago, I've made it a point to meet as many neighbors as possible, gathering their names and exchanging phone numbers. It's a habit that comes in handy when a windstorm nudges a neighbor's back gate open and their dog gets loose, or when someone needs a hand lifting a piece of furniture or jumping a car. When a friend and I planned our first-ever neighborhood block party last year, I joked to my husband that it was really a small act of disaster preparedness.

Of course, we have also tried to do the things that we are supposed to do. To stock shelf-stable food in the pantry, to sleep with shoes and a flashlight under the bed, to keep a small emergency kit in the car, to know where the water and gas shut-off valves are located. And still, there are plenty of proactive things we haven't done. Our documents are stored safely, but I need to make copies of the important ones. Most of our emergency supplies—a small portable stove, water filtration, headlamps, sleeping bags, and a radio—are stored in various hard-to-reach bins in our garage rather than a dedicated go-bag or emergency kit, since they double as camping supplies. Perhaps that's why I so often find myself contemplating disaster when we go camping.

For people living in disaster-prone areas and faced with impossible choices, cooperation may offer a way forward between abandoning their homes or accepting the looming possibility of annihilation. Coastal communities, including on the Long Beach Peninsula where we camped, are now working together to apply for federal funding to build free-standing tsunami towers. In the absence of higher ground, these vertical evacuation structures can fit hundreds of people. By contrast, an individual could purchase a two-person tsunami-proof pod filled with food and supplies to last a week. If it were up to me, though, I'd rather seek refuge with my neighbors than seal myself into a survival capsule.

Disaster preparedness, like climate mitigation and adaptation, is best done in community. As a first step, disaster justice expert Samantha Montano advises people to look up their local emergency management budget and advocate for investment because many agencies are under-resourced and staffed by part-time employees or volunteers. In addition to preventing disasters and eliminating risks, her definition of disaster justice includes "being effective and equitable in how we do preparedness, response, and recovery" and it depends on moving from an individual to a community-based approach.

In her book *Hope in the Dark*, Rebecca Solnit argues that "disaster is a lot like revolution" in the sense that moments of rupture are unpredictable and disruptive and remind ordinary people of their power to act on altruistic ideals. She writes, "Social, cultural, or political change does not work in predictable ways or on predictable schedules . . . We don't know what is going to happen, or how, or when, and that very uncertainty is the space of hope."

As a response to the precarity that marks our present age, writes ethicist Elena Pulcini, "care can become the revolutionary value to counter the challenges threatening humanity and the living world and to build an ethic of the future." There's no denying that children deserve a better world than the one they will inherit, but it may be that our care for them and for each other is a force powerful enough to drive decarbonization, powerful enough to prevent the worst predictions from coming to pass.

That first night we spent camping at Cape Disappointment, I anticipated lying awake, thinking about the earthquake and the tsunami. While our children slept in the camper, my husband and I sat outside on the picnic table and played a card game by lantern light, talking and laughing, keeping our voices low.

I fell asleep easily, but in the middle of the night, I woke to the sound of retching. When I opened my eyes, I saw my husband hunched over a plastic bag. He shuffled out the camper door, suddenly in the throes of the stomach bug my children and I had caught the week previously. He sat, for several miserable moments, in the cool, dark fog in a camp chair beside a bucket. Once he'd returned and I was sure that he was fine, I decided to leave our bed and sleep the rest of the night on the mattress next to our son.

The next day, my husband was recovered enough to join us for a hike to a lighthouse overlooking the treacherous waters where the Columbia River empties into the Pacific Ocean, a stretch of coastline whose shifting sandbars, fog and storms, and rough waters have caused thousands of ships to sink and earned it the nickname the Graveyard of the Pacific.

Along the way, we noticed a small path that led to a sandy cove, so we scrambled down it to the beach. Water rushed into the cove between two rocky, forested headlands and the sun shone between them, cresting over a large rock formation that rose up out of sea, out of which grew a lone tree.

We kicked off our shoes and stretched out in the sunshine. My children ran to investigate a lean-to shack someone had made from driftwood, and they set about continuing the project, dragging logs and moving rocks before scrambling inside their fort. They returned for snacks and then began burying themselves in the sand.

Before continuing with our hike, we walked together toward the surf, where we noticed a beached jellyfish, and then another, and another. Pacific sea nettles, like the ones we've seen many times at the aquarium, that were now dead or dying. I didn't know until we returned to the main trail and read the signpost that the beach we were exploring was known as Deadman's Cove, named for the bodies of shipwrecked sailors, that like the jellyfish, had washed ashore.

When we reached the lighthouse, we looked out at the great expanse of the Pacific, out over the waters that even on a clear, calm day, churned restlessly. This was why we'd come all this way. It was not the camping trip we'd planned, there'd been plenty of rain and illness and even some mechanical issues, but we'd somehow put ourselves in the way of so much beauty, beauty that evidently did not come without significant risk.

Sleeping that night, once more beside my son, I thought of the lighthouse on the cliff, its light flashing both welcome and warning. Listening to the sound of distant waves, I thought of the many ships that had come to rest on the seabed, of the giant fault line not far offshore, of the uncertain future, which felt to me as impenetrable as the fog that had settled over everything.

And I recalled that when I was first deciding whether to become a parent, I'd read a *Dear Sugar* advice column, in which someone asked, "For those of us who aren't lucky enough to 'just know,' how is a person to decide if he or she wants to have a child?" Cheryl Strayed's compassionate response became a guiding metaphor for me whenever I reached a point of indecision. "I'll never know and neither will you of the life you don't choose. We'll only know that whatever that sister life was, it was important and beautiful and not ours," she wrote. "It was the ghost ship that didn't carry us. There's nothing to do but salute it from the shore."

I realized then that I'd made peace with my ghost ships. Whatever else may come, I thought, one arm around my son, this was the life I'd chosen.

Early one morning, while writing this, I was watching a video that modeled how tsunami waves would someday sweep across the bay, flooding our city's waterfront, when I felt the earth begin to shake. I heard the rattling of our home's single-pane windows first and then became conscious of the rocking motion beneath me. I looked around as my grandmother's dishes clinked in our hutch and the doors to the bookcase swung on their hinges.

Was this the start of something bigger?

Thankfully, it was over nearly as soon as it had started. It was a 4.5-magnitude earthquake, the second such temblor in two weeks.

I sat there for a minute, realizing I hadn't dropped, hadn't sought cover, hadn't reached out to hold onto anything solid—I'd just held very still, holding my breath.

After, I walked upstairs, knees shaking, adrenaline coursing.

"Did you feel that?" I asked, crawling into bed beside my husband.

"Yeah," he said. "The shaking woke me."

Eventually my breathing slowed, returning to normal. Soon our son called out for us, and he joined us beneath the covers, warm and safe, as he drifted back to sleep.

I watched the light rise, and when we got up, I held my son in my arms as we pulled back the curtains and looked down at our backyard and across our neighborhood, everything still and quiet, just as it had been yesterday, mercifully unchanged.

It could happen in five minutes, or in fifty years, but for me, these moments together would always be enough.

What to Expect

"Mama, come look."

My two-year-old daughter was holding something in her hand. The tide splashed quietly against her yellow rain boots. I stepped closer to where she was standing near the water's edge and knelt beside her. She opened her fist. There, I was expecting to find a seashell or a bit of sea glass. But in her palm, I saw instead a small fishing weight. It was gunmetal gray and shaped like a falling tear drop. There was an eyelet on top for threading fishing line.

We dried it off and, after inspecting it, she asked me to hold it for her, before toddling off to investigate a tide pool. I placed the fishing weight in my coat pocket and stood beside my husband, watching our daughter, who was watching the water, peering past her own reflection in search of other lives.

On the way to our hike, we'd sung along to "Baby Beluga," one of my daughter's favorite songs. She'd stopped singing at the final verse. Written to commemorate the song's fortieth anniversary, its lyrics were unfamiliar and complicated, calling on grown-up "beluga grads," like me, to honor our children by working toward climate justice. I, too, fell quiet during this verse, thinking about all the ways we burden each new generation with problems we haven't yet solved.

"Will we see a whale?" my daughter had asked from her car seat, looking out the window as views of the bay flashed into and out of focus between the trees.

"I hope so, love, but probably not," I said, turning to make eye contact with her in the car seat mirror. Her third birthday was several months away. It was autumn, mid-morning and chilly, and I was pregnant with our son, having just entered my third trimester.

I reminded my daughter that despite living on the coast of the Salish Sea for a decade, I'd never seen a whale. Still, I knew about the endangered Southern Resident orcas, the names of their matrilineal pods, how their efforts to hunt for fish are hindered by underwater noise pollution and declining salmon populations, how they struggle to bear and raise their young.

When I was pregnant with my daughter, I'd watched with the rest of the world as a Southern Resident orca named Tahlequah mourned her calf, which had died shortly after birth. As she traversed the waters of the coast, she kept her calf's body afloat during a seventeen-day journey of grief that spanned more than a thousand miles of sea. Her pod had escorted her, taking turns holding the calf's body so that the grieving mother could rest. I'd followed along, seeking updates each morning, fearing the day I'd pick up my phone and find that she was, finally, swimming alone.

I had never lost a child, had never known a grief like hers, but I could understand the impulse to hold on and tried to imagine the weight of what she carried.

Shortly after moving to Washington state, I purchased a used field guide to the Pacific coast. It had previously belonged to a young person named Sylvia, according to the sticker on its title page. My own childhood was landlocked—I was eighteen the first time I waded into salt water—so upon relocating, I sought to put language to what I was seeing. Sylvia's former field guide taught me the first rule of hiking: "Before planning an outing, you will want to know what you can expect to see."

I thought of this guidance, during my first pregnancy, when I picked up *What to Expect When You're Expecting* from the library hold shelf and felt the heft of its more than 600 pages. At home, I let the book fall open across my lap, struggling to get comfortable under its weight.

Unlike my coastal field guide's color plates of animals arranged by phylum and class, *What to Expect* mostly cataloged the unpleasant and difficult changes that lay ahead each month. I took note of the many restrictions and warnings. There were so many missteps a mother could make.

I found the book's paternalistic tone and overly familiar language cringeworthy, and there was much else that I objected to, like the sections written just for fathers, which relied on heteronormative assumptions and gendered language. But before I could return the book to the library, I spilled an entire thermos of coffee on it—coffee that likely exceeded the book's recommendations for caffeine intake. Nonetheless, after paying the library replacement fee, the book became mine.

Flipping through its coffee-stained pages, reading over its nutritional guidelines, I contemplated my body's needs in pregnancy, and wondered, what would it mean to think about pregnancy ecologically?

An ecological approach is not well-documented in books for pregnant people, but it's one that biologist Sandra Steingraber seeks in her 2001 memoir *Having Faith*. She writes, "If the world's environment is contaminated, so too is the ecosystem of a mother's body. If a mother's body is contaminated, so too is the child who inhabits it." Encountering this perspective ushered me into a new understanding of my body as a nested ecosystem, a habitat within a habitat, a world within a world. I was not separate from nature, my body was as much a part of the water cycle as the rain that fell over the landscape, the stormwater that flowed out to sea.

On our hike, I'd slipped on the short but steep wooden stairs that led to the beach. For a moment, I was standing on the top step taking in the horizon, looking out at the islands and the vanishing point where so many shades of blue converge, and then I was falling.

It was a cold morning. With each step along the trail, I'd heard the crisp, satisfying strike of our boots on frost. My husband walked ahead with our daughter in the hiking backpack. I could see her head bobbing as she looked around and the small puffs of her breath that hovered in the morning air before disappearing.

We'd emerged from the woods where the railway carves along the coast, then crossed over the tracks toward a small cove. The sun had not yet risen above the foothills, which loomed dark and forested at our backs. The wooden steps down to the beach were still slick. I slipped and, instinctively, my hands went out behind me. I caught myself before I could fall further than a couple steps. I sat for a moment, my hand feeling for the tender spot where my back had scraped against rough wood.

Once assured that I was fine, my husband helped me to my feet, and as I reached up for his hand, I could feel the muscles in my shoulders and neck tighten, already sore from absorbing the shock of my fall. I blinked away tears and rubbed the back of my arms, easing the tension. Gathering myself on the beach, I reached inside our backpack for my reusable water bottle and a silicone pouch of goldfish crackers. My daughter took a handful and crammed them into her mouth. Orange crumbs gathered at her lips, and I wiped at her nose. Still chewing, she toddled away to turn over small rocks.

I palmed my belly and looked out at the sea, breathing deeply and feeling for where I knew our still developing baby was held safely within the fluid-filled amniotic sac, protected in part by water that I had consumed over the course of my pregnancy.

In her book, Steingraber contemplates the origins of amniotic fluid, writing, "I drink water, and it becomes blood plasma, which suffuses through the amniotic sac and surrounds the baby—who also drinks it. And what is it before that? Before it is drinking water, amniotic fluid is the creeks and rivers that fill reservoirs. . . . And before it is creeks and rivers and groundwater, amniotic fluid is rain."

The water cushioning our son, the amniotic fluid moving into and out of his developing lungs, I realized, was only as healthy as our watershed.

Everyone on the planet lives within a watershed, which is, simply, the area which drains into a common body of water, such as a lake, river, or ocean. In the Cascadia region, our watersheds are marked by the rivers, creeks, and streams that flow from their headwaters in forested mountains through agricultural valleys to the ocean.

Whenever I turn on the faucet to fill a drinking glass or bathe my children, the tap water that spills out is drawn from Lake Whatcom. Water from that lake makes its way to the sea by way of Whatcom Creek. Since our home is located within the creek's watershed, all the water that drains from our yard and the surrounding neighborhoods, as well as any pollutants, empties into the creek and out into the bay.

"When we figure our addresses, we might do better to forget zip codes and consider where the rain goes after it falls outside our windows," writes Scott Russell Sanders in *Staying Put*, his book about making a home and raising a family in a manner that reflects his commitment to place. "We need such knowledge. . . . The tilt of land that snares the rain also defines where we *are* more profoundly than any state line or city limit."

Recognizing the importance of how water flows across a landscape is an idea that is central to bioregionalism, a philosophy that focuses on the communities, both human and nonhuman, formed by the natural boundaries of watersheds. Environmentalist Peter Berg and biologist Raymond Dasmann define a bioregion as referring "both to geographical terrain and a terrain of consciousness, to a place and the ideas that have developed about how to live in that place."

In graduate school, I realized how little I knew about my new bioregion while reading an article about sustainable teaching practices. It described a place-based writing assignment in which students were asked to research their university's watershed. I realized, then, that I couldn't answer the assignment's most basic questions.

I learned that Whatcom Creek, at the heart of our local watershed, is central to our city's history of colonization and extraction. It's where Euro-American settlers landed and made first contact, as well as the site of the original lumber mill that, along with the fishing industry, fueled the area's development, including perhaps the construction of our own home with its century-old fir floorboards—the floors upon which my children have learned to crawl and whose rough edges have left slivers in my children's bare feet.

"Only by understanding where I live can I learn how to live," writes Sanders. To understand a watershed is to appreciate how everything, including our bodies, is connected, how the past flows into the future, how all that happens upstream affects all that happens downstream, how even political boundaries cannot stem the flow of water.

As a family, each fall, we lean over a footbridge that spans the mouth of Whatcom Creek and look for the salmon returning to their birthplace to spawn before dying. We look for the flash of a tail, a swift-moving body, and often we see, too, the slick head of a seal as it surfaces, its whiskers gleaming.

At the summer camp my children attend, which is put on by a local nonprofit dedicated to salmon recovery, they learn that salmon are a keystone species. More than 130 animal species have a relationship with salmon, including the Southern Resident orca whales that depend on Chinook salmon as their primary food source. The forests, too, are nourished by the bodies of salmon as they break down and return nutrients to the earth. And it's impossible to overstate the significance of the Coast Salish peoples' relationship to salmon, nor the extent of their efforts to restore wild salmon. As poet Rena Priest, editor of the *I Sing the Salmon Home* anthology and a member of the Lummi Nation, told me, "The lack of salmon has left our people with a lack of physical and spiritual nourishment, and we all feel it. Fishing has been our way of life for thousands of generations and the fishery decline has left a whole generation of fishermen without a livelihood. It's been a crisis in our community, and it's impacted me to see people I love struggle to find a different way of living off the water." Still, Rena insists that the salmon hold lessons on hope. "The salmon's journey itself teaches us hope, because they come back every year, defying all odds," she says. "After all we've put them through over the last hundred years, as soon as you take a dam down, here they come."

At camp, through crafts and songs and trips to the beach, my children are beginning to understand that the health of our ecosystem depends on the health of the salmon, and the health of the salmon depends on the health of our watersheds. My daughter knows that salmon migrate from freshwater to saltwater and back again and can explain why they need access to cool, clean freshwater to spawn, access that is often blocked by dams and failed culverts.

My neighbor, Annitra Peck, who is the nonprofit's executive director, told me that one of its goals is to "increase everyone's sense of place and belonging within this watershed," which she believes will lead to improved stewardship. She says, "It all comes down to water, right?"

And climate change is affecting both freshwater and ocean conditions, threatening the already at-risk salmon. We now experience more extreme rainfall events in the winter, which can lead to floods and landslides that disturb salmon habitat downstream, as well as hotter, drier summers which negatively impact the temperature and flow of the rivers where salmon run. This weather pattern is worsened by industrial logging in the upper reaches of our watersheds, since mature forests regulate the flow of water through watersheds more efficiently. Areas that have been clearcut, fail to capture water in winter and therefore cannot gradually release it in summer.

All you need to understand a watershed is your own two hands, cupped to form a bowl beneath the faucet. To do this is to know how hard it is to hold water, to keep it from slipping away.

If the story of our watershed is the story of colonization and extraction, of salmon decline and recovery, it is also the story of a tragic pipeline failure. Our watershed bears the scars of an oil pipeline that, in 1999, ruptured and leaked 230,000 gallons of unleaded gasoline into Whatcom Creek.

Unaware of the gasoline coursing through the creek, two ten-year-olds were playing with a butane lighter when the vapors ignited and a fireball boomed through the creek bed. The resulting fire destroyed the city's water treatment plant, burned acres of riparian forests and meadows, and killed an unquantifiable number of trees, plants, and animals, including all aquatic life within a three-mile stretch of the creek. It also, tragically, took the lives of the two boys playing on its banks, Wade King and Stephen Tsiorvas, as well as a teen, Liam Wood who was flyfishing.

In the wake of that disaster, the boys' parents became advocates for pipeline safety, supporting the formation of a national nonprofit and testifying before federal lawmakers about the need for regulations to protect against the irreversible destruction of pipeline failures. "I no longer have children to protect. Nothing I do or say about this issue can bring Liam back," said Marlene Robinson, one of the grieving mothers, at a Senate hearing. "I do, however, consider it my privilege and obligation to do what I can to protect the children of this and other communities."

The burn zone was replanted and the streambed restored. Over time, vegetation and aquatic life have returned to the creek, but no recovery efforts could ever return the children our city lost to this pipeline disaster.

Twenty-five years later, a new commemorative sign was placed near where the pipeline ruptured, at the park where my own kids ride their bikes and play on swings. When I read it on a rainy day last fall, I noticed that the final point on its timeline of events is dated 2023, a more recent date than I expected. It marks the day when that same pipeline spilled 25,000 gallons of gasoline into a creek located near an elementary school, a catastrophe that was narrowly averted.

I paused before the sign, with my youngest in my arms and thought of the mothers who'd lost their sons, about the weight of their grief and the way their arms must ache to hold their children.

For all the risks exhaustively covered in the so-called pregnancy bible, rarely does *What to Expect* discuss society's responsibility in addressing environmental concerns. There is increasing evidence for the threat that fossil fuels pose to pregnant people, including how exposure to extreme heat and air pollution increases risks for stillbirth, low birth weight, and preterm birth—risks which are more likely to impact people of color and are worsened by environmental racism. But in the pregnancy book's revised fifth edition, there are just two references to climate change, one which recommends preparing for natural disasters and another in the section on extreme heat. Remarkably, climate change isn't included in its seemingly exhaustive index, which lists everything from clay eating to snowboarding. Instead, pregnant people are advised to take individual precautions, like using an air purifier and testing tap water for lead. There's little emphasis on the kind of federal and state regulations that would ensure pregnant people, let alone children and everyone else, equitable access to clean water and clean air, as well as a stable climate and healthy ecosystems in which to live and grow.

The summer I was pregnant with our son, a once-in-a-millennia heat wave known as a "heat dome" settled over the Pacific Northwest. Our home, like many in the region, was built without central air, so as temperatures climbed toward 100 degrees Fahrenheit, we ran box fans and installed air conditioning units in bedroom windows. I cooled my feet and did my best to stay hydrated while my daughter splashed and played in a kiddie pool in the backyard.

But I worried about what the extreme weather might mean for the child I was carrying.

There were reports of melting power lines and buckling pavement, and hundreds of people died, including elderly people and farmworkers. The heat was followed by weeks of wildfire smoke, which choked our skies and cast orange slants of light across the floorboards.

I skimmed research articles about the maternal-fetal health impacts of extreme heat and wildfire smoke, before I became overwhelmed, bookmarking them for later. I learned that air pollutants from wildfire smoke can cross the placenta, leaving black carbon particles on the fetal side. Studies also suggest that exposure to extreme heat can alter blood flow and weaken the placenta, increasing the risks of preterm birth. A researcher who studies the human placenta calls it the "chronicle of intrauterine life." It's an organ, she says, that "tells the story."

The unprecedented extreme heat called to mind the summer that I was born. It was 1988 and the hottest and driest year on record. From the town where my parents lived, some 50 miles west of Chicago, wildfire smoke was visible from fires burning in Yellowstone National Park. Farmers prayed for rain, and the river that cut through town ran low; further north, several rivers evaporated completely. That June, climate scientist Jim Hansen testified in a Senate hearing that "the greenhouse effect has been detected, and it is changing our climate now." The front page of the *New York Times* ran a headline declaring, "Global Warming Has Begun."

I was born later that summer, six weeks premature and weighing just over five pounds, but with no other complications.

The next year, the United States would come close but ultimately fail to sign the kind of binding international agreement that would have addressed climate change. These efforts were thwarted by a small group of skeptics and deniers, including politicians and fossil fuel executives who funded ad campaigns intended to cast doubt on climate science.

Since then, warnings about climate change have largely gone unheeded and warming has only accelerated.

Several months after the heat dome, on our hike to the beach, I looked out over the shoreline and tried to comprehend the staggering loss of billions of intertidal invertebrates that were killed by the extreme heat and feared for the people and places I love, including the salmon populations threatened by warming waters. A changing climate is testing the resilience of marine life, leading some researchers to speculate that, in time, the Pacific Northwest's coast could come to resemble the places where certain intertidal organisms die off completely each summer.

In my field guide, I read that the creatures living at the water's edge must adapt to their habitat's extreme fluctuations: "Somehow they must manage."

From where we stood on the beach that day, our youngest still within my womb, you could follow the coastline north some three hundred miles to where two adults and a small child left footprints on the shore, footprints which were hidden in sediment beneath the surface for 13,000 years. You would think footprints on the coast, subjected to wind and waves would be impermanent, but shifting shorelines, where sand can fill impressions left in hard, wet clay, are prime locations for finding trace fossils of human activity.

In coastal regions around the world, the rising seas and raging storms of a warming climate are exposing the record of ancient humans. Thousands of years from now, I wonder what our own footprints might reveal.

While pregnant with my son, I brought my daughter to a prenatal appointment. The visit progressed in fits and starts as my midwife paused to answer my daughter's many questions.

When it was time to listen for the fetal heartbeat with the handheld doppler, my daughter helped. The midwife guided her hand as the doppler arced over my abdomen. I liked to imagine this doppler was sounding my depths like how orca whales use sound waves to find fish in the dark. We listened together to the reassuring rhythm of my son's heartbeat and to the slower, more distant sound of my own.

At the end of my prenatal appointment, my daughter pointed to a plush doll on top of the clinic's bookshelf. My midwife handed it to her and showed her that the doll was pregnant and could demonstrate how a baby is born. My daughter's eyes lit up at the emergence of the baby. Next came the placenta, which looked like a bright red felted pancake. The midwife held the placenta in her palm, and explained, "The placenta is what feeds the baby."

After I was born, my mother struggled to deliver the placenta; it would not yield. Placenta accreta is an invasive placental disorder, a potentially life-threatening condition, in which the placenta attaches too deeply. When my mother's doctor finally forced the placenta from her uterine wall, she began to bleed. She bled until she lost so much blood that she required a transfusion that saved her life. I still don't know what it means that my beginning was nearly her ending. It was a thought too heavy to contemplate during my own pregnancies.

I'm not sure how much time elapsed between my daughter's birth and when I labored to expel her placenta, but I was grateful for the shot of Pitocin that hastened contractions. I was so completely absorbed in the sensations of holding my daughter that I barely remember that stage of labor except for the relief I felt when it was finally over.

Seated on the foot of the bed, my midwife had lifted the amniotic sac from a pink plastic receptacle to point out the gaping hole where my water had broken open. Then, she showed me my daughter's placenta with its dangling umbilical cord. I was looking at three things that were once submerged, three things that had now surfaced: my daughter, her amniotic sac, and her placenta.

Now, my daughter was seated beside my midwife, holding an umbilical cord of braided red yarn, and when it came unsnapped from the doll she uttered a shocked, "Uh-oh."

A temporary organ that supports a developing fetus, the placenta attaches to the uterine lining on one side and on the other to the umbilical cord. It allows for the exchange of oxygen and nutrients and the removal of waste and plays a crucial role in protecting the developing fetus from infections and toxins. But some environmental contaminants can cross the placental barrier, including heavy metals found in fish and water, microplastics, air pollution particles, endocrine disrupting chemicals and the so-called forever chemicals in drinking water. The full story of my children's exposure to toxins began while my egg cells were developing when I was a fetus in my mother's womb. The pesticide, DDT, for example, can affect up to three generations after the initial exposure.

As in a watershed, what happens upstream affects everything

downstream. There were some things that I, as an individual pregnant person, could do to limit my exposure, but mostly I had to come to terms with the reality of our ecological interdependence, to learn to hold it.

My daughter reached for the little metal snap at the end of the umbilical cord and tried to press it to the corresponding snap on the doll's belly button. As my daughter's fingers fumbled with the snap, I moved my hand to my own belly button, which was protruded in pregnancy, and thought of the cords that had connected me to my mother, then to my daughter, the cord that, at that moment, bound me to my son.

Months later, my midwife would lift my son from the waters of the birthing tub, would lift him like a fish on the line, and place him on my chest, the waters lapping against us, the umbilical cord still pulsing.

Standing on the shoreline recently while my husband and children explored tide pools, I considered, as I often did, the more than one trillion pieces of plastic that were at that moment swirling in the Great Pacific Garbage Patch, atop a seafloor heaped with unknown amounts of trash. I thought of all the pieces of plastic my family and I have used and discarded and which will never fully break down.

I know that there are likely microplastics in our food and drinking water, just as there were likely microplastics in my amniotic fluid and placenta, microplastics in my breast milk and the meconium our newborns passed shortly after birth, microplastics seemingly everywhere.

There's a photograph of the impacts of marine debris at the Marine Life Center, a small educational aquarium that my children and I like to visit on rainy days, where fishermen bring bycatch, most recently a giant Pacific octopus, to recover before being returned to the sea.

Hanging on the wall beside the tank is a large, framed print of a dead albatross chick, its midsection cut open to reveal a spill of discarded plastic items. Beside it, these startling stomach contents are laid out to form a full circle of trash. The artist statement reads: "An albatross chick is unknowingly fed plastic by its parents, who scoop food from the ocean surface. . . . Each year, millions of tons enter the ocean, accumulating in giant patches called gyres."

Often when I take out the trash and the recycling, the albatross photograph comes to mind. The detritus of everyday life spilling out of the chick's belly, and my own children looking up at the photographic evidence of it all.

I know that, like the albatross parents, I too am inadvertently exposing my children to microplastics and other pollutants, that I am caught up in the web of suffering that degrades the environment and that I am largely unable to protect my children from such threats.

Like everything else, for better or worse, we are part of our watershed.

At our neighborhood elementary school, there's a playground panel that depicts the water cycle. My children and I can follow its arrows with our fingers, arrows that track the flow of water as it evaporates from the sea into a cloud that drifts over the landscape until it reaches a mountain range and falls as snow and rainwater. Arrows point the way as rivers flow through the landscape, returning the water to the sea.

But where did all this water come from, my children wanted to know, where did it all begin?

As it turns out, before our planet was formed, much of the water molecules that now make up our oceans and drinking water may have existed as ancient specks of ice that drifted through space in interstellar clouds, ice that survived the birth of our solar system, ice that went on to wash our young planet in water.

How improbable, I thought later, that the same water that protected my children in utero and fills their water glasses, that nurtures the spawning salmon and the calves of orcas, that splashes through Whatcom Creek and circulates through our bodies and around the globe endlessly, is older than the sun. How essential that we protect it.

On our hike back from the beach that autumn morning, I carried my daughter in my arms, her legs wrapping around my pregnant belly. When I set her down near the trailhead, she looked up at me and asked, "Mama, you have the heaviness?"

She pointed to my jacket pocket. I'd forgotten about the fishing weight.

I put my hand to it, felt it smooth and cold and heavy, an unexpected weight that I was carrying for her.

"Can I hold it?" she asked.

Handing it to her, I was keenly aware of its purpose: to sink, to pull a line to the desired depths, to stay the hook to catch in the mouth of things that swim. And it was startling to hear her name the heaviness, to bear it together for a moment, our hands touching.

The Looking Glass

Rain was falling while I carried my two-year-old and her tricycle home from the park. Her legs, galoshes swinging, straddled my pregnant belly. One slick rubber tricycle wheel bumped against my shin with each step, the other spun on its axle.

At that moment, I didn't know about the approaching atmospheric rivers, about the flooding that would soon overtake parts of our county. I only knew that it was raining, and my daughter wasn't feeling well. My arms were wrapped around her fox raincoat; its orange tail swished back and forth. She rested her head on my shoulder, and a wet fox ear nuzzled my cheek.

Once inside, I shuffled us out of our raingear and over to the sofa, where I hoped we both might nap. I could hear the rain striking the windowpanes, fiercer than late autumn's usual subdued drizzle. With my daughter curled against me, I covered us with a blanket, scrolled on my phone for audio to stream quietly, and landed on a playlist of fairy tales read aloud by a British nanny whose voice crackled with kindness.

I closed my eyes and listened as a music box unwound its thin notes, a prelude that transported us. It was as if I'd opened a pop-up book that still smelled of the primeval forest from which its pages were milled. We'd entered the deep, dark woods in a time long ago and a land far away. We could hear someone at the door knocking, a princess with wet hair and sodden clothes.

Soon the princess would be tossing and turning in her bedclothes, bothered by a pea placed beneath a pile of feather beds. Soon my daughter would be dozing beside me, her cheeks flushed with fever. Soon I would be lost in the woods, realizing I could no longer hear these stories as I once had. I wasn't a child casting breadcrumbs to find my way home. I was a mother and unsure where that left me.

Mothers rarely figure in our culture's most reproduced fairy tales, except as backstory. These missing mothers are usually dead and gone long before the utterance of "once upon a time" sets the narrative clock in motion. And those few living, breathing mother figures, well, they often treat their children monstrously, making catastrophic bargains or meting out cruel punishments.

I tried to remember, were fairy tales regressive or subversive? I read once that fairy tales began as a domestic art—stories that women shared to instruct the children in their care or to entertain each other while they worked—that the writers who aspired to make literature of folklore had tamed the tales they took from the mouths of women. Thus, sanitized of questionable humor and enriched with morals, the tales were circulated in national collections and praised for their "civilizing" influence on children.

Since then, fairy tales have played a formative role in the imaginations of children. "Where else could I have gotten the idea, so early in life, that words can change you?" wrote Margaret Atwood of her early encounters with the *Grimms'* tales, with a nod to both magical spells and the transformative power of stories.

Even so, the cultural status of the fairy tale, as a genre, has been debated, simultaneously undervalued and overvalued, marginalized and mythologized, a bit like motherhood.

In those days of fairy tales and floodwaters, I was reading *Arts of Living on a Damaged Planet,* an anthology that asks how humans and other species can continue to coexist in a time of human-caused climate change. The editors suggest that "sensibilities from folklore and science fiction" may help us navigate a planet made strange by environmental damage. Seeking to challenge both the "fable of Progress" and the "conceit of the Individual," the editors argue that "ghosts and monsters unsettle *anthropos*, the Greek term for 'human,' from its presumed center stage in the Anthropocene by highlighting the webs of histories and bodies from which all life, including human life emerges."

Its essays were assembled around those narrative figures: ghosts and monsters. Think: the ghosts of haunted landscapes and discarded tires, of extinct megafauna and radioactive waste, of death and deep time. In these pages, I encountered grief, but also forms of brilliant resistance, like the shimmering presence of endangered flying foxes who, though hunted, persist in their night flights through the Australian bush, seeking nectar from flowering trees and playing a vital role in pollinating eucalyptus trees.

Then, I flipped over the double-sided book, balancing it atop my rounded belly, to read of monsters both wondrous and terrible, of nested ecosystems and symbiotic entanglements, of multispecies relationships like coral reefs and lichen, and of microchimerism, the phenomenon in which fetal cells pass through the placenta and persist in maternal tissues long after pregnancy.

In my third trimester, I was uncomfortably aware of my body's entanglements but felt a newfound appreciation for this exchange of cells—the fetal cells that would become, forevermore, part of my genetic makeup, and the cells my child would inherit from me. It pleased me to realize that among the many ways motherhood had changed me, on a cellular level, it had also made me a bit monstrous.

As I read about ghosts and monsters, my thoughts returned to fairy tales. What lessons might these stories hold for making a life on a warming and damaged planet?

By bath time, that night, the wind howled at the eaves and rainfall pelted the skylights. My daughter slept fitfully, and each time we woke to tend to her fever, I was startled by the rain's insistence. The next morning at the kitchen table, we heard the constant whooshing of the sump pump in the basement straining to keep the rising waters at bay.

Shortly before my family moved in, the woman who previously lived in our house beckoned me to follow her into the unfinished basement and warned me to make sure the sump pump remained operable. Although the house had never flooded, she offered me a vague warning—based on her observations of the neighborhood's oldest trees and a historical map she wasn't able to produce—of a creek that was rumored to have flowed where our century-old home now stood. It was as if she were telling me a ghost story. The thought of this creek would haunt me as I peered outside, looking up at the tall trees through the rain.

Forced to remain indoors, by rainfall and illness, my daughter and I returned to the enchanted forest. The stories were as strange and disturbing as they were comforting. The fairy tales came to us through my phone, and so, too, did weather reports about atmospheric rivers and historic rainfall. While we listened, I swiped the glass of my touch screen, a portal that transported me to familiar places made strange by the swift currents of muddy water.

A boy climbed a beanstalk to the sky. Drone footage captured kayakers paddling city streets alongside abandoned cars, stormwater swallowing parks and neighborhoods as it coursed toward the sea. Two hungry children followed a trail of breadcrumbs home. The river pushed northward, threatening to overwhelm a pump station that drains thousands of acres of farmland. A wheel that spins straw into gold came at a great cost. The floodwaters rose, displacing hundreds and stranding families in their homes, awaiting rescue. A mother played a guessing game to keep her firstborn child.

We were still in the middle of our story, and it was too soon to say what it would all mean, but one thing was becoming certain: there was too much rain falling all at once on a landscape haunted by a river that could no longer be controlled.

Reading stories with ghosts, monsters, and other folkloric creatures is one way to unsettle humans from center stage. Another is to read stories with talking animals. Anna Lowenhaupt Tsing, an anthropologist and one of the anthology's editors, suggests that it is cultural bias that marginalizes stories with talking animals, relegating such narratives to the children's shelf. She writes, in her book *The Mushroom at the End of the World*, that this bias is based on "a cultural agenda tied to dreams of progress through modernization." But, if we silence animals, she writes, "[W]e imagine well-being without them. We trample over them for our advancement; we forget that collaborative survival requires cross-species coordination. To enlarge what is possible, we need other kinds of stories—including adventures of landscapes."

In response to environmental damage, Tsing calls for stories in which plants, animals, and ecosystems speak, in which they might be figured as protagonists of their own stories. One effect of such stories might be to generate empathy and understanding across species, transforming our ability to care. Stories that challenge anthropocentric perspectives should be taken seriously across genres, neither consigned to children's literature nor to works of fantasy, folklore, or science fiction.

It isn't strange in a fairy tale for a river to speak, to turn into gold or poison, to ferry wayfarers to other realms. Fairy-tale scholar Kate Bernheimer identifies "normalized magic" as one of the genre's key elements. "The natural world in a fairy tale is a magical world," she writes. "The day to day is collapsed with the wondrous. In a traditional fairy tale there is no need for a portal." For me, caring for my young children wasn't a fairy tale, but it was a portal through which I was reintroduced to the everyday enchantments of the natural world.

My children encountered the living world in ways that weren't bound by the binaries that shaped how I saw the world, the sharp divides between human and nonhuman, animate and inanimate. I have never been more charmed than when my son would chatter through the open window to the crows perched on the wires. The sound of his cawing and the word "crow" were among his first discernible speech. Or when my daughter knelt on a hiking trail to peer into the undergrowth and greet a mouse my husband and I had overlooked. "Hi, mouse!" she said, prompting us to look about for what we'd missed.

Research confirms that young children commonly animate their surroundings, ascribing liveliness to animals and plants, trees and stones. It would be a mistake to view this habit of mind as something children naturally outgrow, but this is the view advanced by Jean Piaget, the developmental psychologist whose theories have profoundly shaped educational practices in the West and who disparaged such thinking about the natural world as "primitive." Piaget's bias reflects a dominant worldview that fails to recognize the relationships between all living beings.

According to early childhood education scholar Jane Merewether, the tendency for children to animate the nonhuman world can "create conditions for curiosity, wonder and a sense of *worldly embeddedness* that ignites possibilities for more responsive and attentive ways of living with an increasingly damaged Earth." By sensing that the world is alive, young children are better able to relate to it in ways that challenge the calcified hierarchies that many adults, and even older children, take for granted.

When I spoke with Merewether, who worked for years as an early childhood educator before earning her doctorate, she recalled a common classroom exercise in which young children are presented with a tray of objects and asked to classify them as alive or not alive. Yet, at the beginning of her teaching career, whenever she tried it with her own students she was left pondering questions like, at what point does a leaf or a stick cease to be alive?

During her doctoral research, Merewether revisited Piaget's earliest works and found many observations of children's animism. As she read, she grew dismayed by his view of young children, his belief that their reasoning powers were unsophisticated and simple. Even more disturbing was the colonialist lens that shaped his stage-based theory of cognitive development, which positioned Euro-western worldviews as superior to those of Indigenous peoples. Much as Min Hyoung Song observes in *Climate Lyricism*, the hierarchy that "privileges the well-being of the human over the nonhuman" also "overrepresents some humans at the expense of others."

Merewether's objections to Piaget's perspective led her to research how children interact with nature, proposing that "speculative and playful animism can be a matter of care, as it allows children to relate to the world in a spirit of companionship and kinship."

When I first encountered her research, I became curious about how parents could nurture their children's relationships to the more-than-human world in ways that challenge the dominant paradigm. Merewether encourages parents and educators to practice what theorists call "cultivating the art of noticing." She told me that this begins with modeling for our children how to slow down and pay attention to the world around us. "Rocks, trees, wind, insects," Jane says, "just noticing them in the first place is the first thing. Then, recognizing that they are participants in our shared world."

Just as important as *what* we notice, is *how* we notice.

During our conversation, when Jane recommended that parents "resist the urge to explain everything," I winced, and we laughed. An alternative to explanation, says Jane, is wonder. She suggests asking children questions like: "What might the tree be feeling on this really hot day? What story might this bird be telling?" This is not the stuff of superstition or magical thinking, but rather it is a form of inquiry that challenges the biases of Western thought. Questions like these invite children to recognize that other beings have agency and to treat them as such. "I feel that those small acts of wondering open up a space for relationality rather than control," says Jane.

Following our call, I made a conscious effort to wonder aloud rather than to explain what we were seeing. My children and I were flying paper airplanes off our back deck, when we looked up and noticed several seagulls shrieking at a bald eagle, swooping and diving at it. "Why do you think the gulls are doing that?" I asked.

"I bet they're protecting their babies," my daughter said.

"Could be," I said. "How do you think they know to work together?"

"They're talking to each other," she said. "Everything can talk!"

I am learning to help my children imagine the world from the vantage point of other species. In this, I'm inspired by mothers like Elizabeth Rush, who writes in *The Quickening* of her efforts to change who acts in her sentences. When speaking to her son, she might say, "The tupelo trees are greeting you; the Narragansett Bay swims by." Reflecting on these efforts, she writes, "I was walking on the beach and realized I didn't have to try anymore to think about this ocean as a person: it just was and is."

When we objectify nature, suggests Robin Wall Kimmerer, exploitation follows, but when we speak of other beings as persons, we cultivate "ecological compassion" for them, bringing them into our "circle of moral responsibility." Writes Kimmerer, "To become native to this place, if we are to survive here, and our neighbors too, our work is to learn to speak the grammar of animacy, so that we might truly be at home."

After the atmospheric river, once the floodwater began to recede and families were able to return to the homes they evacuated, my phone was inundated with fundraising campaigns, many reporting catastrophic losses insurance could not or would not reimburse: renters who discovered their policies didn't cover flood damage, organic farmers whose farm insurance didn't extend to equipment damage and crop loss from flooding, people who operated small businesses from homes that were now-destroyed along with their source of income, homeowners who'd been assured by loan officers their flood risk was minimal.

So, they posted their stories of displacement, documenting the storm's impact and including photos of their beautiful, smiling-despite-it-all children sharing pizzas in hotel rooms, in hopes that strangers, like me, would donate.

From the comfort of our kitchen table, I scrolled through images of submerged minivans and front porches, of toppled over cribs and highchairs covered in silt and recalled how my daughter had tossed with fever upstairs in her bed while nearby children woke to muddy waters sweeping away their sense of normalcy. I sent money and grappled with the commingling of relief and guilt at having been spared as I read stories of families whose rescue came not in the form of a beanstalk or a braid unfurled from a window, but a stranger's boat, a neighbor's tractor.

In the aftermath, attention turned to preventing future disasters. The region's topography suggests that at some point within the last millennium the Nooksack River used to flow northward over what would become the U.S.-Canadian border, and during the 2021 floods, the floodwaters followed that same path across the border, spilling into a manmade agricultural region created when Canadian settlers drained Sumas Lake—a lake which formed thousands of years ago and had been vital to the culture and food security of the Sumas First Nation.

Now, even though the prairie produces food for the region and many people make their homes there, some researchers are calling for managed retreat after finding that rebuilding would cost more than twice as much as restoring the former lake. Buying out properties could offer homeowners, many whose residences are now uninsurable, a financial lifeline while minimizing the risks from future floods. But the region's economy and food supply are now built around the agricultural land, and it's an option many officials are unwilling to consider, though it could restore habitat for salmon and other at-risk species and advance reconciliation efforts by returning land rights to the Semá:th people.

"Some people find it a lot easier to throw their support around the idea of some built infrastructure versus letting the water come in," said Chief Dalton Silver, who also expressed concern for his family and friends who live in the prairie, in an interview with *The Narwhal*, "It's not our way as Semá:th people to be fighting nature."

Choosing whether and how to rebuild in the wake of disaster is just one of the many difficult decisions communities and families face as a changing climate changes the landscape. Across the border, in the United States, efforts to rethink flood management and reduce risks are also underway. Flooding is a story that repeats itself across the landscape. We've built infrastructure to restrict the flow of water in order to construct homes and farm fertile low-lying areas, but water ultimately cannot be tamed. "'Floods' is the word they use, but in fact it is not flooding; it is remembering," wrote Toni Morrison, perhaps ascribing personhood to the Mississippi. "Remembering where it used to be. All water has a perfect memory and is forever trying to get back to where it was."

Increasingly, nonhuman entities, like rivers, are being granted personhood and legal standing. This means the rivers cannot be owned, and polluters who harm a river can be sued on its behalf. "In

Bangladesh, the river is considered as our mother," environmentalist Mohammad Abdul Matin told NPR, following the 2019 passage of a landmark ruling that recognized the country's rivers as living entities with the same legal standing as humans. Though enforcing these legal protections is challenging, the "rights of nature" movement is growing, with rivers and forests gaining legal status in many countries, including in the United States, where Ohio voters approved the short-lived Lake Erie Bill of Rights before it was struck down by a federal court.

In 2019, the Yurok Tribe granted personhood to the Klamath River, which flows from Oregon to northern California, making it the first river in North America to be granted legal rights. The tribe's general counsel, Amy Cordalis, explained its impact on water flow and salmon runs, in an interview with NPR, saying, "[I]t gives the right to the river to exist, to flourish and to naturally evolve and a right to a stable climate free from human caused climate change impacts."

One way to prepare for and adapt to climate change's impacts may be learning to heed the memories of rivers, to rewild landscapes in ways that respect personhood and challenge the fables of progress, to let the landscape speak.

In her book *Women and Other Monsters*, cultural critic Jess Zimmerman revisits her childhood copy of *D'Aulaires' Book of Greek Myths* to reconsider mythological monsters through a feminist lens. "Women have been monsters, and monsters have been women, in centuries' worth of stories, because stories are a way to encode these expectations and pass them on," she writes.

I didn't grow up on *D'Aulaires*, but on Disney, and learned many of the same lessons about monstrous women. In grade school, I was spellbound by *The Little Mermaid*. I rewound our VHS copy and watched it over and over again, rapt. When I return to it now, I'm fascinated by what the story implies about the hierarchy between humans and nonhumans. The way Ariel gives up her voice, everything, for the chance to become human.

My children have not yet watched the Disney films I grew up on, and I'm hesitant to revisit them until they're much older. But recently, during another atmospheric river, we stayed indoors and watched *Shrek*, a movie I hadn't seen in decades.

Just as the fairy-tale creatures invade Shrek's swamp, arriving at his doorstep after being forcibly displaced by Lord Farquaad's efforts to outlaw magic, recognizing the threat enchantment poses to his perfectly orderly concrete kingdom—I looked over at my children. They were giggling and reaching for handfuls of popcorn without taking their eyes from the screen. I wondered which of these characters they might recognize. I can't know what it was like to watch the parody without having seen the source text, but what I saw in the film was the reversal of a familiar plot.

In *Shrek*, Princess Fiona is cursed to be human by day, ogre by night. She fantasizes that someday a prince will rescue her and grant her true love's kiss, finally breaking the curse and allowing her to remain human. Instead, she falls in love with an ogre and comes to embrace, in the end, her monstrous form. Her happily ever after is found not in being human, but in embracing her monstrosity, returning to the forest with the talking animals and other enchanted creatures.

Perhaps we cannot outrun into adulthood the stories that haunt us in childhood. But the thing about folktales and fairy tales is that they have been made and remade for centuries. As Zimmerman writes, "[T]he stories we're given can be rewritten, reconceived, even redacted—and nobody redacts like a monster. Imagine tending your terrible children until they're strong enough not only to leave the cave, but to rip out the heart of the story. Imagine nurturing them until their little claws grow sharp enough to shred the old sentiments, the old sentences."

Rewilding our storytelling, like rewilding the landscape, may help us work out the tensions inherent to bearing, and sustaining, life on a planet that's imperiled, to hold our griefs and shape our hopes.

As a mother, I'm most interested in telling my children stories that will help them live on a damaged planet, stories that help them to recognize all their many entanglements and to imagine possibilities for mutual well-being. I want to teach them to sharpen their claws, to sniff out the stories that need to be shredded in order for new ones to emerge.

Little Apocalypses

The morning after the winter solstice, it was dark and I was still in bed, tossing and turning through the contractions of false labor, when I heard my daughter's footsteps in the hall. She appeared at the doorway to our bedroom, a small figure backlit by the night light. "Come cuddle," I whispered, as I did most mornings.

She crawled into bed and settled into the space between us. I draped an arm over her shoulders, the round moon of my belly curving against the small of her back.

She lay still for a few minutes, breathing heavily, and part of me hoped we might fall back to sleep, until she turned to face me, placing her palms on my cheeks, to ask for a story.

I closed my eyes, leaned forward to touch my forehead to hers and breathed out as my abdomen tightened once more. With my due date approaching, all I wanted was for the longest night of the year to last just a little longer.

I heard the rustle of sheets and then the quiet click of a flashlight, and when I opened my eyes again, my husband was shining a small beam of light at the eaves. Into that bright circle, hopped a bunny, which morphed into a crab, which morphed into a bird, then finally into a frog that was identifiable only by its croaking, much to our daughter's delight, before it, too, crumpled into darkness.

"Your turn," he whispered, handing her the flashlight.

My daughter pointed it at the ceiling and wiggled her fingers behind it. The spotlight remained empty. "Want me to show you?" I asked, before forming her two fingers into bunny ears and bringing her small hand into the light.

In my early twenties, I went to a spiritual director who guided me through the unraveling of my faith. Each time we met, she sat across from me and lit a candle, blowing out the match and tucking it into a little matchbox. Sometimes we sat quietly, listening to the flame hiss and crackle, while I searched for something true to say.

As a child, I had been given a set of stories about myself and about the world, stories that, my evangelical church told me, had all the answers. As a teenager and young adult, I spent years rereading and reinterpreting those stories in search of different answers, before finally beginning to read, instead, for questions and for silences.

When I spoke, my spiritual director listened to all that was unresolved within me with a gentleness I could not give myself. I needed to grieve the harm those stories had caused in the hands of powerful people, to grieve the sense of betrayal I felt toward those I'd found to be unreliable narrators.

Once—after telling her that I felt pressure to arrive at answers to my deepest, most perplexing questions before becoming a mother, that I worried about raising children without the certainties, theological and otherwise, that had shaped my own upbringing—she'd held out her hands, one open, one closed. She raised her closed fist over the palm of her open hand and unfurled it, as if releasing something into it, letting it go. "Whatever parents pass on to their children is like a hunk of clay," she told me, curling her fingers around the imaginary clay. "And children are free to mold it into shapes of their choosing."

Hearing this, I thought of a definition of fundamentalism that I'd read in Rachel Held Evan's writings about leaving evangelicalism:

"holding so tightly to your beliefs that your fingernails leave imprints on the palm of your hand."

By then, I'd loosened my grip on my beliefs so much, I wasn't sure what, if anything, remained. What stories would I someday tell my children about the beginning of the world and about its end, I wondered, knowing that my children would also be listening for what these stories told them about humanity, about the more-than-human world, and about themselves.

I want my children to be familiar with the narratives that have shaped much of our culture, and indeed my own life, but I don't want to burden them with belief. I didn't want to hand my children the stories I'd been given, but still I wanted to give them something with which to shape their own.

Both my children were born in mid-winter, which means that, twice, I have spent the holiday season waiting, sometimes impatiently, to give birth.

When I was pregnant for the first time, a friend sent me a small Advent book about how woodland animals prepare for and adapt to winter, a season that confronts us with the realities of death. That Advent occurs during the darkest weeks of the year makes the ritual lighting of candles both a poignant reminder of the gifts of darkness and a promise that the light will return.

In the final two weeks of that pregnancy, time slowed, and I greeted each dim morning with stories of animals, like black-capped chickadees, who spend cold winter days foraging for food to keep up their fat reserves, and painted box turtles, who bury themselves in mud beneath frozen ponds, holding their breath until spring. Day after day, animal after animal showed me how to prepare, how to adapt, how to wait—by slowing down, focusing on my breath, and finding stillness.

In my third trimester, I'd worked diligently for weeks, carefully managing my time to submit final grades and complete my other work, so that after giving birth, I could take twelve weeks of unpaid leave. But once winter break began, I napped. I lay in bed listening to guided meditations, visualizing giving birth. My husband and I took rambling hikes through the woods. I paced the boardwalk, squinting out at the horizon against the misty rain, anticipating the contractions that would come like waves.

During my second pregnancy, between work and caring for a toddler, it was more challenging to do what I felt I most needed to ready myself for giving birth. When I once again picked up our Advent book as my due date approached, I read to my daughter the story of the black bear's hibernation—how a mother bear sleeps soundly through the winter and rouses in spring to find she has birthed and nursed two cubs, all without waking up—I thought, *must be nice*, and resolved to, at least, try to take a nap.

I've taken to keeping this book of animal stories in our box of winter decorations. I read it aloud to my children as the solstice approaches, appreciating how it invites us to observe the holidays in ways that are neither overly religious nor consumeristic, but instead attuned to the seasonal rhythms that once structured our experience of time.

There is something quietly subversive, in a dominant culture that requires the relentless churn of productivity and profit in all seasons, about stories that remind us of our soft animal bodies, of the need to gather in the dark, to make space for rest.

In her book *Wintering*—about those long, dark winters of the soul, like illness, loss, and depression, which ultimately transform us—Katherine May also takes lessons from the natural world. "Plants and animals don't fight the winter; they don't pretend it's not happening and attempt to carry on living the same lives they lived in the summer. They prepare. They adapt. They perform extraordinary acts of metamorphosis to get them through," she writes. "Wintering is a time of withdrawing from the world, maximizing scant resources, carrying out acts of brutal efficiency and vanishing from sight; but that's where the transformation occurs. Winter is not the death of the life cycle, but its crucible."

In my experience of giving birth, I came to see that it, too, is a crucible. That labor often begins in the dark of night, and, in the face of its extremes, I sought a quiet, safe place to transform. Breathing into the brutal power and pain of childbirth is to know that to be human is to live and to die, that the guttural wailing of grief is nearly indistinguishable from the wailing of labor, but that on the other side of all that work, there is no sound on earth quite like the cry of a newborn baby.

Yet, we live in a culture that professes devotion to mothers and babies, all the while systematically denying people who have given birth the right to withdraw, to rest and recover, to transform. As Jacqueline Rose writes in *Mothers: An Essay on Love and Cruelty*, "Mothers require protection, solace, and support from the first moment they find themselves the bearers of new life. Instead, you would think that mothers were the danger against which the workplace needs to protect itself."

The same forces that deny birthing people care and support are stressing planetary systems, pushing the Earth to the brink by disturbing and disregarding its natural cycles and processes, and pressuring people and the more-than-human world to produce as if nothing has changed.

Now, when my children and I read our Advent book each year, I think, the wisdom of animals in winter may contain more than just insights into accepting our limitations and living with the seasons, but also wisdom for learning to live within a changed climate; rather than carrying on with business as usual, we can instead prepare, adapt, and transform.

According to church tradition, Advent is the four-week season of hopeful anticipation preceding Christmas, a time so significant that it marks the beginning of the liturgical new year.

Because most evangelical churches, like the one I grew up attending, don't follow liturgical rites, I was surprised when, years ago, I visited a friend's Episcopal church during Advent and heard scripture readings that included the apocalyptic teachings of Jesus, prophecies that warn of cataclysmic upheaval and cosmic darkness—hardly tidings of comfort and joy. Ever since, I'd wondered, what did end-times prophecies have to do with anticipating the birth of a baby?

Once I knew what it was like to await my child's birth while reading the latest climate reports and contemplating the end of the world as we know it, it didn't seem so strange. When I mentioned my fascination with these apocalyptic texts to a friend who is a pastor, they told me that in contrast to the "big apocalypse" that is the Book of Revelation, the apocalyptic teachings read during Advent are collectively known as the "little apocalypse."

I laughed, at first, because when you put it that way, it makes the trials and tribulations of civilizational collapse sound slightly more manageable, kind of adorable even. Like when something sort of bad happens, and you attempt to put it into perspective by saying, "It's not the end of the world." Only, in this case, it really is.

I began to wonder if we all experience little apocalypses—diagnoses and disasters, births and deaths, and all the many human dramas that cleave our lives into before and after stories—that shake the ground beneath us and cast the light of familiar stars into darkness, revealing the glorious, heartbreaking world as it is, and meanwhile all around us people, even those who love us best, are carrying on with their everyday lives.

The Magnificat is another text read during Advent—the revolutionary hymn attributed to Mary. Composed during her pregnancy, it expresses her longing for the end of one world and the beginning of another. In it, Mary casts a vision for a world in which the powerful forces of empire are overthrown and the rich are turned away emptyhanded so that the hungry may feast. It's a call for justice so radical that, historically, the singing of her song has been banned at least three times by nations seeking to prevent mass uprisings. Reverend M Jade Kaiser's modern interpretation of the Magnificat puts fresh language to it. They write: "God is a feast for the hungry. God is the great redistributor of wealth and resources. God is the ceasing of excessive and destructive production that all the earth might rest."

Amidst the singing of carols and lighting of candles to herald the birth of a baby, an invitation to contemplate a world transformed by justice.

During my first pregnancy, the doula who taught our childbirth course recommended an exercise in which we were to hold an ice cube in our hands for 60–90 seconds—the length of an average contraction.

It was an invitation, she said, to consider our ability to bear pain.

Though it seems silly now, when I returned home, I couldn't bring myself to try it. It was not as if I'd never experienced physical pain before, but something about the exercise felt too deterministic. I feared, almost superstitiously, what the practice might reveal about me and my ability to cope with labor. I didn't want to open my hand and find myself wanting.

Though I'd chosen to give birth attended by midwives, I hadn't bothered to write a birth plan, accepting that childbirth was an experience I could prepare for but, ultimately, would be unable to script out in advance. Instead, waiting to give birth for the first time, I read and listened to hundreds of birth stories. Stories of home births and hospital births, emergency C-sections and still births, premature births and induced labor, surrogate births and twin births, stories of trauma and transformation, stories that held insights and warnings, stories that helped me understand the stakes and the scope of what was possible. Everyone is born, I realized, but there are so many ways that birth can go.

Aside from the handful of birth stories I'd heard from family and friends or read on blogs or social media posts, the birth story, as a genre, was largely unfamiliar to me until I became pregnant. I'd encountered few literary accounts of giving birth, and the stories I read in childbirth books, podcasts, and message boards were an affront to what I had observed in film and television depictions of labor and delivery, which all seemed determined to compress time—to skip over the long days of waiting, uncomfortably, for labor to begin, the long hours of early labor, the even longer minutes of pushing—and jump cut to the skin-to-skin triumph of a crying baby held to a bare chest.

Despite the relatively few representations of birth in fiction and on-screen, humans seem to find narratives of beginnings as well as endings particularly animating, and the most ancient of these, are stories about the beginnings and endings of the world itself. Often these stories are joined in figures who represent both birth and death, as with the Hindu goddess Durga, who is both a creative and destructive force, and Pele, the Hawaiian volcano deity who creates new land by destroying what came before.

As environmental writer Kate Weiner notes in her introduction to *Waking the Ground*—a double-sided magazine issue on the duality of birth and death—thinking about our relationship to birth invites all of us to remember our embodied relationship to natural cycles of beginnings and endings and to consider the process of letting old stories die and birthing new narratives. She writes, "To give birth is to put one's body on the line, and when so much is at stake—our climate, our culture, our children—(re)membering what it means to put our bodies on the line is vital."

To bring a child into the world is quite literally to reckon with the mortal risks of pregnancy and childbirth. In her book *Like a Mother*, Angela Garbes writes, "Childbirth is beautiful, but it is not pretty. It is grisly and life affirming, glorious and deadly. It requires you to open, to rip apart both physically and emotionally, and allows the scent of death to seep through those tears and fissures. Whatever form it takes, however long it takes, it is also the means to an ecstatic end."

Giving birth in the United States is especially perilous given the maternal health crisis, which is likely to worsen as states restrict access to reproductive care. Already, it is the country with the highest maternal mortality rate among industrialized nations, with racism and sexism placing Black and Indigenous women most at risk. The medical system, like so many systems, very often does not listen to women, especially to women of color. Yet, many people still choose to give birth—and it must remain a choice—putting their bodies on the line because they believe that the risks are worth it.

But birth is just one metaphor for thinking more deeply about how we participate in the act of bearing worlds. Weiner continues, "We put our bodies on the line through direct action, committed relationship, daily labor . . . In this way, our bodies are vessels for new worlds to flow through. What kind of vessel are you? What is flowing through?"

Stories, too, are vessels through which words and worlds flow. These days, I find myself turning over stories about beginnings and endings much the same way my children pick up small rocks on the beach, just to see what lives there.

The faith tradition I was brought up in offers several stories of creation and destruction. Of the latter, the most famous of these is the apocalypse foretold in Revelation. A fever dream of a book, written by John of Patmos, it's dense with violent, hallucinatory prophecies of global suffering, and in Western culture, it has seeded our most potent and persistent ideas about the end of the world—which means that even when I left the church, I was unable to fully leave its stories.

When I read Revelation as a teenager, I was alarmed by the description of Christ as a militant warrior king, riding in on horseback, clad in a blood-dipped robe; it was a stark and disturbing departure from the carpenter Jesus who rode a humble donkey and taught his followers to give their possessions to the poor, to welcome strangers, to love their neighbors and forgive their enemies.

In his book *Life After Doom*, Brian McLaren, a former English professor and pastor, attempts to summarize Revelation, writing, "At the end of the Christian Bible, an old mystic, banished to an island, writes a work of apocalyptic fiction in which civilization collapses in an orgy of economic desperation, religious corruption, desperate political violence, and ecological catastrophe—the same macabre mixture of environmental and social collapse that produce our sense of doom today."

Perhaps it's because the manifold doomsday scenarios foretold in Revelation are devastatingly predictable—earthquakes, plague, famine, injustice, and war—that they have resonated with readers for thousands of years. It's not exactly comforting to know that nearly every generation has feared it could be the last, brought to an end by some great catastrophe or another, but it does offer some perspective.

Dorian Lynskey, in *Everything Must Go*, traces the development of apocalyptic stories from the Christian apocalypse to its secularization in the nineteenth century, demonstrating how existential threats have shaped contemporary film and literature, politics and culture. Even apocalyptic narratives that don't acknowledge Revelation as a source text are beholden to it because it has so shaped our collective imagination of disaster and civilizational collapse. Whatever the threat fueling contemporary apocalypses—be it the atomic bomb or uncontrollable artificial intelligence or climate change—the central anxiety seems to be that humans have made a mess of things. In that sense, not much has changed.

At the time of John's writing, Revelation was just one of many apocalypses in circulation. As Lynskey notes, "Before it became a synonym for the end of the world in the nineteenth century, *apocalypse* described a genre rather than an event; it was a form of storytelling."

I find it telling that, as a genre, apocalypses are far more well-known and widely regarded than birth stories. I struggle to imagine a world in which birth stories evince the same cultural and political impact.

Because stories about the end of the world exercise such force, particularly in Western culture, Catherine Keller argues for what she calls "apocalyptic mindfulness." She warns that the overuse of apocalyptic rhetoric within climate discourse may lead to unproductive responses in the form of climate denial, on the one hand, and climate doom, on the other. She writes, "If apocalypticism cannot be erased, it must be *minded*: used *mindfully*, that is not for mindless fright or melodrama, not for supernatural or sci-fi flight. To attend to its actual meaning becomes key to redirecting its present energies."

In other words, if we can't escape these stories, and if we can't escape the planet, then we must become skillful at recognizing and transforming apocalyptic rhetoric. Learning to cultivate apocalyptic mindfulness, Keller writes, may "keep us from acting it out in private despair or collective inevitability, playing it out subliminally in our economic habits, democratic disarray and ecological suicide."

Keller emphasizes the creative potential of facing the apocalypse, writing, "It means to confront the forces of destruction: to crack open, to disclose, a space where late chances, last chances, remain nonetheless real chances." Likewise, Lama Rod Owens writes: "To meet the apocalypse, you must embody an intention that this experience will not consume you, that this experience is calling you into a deeper labor of transformation and creativity." To crack open, to labor, to make space for transformation—this sounds to me like the work of giving birth.

But, for many of us, minding the existential threat of climate change is easier said than done. When we aren't doomscrolling or personally contending with its disastrous effects, it can be difficult to think about the climate crisis, let alone talk about it.

In an essay about climate anxiety, *New Yorker* writer Jia Tolentino observes, "It may be impossible to seriously consider the reality of climate change for longer than ninety seconds without feeling depressed, angry, guilty, grief-stricken, or simply insane." At ninety seconds, my thoughts returned to the ice cube test and my inclination to avoid the pain of facing reality as it is, my reluctance to open my hands to it.

The other day, just to see what it felt like, I stood at the kitchen sink holding an ice cube in my palm, watching it slowly lose its shape as the seconds ticked by, as melting water dripped between my fingers and down the drain.

Despite all that medicine can tell us about human reproduction, we still don't know exactly what causes labor to begin. The best theory is that it's triggered by an interplay of fetal and maternal hormones and influenced by genetics and environmental factors.

I knew all this from my first pregnancy, but as my due date approached, that didn't prevent me from spending a portion of each appointment asking my midwife to review the symptoms I should watch for, to speculate as to when she thought labor might begin.

It was maddening to anticipate such rupture and change, not knowing where or when or how it would begin. As time ticked on, I was often impatient, short-tempered, and exhausted. I was on edge, reading my body's signs, alert to any possibility that my water might be breaking, that my false contractions might suddenly become true.

People try to offer helpful advice. Rest now, they say, while you still can, even though I was so uncomfortable I could barely sleep. But also, distract yourself by staying busy. I made freezer meals, washed and folded baby clothes, packed an overnight bag—these were all useful things to do, but in my experience, even the most careful of preparations cannot ease the pressure of all that waiting.

In his apocalyptic sermons, Jesus warns his followers that they are living in an in-between time and implores them to remain alert, vigilant in waiting for the apocalypse to come. But this is an impossible way to live, and those who actually manage to conduct their lives as if the world's end is imminent, are often found to be under the sway of the warped group think of a doomsday cult.

But, in a sense, waiting to give birth, is sort of like sitting around waiting for the apocalypse to come. While not as imprecise as the long history of failed Doomsday predictions, due dates are misleading in their own way because a full-term birth can happen any time in a roughly five-week window. For those caught in the in-between time of waiting, time plays tricks.

In her memoir of receiving an incurable cancer diagnosis—a

very different kind of in-between time—religious historian Kate Bowler explains the Christian tradition's language for time: pastoral time, tragic time, and apocalyptic time. Pastoral time describes the unremarkable, but unspeakably good, experience of going about our ordinary, everyday lives, following the seasons and rhythms of the natural world. Tragic time describes how pain, suffering, and death can trigger an existential awareness of mortality. Apocalyptic time describes those world-shattering moments of awakening when we see the world, with its deeply unjust systems of exploitation and oppression, as it has always been. "There is a wonderful and terrible clarity to apocalyptic time," Bowler writes. "The last chapter has been read, and now that it is too late, all the hidden facets of our stories are beginning to reveal themselves."

It seems to me that we live in a dominant culture determined to deny all three modes of time—refusing to abide by the limitations of the natural world, preferring distractions to the realities of pain and death, and obscuring the systems that structure our lives and communities.

In my experience of childbirth, once labor finally began, it was as if time collapsed. I found it cyclical, painful, and revelatory.

Sometimes I try to imagine what stories we would tell about the climate crisis if apocalyptic rhetoric weren't readily available, if our collective imagination had not been so profoundly shaped by the sense that the ending has already been written. It's not that I think we need more hopeful stories, it's that I think we might need more helpful stories. What if we were to open our clenched fists and let go of old stories so that we might shape new ones with the materials we've been given?

Perhaps we might look to the natural world and its cycles and rhythms. Perhaps we might even look to our own bodies, to our experiences of dying and giving birth, for other narrative shapes, other metaphors, other ways of plotting time.

Because most of us have few direct experiences witnessing death and birth, this suggests that the people who provide care for dying and birthing people may be among our wisest storytellers in this era of change and loss.

In a conversation with palliative care physician Kathryn Mannix, Bowler describes the kinds of choices that people living with advanced illnesses can make. In the space between everything is possible and nothing is possible, is what she calls "limited agency." In response, Mannix says, "Do everything is a hope that's pinned on cure. And do nothing is despair. But actually there's do what you can and let your hope evolve. It's somewhere in the middle of that continuum, isn't it? And so what do you hope for if you can't hope for a cure?"

While Mannix is talking about the kinds of decisions a person can make about treatment options or managing symptoms, the language of "limited agency" may help us to hold open the space between hope and despair so that we might talk more productively about what's possible, about developing a framework for equitable climate adaptation and mitigation.

As a culture, we seem to be fairly averse to thinking and talking about death, but we may be even less skillful at thinking and talking about birth. Yet, in childbirth, wherein fear and love, pain and strength are concentrated in the intense, embodied experience of bringing a new life into the world, perhaps, we might find alternative metaphors for conceptualizing the climate crisis.

In an interview with *YES!* magazine, adrienne maree brown draws on her experiences as a doula to explain the persistence required for bringing about social change. She describes the moment when birthing parents reach the point of painful exhaustion and realize they cannot quit:

I know there's something miraculous coming but I've been pushing a long time for it, and what I want to do is rest my body and my mind and my spirit. And it's like, how do I take in breaths that give me rest, knowing that there are still several more pushes before this new world, this next phase, this next era that we are responsible for bringing into existence, actually comes into existence?

Reading this, I can remember deep in my body, what it felt like to reach that point of exhaustion, and to keep going. I remember how important it was for me to feel supported by my midwives as I made decisions about when and how I wanted to push.

As in palliative care, the choices that birthing people make are important. The feeling that they have agency, or the ability to make choices even if things don't go as planned is one of the things that can lead birthing people to feel good about their birth experiences.

Once birth begins, anything can happen. Feminist philosopher of motherhood Sara Ruddick wrote, "Birth is a beginning whose end and shape can be neither predicted nor controlled. Since the safety of human bodies, mortal and susceptible to damage, can never be secured and since humans grow variously, but always in need of help, to give birth is to commit oneself to protecting the unprotectable and nurturing the unpredictable." This is exactly what responding to the climate crisis asks of us, to make ourselves vulnerable to the experience of "protecting the unprotectable and nurturing the unpredictable."

In an era of rising pro-natalism and alarming attacks on reproductive freedoms, I wonder what would happen if we actually listened to birthing people, affirming their agency in making choices about their bodies and their medical care, if we made both abortion and childbirth safer, more comfortable, more comprehensively supported experiences, if we made space for all the many birth stories, including those of miscarriage and loss, that unfold every day? By attending more carefully to the bodies and stories of birthing people, we might find a path forward into the start of something new.

Jennifer Banks, in *Natality*, a philosophical investigation of birth, writes, "Death has been humanity's central defining experience, its deepest existential theme, more authoritative somehow than birth and certainly more final." In contrast with mortality, Banks endeavors to recover the term Hannah Arendt coined to describe the human condition of having been born: natality. She writes, "Because we were all born, Arendt believed, we are always all capable of beginning again, of starting something new through each human action—the most prized of capabilities, in Arendt's estimation." Likewise, Jaqueline Rose observes that for Arendt, "every new birth is the supreme anti-totalitarian moment" and that "freedom is identical with the capacity to begin."

By reimagining the stories we tell about the end of the world, by insisting that we can begin again, we take back our power to remake the world.

Climate activist Thelma Young Lutunatabua put it this way: "As a mother, cynicism is not an option. My hope is tied to an existing practice of refusing to allow apocalyptic prophecies of the future to come to pass. . . . There is no choice for me but to ensure as many families as possible can safely make it through this rebirth."

Holding open my hand, I think, when the big stories become too hard and heavy to work with, the little stories are what I can offer my children. We are born and then we die—and what happens in between those moments is everything. That's the beauty and terror of it.

As Rebecca Solnit writes in *Hope in the Dark*, "But again and again, far stranger things happen than the end of the world." Of the uncertain future, she writes, "The future is dark, with a darkness as much of the womb as the grave."

Twice, I have breathed through labor pains that would not cease until the work was done, pushed through the realization that I could not quit. And each time, I did not quit pushing until I held a slippery and squalling newborn and felt the warm weight of bringing a new life into the world.

I am beginning to think the struggle to bring into being a more just and livable world may also be something like that, and that's something I hold onto, as I hold onto my children. It's the miracle that begins again each morning when I hear my children's quiet footsteps in the hallway, the miracle I celebrate each winter when I tell them the stories of their births, the miracle I celebrate each summer when we make sun prints on the solstice to mark the astonishing return of the light. Like the truth at the heart of the animal stories in our Advent book, "the dark is not an end, but a door. It's the way a new beginning comes."

Mother Nature

"Babies aren't robots." This is probably the only bit of original parenting advice I offered my sister when I visited after she gave birth. Surely others have said as much, but the realization came to me one evening, years earlier, when my husband and I were comparing notes on rocking and shushing techniques after a particularly drawn-out bedtime routine. We were so eager for sleep that we'd become exacting in our efforts to replicate whatever conditions had previously helped soothe our five-month-old daughter. We weren't consciously trying to program our baby for sleep, but we felt bewildered when our efforts to follow best practices failed, suggesting that maybe, in fact, we were. Soon after, we took to reminding each other, whenever one of us was spinning out over the vagaries of parenting, "She's not a robot!"

It was a comforting thought, one that made it easier to shrug our shoulders over the unexpected, the variable, the ever-changing conditions. Infants develop so rapidly that as soon as it felt like we had things figured out, our daughter would enter a new stage. Sometimes our daughter was hungry or tired or teething, but just as often there wasn't a problem to solve, sometimes she was just growing, sometimes she just needed to be held. As she changed, we changed.

There's so much good information out there now, my own mother has observed, about contemporary parenting. And it's true, I'm grateful for the resources always at my fingertips, but as we emerge from the baby years, I find myself limiting the amount of expert parenting content I take in. What was it like, I've wondered, to parent without the proliferation of word-for-word scripts for every conceivable child-rearing situation, without social media feeds filled with coaches modeling exactly what to do and what not to do, without so many faces scrutinizing my efforts from the screen of my own phone.

It took years of parenting for me to arrive at a related realization: a mother is not a robot. I could no more program myself to perform motherhood perfectly than I could program our children for childhood—nor would I want to.

Recently, we settled in for a family movie night to watch *The Wild Robot*, the story of a robot who becomes a mother. Set in the distant future, it's based on Peter Brown's middle-grade novel about an intelligent robot called ROZZUM unit 7134, or Roz, for short, who is shipwrecked on an island in the Pacific Northwest.

When some curious sea otters accidentally press her power button, the task-oriented automaton boots up. With no discernible task to complete, Roz sets out to learn as much as she can about the island and its wildlife, including how to communicate across species. After she's involved in an accident that kills a family of geese, it falls to her to adopt the lone survivor, an orphaned gosling who imprints on her.

Roz, voiced by Lupita Nyong'o, complains about the difficulties of new parenthood: "That gosling stalks me, and makes noise and makes simple tasks more complicated, or impossible." But Roz comes to care about the gosling, whom she calls Brightbill, and commits to the work of teaching him to eat, swim, and fly before migration.

She accepts this role with some hesitation and self-doubt. "I do not have the programming to be a mother," Roz says to an opossum named Pinktail. Voiced by Catherine O'Hara, Pinktail, whose own litter of joeys numbers seven, replies, consolingly, "No one does. We just make it up."

It's the kind of admission from a fellow, more experienced mother that is as unmooring as it is reassuring. I was sandwiched between my children on the couch, nodding my head, when it occurred to me that I was commiserating with animated characters. Human, opossum, robot—all of us contending with the confounding, life-altering experience of caring for our young.

Philosopher Sara Ruddick wrote in her 1989 feminist classic, *Maternal Thinking*, "Anyone who commits her or himself to responding to children's demands, and makes the work of response a considerable part of her or his life, is a mother." So much about motherhood that we are led to believe is instinctual, is natural, is biological, a matter of programming, is really just a matter of making it up, of committing to the work of care and opening oneself to being changed by the experience of caregiving.

Emerging research on the plasticity of the parental brain demonstrates how caregiving changes us—it rewires the brains not just of birthing parents but also of fathers, co-parents, adoptive parents, and foster parents and other care providers in ways that affect long-term physical and mental health. "Birthing a baby doesn't simply turn on a long-dormant circuit marked for maternal instinct and specific to the brains of females," writes Chelsea Conaboy in her book *Mother Brain*. "Researchers studying the neurobiology of parents have begun documenting the many ways having a child reorganizes the brain, altering the neural feedback loops that dictate how we react to the world around us, how we read and respond to other people, and how we regulate our own emotions."

While I don't have the fMRI scans to prove it, I suspect that among the myriad ways caregiving has changed me is that it has brought me into a deeper relationship with the place we call home.

Roz's efforts to survive in the wilderness reminded me of a show we watched in the first few weeks after bringing our son home from the birth center, when so much of my time was spent breastfeeding on the couch.

After our daughter, who was three at the time, was tucked in and asleep for the night, my husband and I would sit in the darkened living room holding our newborn and eating dinner in front of the television. I was in the mood for something slow and quiet, something with few characters and little dialogue or plot, and, somehow, we started watching *Alone*—a reality competition that became popular during the pandemic, in which contestants film their efforts to live in the wilderness in total solitude.

Roz's island bore a striking resemblance to the remote area of Vancouver Island, on the traditional territory of the Quatsino First Nation, where the contestants were dropped, by boat or by helicopter, with camera gear, ten tools of their choice, first aid equipment, and a satellite radio with a GPS tracker and tap-out button. As they went about building shelters and gathering firewood, I recognized the persistent rain that fell over everything, just as it was falling outside our windows while we watched. I recognized the distinctly Pacific Northwest landscape, the rocky shorelines, the Douglas fir and western red cedar, and the cloud-covered mountains, but instead of the cleared trails I was accustomed to hiking, I saw only the thick, nearly impassable underbrush of sword ferns and salal.

Whereas Roz survived unencumbered by the physical needs of a body, the contestants on *Alone* were forced to spend most of their time and energy searching for food. Some I judged to be former military or prepper types who framed the experience in terms of the man-versus-nature conflict, while others seemed to be back-to-the-land homesteaders who were eager to live cooperatively with nature. Most were white, a few were women, and all the participants were motivated by prize money to outlast the other competitors.

I was so bleary-eyed from cluster feedings, at the time, that I don't remember much about the show, or even who won the seasons we watched, but something about the isolation and physical demands, punctuated by moments of intense beauty, resonated with my postpartum experience.

I wasn't alone, of course—friends and neighbors delivered meals, and my husband, who took parental leave, provided constant support, making my favorite foods and taking our daughter on outings—but I'd stepped back from work and social life and I was alone in a body that was healing from childbirth while waking to feed our son every two hours.

While, on screen, contestants foraged for limpets, I held my sleeping newborn in my arms, stroking the bridge of his nose and the side of his cheek with my fingertip, watching his lips turn instinctively toward my touch, rooting for nourishment—and I contemplated attachment, both between parents and children and between people and places.

What did the *Alone* contestants' efforts to survive in isolation in the wilderness—and our own efforts to do right by our children in early parenthood—suggest about our reciprocal relationships to the people and places that care for us?

When I was still teaching, I used to assign my college writing students to read about place attachment—the idea that humans form significant, intimate bonds with landscapes.

Early nature writing extolled the virtues of spending prolonged periods of solitude in wild places, time spent making careful observations about the landscape and wildlife while engaging in personal reflection. More recently, environmental writers have challenged this somewhat narrow view of place attachment, but thrumming throughout this literary tradition is the sense that our ability to form connections to place can be a deeply meaningful part of being human and that such attachments may prove vital to healing ecological crises.

As scholar Jennifer Case concludes, "While we can question how much to celebrate place attachment in an era of globalization and climate change, and although we can complicate experiences of place through gender, race, class, and sexuality, we seem to keep coming back to it, indicating the ways in which place attachment remains integral not only to environmental nonfiction, but also the human experience."

It wasn't until after having children of my own that I began to think about place attachment in terms of the attachment theories put forward by developmental psychologists. Perhaps this is because stories of parenting young children aren't included often enough in what gets called nature writing, or perhaps it's because I simply hadn't thought that all that much about attachment until becoming a parent, at which point establishing a secure bond with my children felt paramount—the stakes, or so I'd heard, were nothing less than their lifelong ability to form healthy relationships.

The set-up of *Alone* struck me as a psychological experiment not unlike the Strange Situation assessment devised by researcher Mary Ainsworth, who first identified the attachment styles—secure, anxious, avoidant, and disorganized—that have become ubiquitous in popular psychology. In the Strange Situation, a mother and baby enter a playroom with a stranger. They play for a while before the mother walks out of the room. Researchers assess how the baby reacts to the mother's departure, to the stranger's attempts to interact, and to the mother's eventual return.

When I watched a recording of a Strange Situation assessment, my initial reaction was one of confusion. It seemed too random, too brief, too incomplete an encounter to meaningfully evaluate the quality of a relationship as complex and nuanced as the one between a mother and child. I felt moved with concern for the women who'd subjected the quality of their parenting to the judgments of observers concealed behind a wall of one-way mirrors.

In *The Good Mother Myth*, Nancy Reddy suggests that there is reason to question much of the science that shapes our ideas about attachment and what it means to be a good mother. For instance, Ainsworth only conducted two real-world observational studies on attachment styles and, upon reexamination, both show evidence of cultural biases and flawed research design.

In a yearlong study based in Baltimore, rather than using established sampling methods for qualitative research, Ainsworth selected 23 middle-class white families based on the recommendations of their pediatricians. Graduate students who observed these households only visited during daytime hours, when fathers weren't present, and at least one observer took months to write up her notes following these visits. "All of attachment styles research is perched on top of these imprecise records of a narrow, haphazardly selected group of white women from midcentury Baltimore," concludes Reddy.

Nor has this research adequately recognized forms of caregiving that are practiced outside the mythical norm of the white, middle-class nuclear family headed by a single income earner. Instead, it has reinforced an exclusionary ideal that ignores the experiences of most American parents, especially single parents, same-sex parents, trans or nonbinary parents, and parents raising children in multigenerational households. As Conaboy writes, "The 'good mother ideal' never has been fully extended to women of color. Or to women in poverty. Or to anyone less likely to hew to the 'angel in the house' model because they have to work or because they choose to. Or because it is important to them that their children be raised by a circle of family and friends that stretches beyond themselves."

Attachment theory research also hasn't led to structural changes, like paid parental leave and access to early childhood education, that would support parents and families. Instead, as Reddy points out, in the United States, our ideas about attachment are often implicated in recommendations that undermine working parents. John Bowlby, the founder of attachment theory, for instance, campaigned against daycare.

The problem with much of the thinking around attachment isn't that it emphasizes the importance of the parent-child relationship, instead it's how this research is used to perpetuate a narrowly defined ideal of good motherhood, as well as the expectation that mothers, alone, bear the responsibility for their children's healthy development.

Like the young children in the Strange Situation, who were left in the company of an unfamiliar caregiver, the *Alone* contestants were left in an unfamiliar place.

Not only were contestants tasked with survival, but they were also required to film themselves constantly, recording monologues, which, as the days wore on, became increasingly personal. They spoke about the children and loved ones they left behind, shared their motivations for pursuing the prize money, and mused about personal failings and dreams deferred. The competition was billed as a physical challenge, one that tested bushcraft and shelter-building skills, but it arguably posed a more arduous psychological challenge, as contestants sought to make meaning of their wilderness experiences with only the imagined audience of the camera for support.

Upon tapping out, contestants were relieved to return home, but they also nearly always expressed appreciation for the place that had nourished them. They'd learned to read their surroundings for signs of predators, prey, and edible plants, for how wind and water moved across their campsites during storms, for how tides and currents affected fishing and foraging, and, in the process, forged a bond to the island.

Like early nature writing, *Alone* reinforces the thinking that place attachment occurs primarily between people and the wild places they experience in solitude. But while the competition may take place in nature, its emphasis on independence over interdependence seems, to me, profoundly unnatural. We need each other for survival; we weren't meant to live alone.

Despite its grueling premise, participants never fully dropped out of society. They were tracked and monitored by the production team, which was always a boat or helicopter ride away. Whenever someone was seriously injured or became ill, they were promptly transported to a nearby hospital for care, and all were periodically visited for medical checks to ensure their safety and well-being.

These precautions remind me of how, during the time that Thoreau spent at Walden Pond, his mother and other family members may have visited to do laundry and bring food. While many have disparaged Thoreau for this, sometimes to humorous effect, especially online, part of me loves knowing that he had help. Not even Thoreau, who wrote of solitude and self-sufficiency, lived in isolation, but instead supported his mother and sisters, including by hosting a meeting of their abolitionist organization at his cabin, and, in turn, they supported him. In *Walden* there are chapters on visitors and the nearby village, as well as sustained engagement with social and political issues. In other words, Thoreau did not seek a hermit's life in the woods.

I'm not a survivalist, nor have I ever understood the bunker mentality that motivates some preppers, but I'm certain that I wouldn't want to bug out to a remote location or emerge with my family from a hold deep underground, after some apocalyptic disaster or another, to find ourselves the lone survivors—though this distorted version of self-reliance seemed to be a motivating fantasy for some of the show's contestants.

Watching comfortably from my couch with my sleeping son curled atop my chest and my belly full of soup that neighbors had dropped off for dinner, I began to wonder if cash-fueled reality competitions like *Alone* are the product of a profoundly lonely culture, a people disconnected from both the natural world and from each other.

Though I don't doubt the transformative potential of solo wilderness journeys, some of my most meaningful outdoors experiences have been those I've shared with family and friends much closer to home. Every summer, we camp at a state park on a nearby island, where in addition to acres of public lands with hiking trails through old-growth forests, there is also a lakeside ice cream shop, a large playground, and campsites we reserve on a loop alongside friends with similarly aged children.

In other words, we're hardly roughing it and not even close to alone. But having left our houses and other responsibilities for the weekend, our boundaries become more porous—we exchange walls for tent screens, fenced backyards for the woods. Our children run back and forth between campsites, helping themselves to juice boxes and snacks and being parented by the nearest adult—all of us taking turns to issue reminders about helmets and sunscreen, settle minor disputes, and distribute sandwiches. It's the kind of communal care I wish we had more access to back at home.

Last year, while we were setting up camp, the kids were biking and riding scooters in circles around the campsites, when I heard my daughter, who was five at the time, shout out, "Truck!" She shooed the other kids, including her two-year-old brother, into the grass as a park ranger pulled over to chat with a few of the adults. I walked up just as he was handing out paper booklets to the oldest children, explaining that upon completing its coloring and activity pages they could become official junior park rangers. Immediately, my daughter and her friend got to work, spreading out their booklets and crayons atop a picnic table and calling me over to help with a nature-themed word search, letters that spelled out words like beach, canoe, river, and fish.

We spent the next few days swimming in the lake and taking beach walks, including a hike at low tide to a small island offshore, where we saw hundreds of ochre sea stars clinging to the underside of rocks. We ate meals at a picnic table beside a shallow creek, and at night sat around a campfire while bats swooped overhead and frogs called out. In all the moments in between, my daughter worked diligently on her booklet, determined to earn her junior park ranger badge.

Before returning home, we stopped at the ranger station and the kids showed the ranger on duty their completed booklets. He brought out a box with little wooden badges and knelt to distribute them with a word of caution, "Careful!" he said, "These pins are sharp, so have your parents help you."

He then invited the kids to repeat after him as he conducted the junior park ranger swearing-in ceremony. We stood there, capturing the moment, while our children offered their pledges,

Watching them, it occurred to me that I have only exchanged vows with my husband, but the bond I feel to my children, and indeed, to the place I call home, are no less significant, just as deserving of my sworn commitment.

On the final page of their booklets was a space for children to write their own oaths. The pledge my daughter dictated to me was this: "I love the world, and I will always take care of wildlife."

While talking about *The Wild Robot* with my kids and answering their questions about how goslings like Brightbill imprint on the first animal, or robot, they see upon hatching, I thought about the work of Austrian ornithologist Konrad Lorenz, whose research on imprinting has shaped much of our thinking about maternal instinct. Conaboy notes how much "popular thinking about parenthood and especially motherhood comes from what we see as 'natural.'"

Working in the 1950s, Lorenz's research on how birds imprint led him to make claims about instinctive behaviors across species, including about the attachment between human mothers and babies. He believed maternal instinct was inherited and operated through a machinelike mechanism—in other words, that mothering was a matter of programming.

Despite having joined the Nazi Party in 1938 and being accused of spreading racist ideology in his work, Lorenz was eventually awarded a Nobel Prize for his research on genetics and behavior. As Conaboy reports, though Lorenz got some things right, later researchers would come to show that genes aren't the only determinants of maternal behavior and that the parental brain is influenced by a person's caregiving experiences as well as their social and physical environment.

In her book, Conaboy demonstrates how scientific evidence came to supplant religious doctrine in shoring up belief in the maternal instincts that make women biologically suited primarily for caregiving and not much else. The theory of evolution, for example, may have revolutionized how we think about human nature but it did not change how we think about the nature of motherhood. According to Conaboy, Charles Darwin "wasn't really trying to dispel the biblical notion that men rightfully dominate women . . . He simply shifted the focus from faith to biology." From there, many scientists, with the exception of Darwinian feminists, continued to look to the natural world for evidence to support patriarchal assumptions.

Lorenz and other midcentury comparative psychologists—like Harry Harlow, whose experiments with infant rhesus monkeys also bolstered support for attachment theory—often studied maternal behavior in animals who were kept in laboratories, alone, with their dependent offspring. "Those caged mothers had no chance to forage for food or compete for status. They had no other mothers with whom to share the caregiving," observes Reddy. "The scientists had made a caged paradise for them: mother, baby, freed even of the need to secure their basic needs."

We now have ample reason to question the assumptions about motherhood drawn from this research, including evidence from neuroscience and more recent studies of animal behavior, but its impact on parenting culture persists. When I became a parent, years after leaving the church, I didn't expect to find religious ideas about gender and motherhood repackaged as evidence-backed parenting advice. Yet claims about natural parenting practices, including attachment parenting practices that put undue pressure on mothers, are as attractive as ever, and this is likely due in part to our culture's strained relationship to the natural world.

"[T]he use of *natural* as a synonym for *good* is almost certainly a product of our profound alienation from the natural world," writes Eula Biss, describing why, despite its risks, natural immunity rather than immunization appeals to some mothers. Biss quotes naturalist Wendell Berry who observes that "the more artificial a human environment becomes, the more the word 'natural' becomes a term of value." Both writers object to this binary framing. Berry argues, "The wild and the domestic now often seem isolated values, estranged from one another. And yet these are not exclusive polarities . . . there can be continuity between them, and there must be."

The separation between the wild and the domestic is related to other binaries that need troubling, like those of mind and body, man and woman, technology and nature, public and private. Ursula K. Le Guin questions the idea that humans are separate from nature, linking her critique to feminism, writing, "Nature is a construct made by Man, not a real thing; just as most of what Man says and knows about women is mere myth and construct," she writes. "Where I live as a woman is to men a wilderness. But to me it is home."

Reading this, I think about how my experiences of pregnancy, birth, and early parenthood disrupted many of these dualisms and compelled me to confront some of our culture's most persistent myths—about mothers and about the Earth.

Environmentalists are right to advocate for the protection of wildlife and wild places, now more than ever, but it's possible that designating land as "wilderness" has had the unintended effect of reinforcing the idea that humans are separate from nature—a distinction that emerged through the colonial logics of European and American settlers and that has shaped dominant narratives about how humans relate to place.

As William Cronon writes, "Only people whose relation to the land was already alienated could hold up wilderness as a model for human life in nature." In his essay, "The Trouble with Wilderness; Or Getting Back to the Wrong Nature," Cronon endeavors to show how the concept of the "wilderness" comes to us, in part, from religious beliefs, which then carried over into the environmental movement. I can't help but notice how the emergence of this ideal follows a familiar path—like how dominant ideas about motherhood emerged from theology that then influenced the work of scientists. Perhaps this is why cultural ideals about motherhood and about wilderness are widely held as sacred.

In the Bible stories I recall reading in my childhood, the wilderness was where Adam and Eve went after being cast out of the garden, where Moses and his people wandered for forty long years after their Exodus from Egypt, and where Jesus faced temptation. According to Cronon, it wasn't until the nineteenth century that the wilderness ceased to be associated with a harsh and frightening wasteland where one faced spiritual trials and tribulations. Through the Romantic movement's idea of the sublime, the wilderness came to be seen as a pristine place, untouched by human activity, where one might encounter God and seek enlightenment.

In landscape paintings, as well as in literature, the wilderness took on greater meaning in art that explored the sublime. But writer Erin Sharkey connects the emergence of nature writing in the eighteenth century to colonization. The genre "grew out of an effort to describe and categorize the attributes of birds, animals, and insects—a list that grew as more of the world was 'discovered,'" she writes. "This discovery was violent because it was a tool of colonization, with 'explorers' conquering new land, and with it, nature that was unfamiliar to them."

The American wilderness was not empty of humans, and any appearance that the land was unoccupied was the result of the violence colonizers inflicted on Indigenous peoples. In the fifteenth century, a series of papal bulls that came to be known collectively as the Doctrine of Discovery, authorized colonial powers to seize land so long as the people living there were not Christians. Under this mandate, Europeans colonized lands in Africa and the Americas, subjugating people in the name of converting them. This doctrine was used to justify everything from the enslavement of African people to the forced removal of Indigenous children from their families to be placed in church-run residential schools intended to strip them of their cultures. These religious decrees were then cited in the formation of U.S. property laws.

As more land was settled and as people relocated to cities during the Industrial Revolution, the wilderness became a place for elites to escape civilization and to recreate, often pursuing frontier fantasies of rugged individualism on their vast cattle ranches and countryside estates, pursuits that required both time and resources.

Throughout the twentieth century, much of what was considered nature writing was produced by people, especially white, cisgender men, who had the means to embark on solo wilderness excursions and then write about their experiences. But Sharkey and other editors of color have sought to redefine the boundaries of environmental literature, expanding the genre to include work by writers who push against this dominant narrative to show that relationships to place can be as varied and complicated as our relationships to each other. They also argue for the importance of relating to places beyond those designated as wilderness.

The problem with idealizing the wilderness is that it can lead to the mistaken conclusion that the environments where we live and work and raise our families are less worthy of our care and attention. This can perpetuate what's called the nature gap, which names how environmental racism and other factors lead to people of color and low-income communities having unequal access to nature and green spaces. Writes Cronon, "Idealizing a distant wilderness too often means not idealizing the environment in which we actually live, the landscape that for better or worse we call home. Most of our most serious environmental problems start right here, at home."

The wilderness ideal also functions to obscure the history of land theft and violence of colonization, which is one reason why answering calls to return public lands to Indigenous peoples and supporting Indigenous self-determination is such an important step toward climate justice. Another is that any attempts to restore connections between people and nature should be led by the people with the closest ties and the ancestral knowledge to manage land sustainably. In his argument for the Land Back movement, Native Hawaiian Kaniela Ing writes, "Climate justice requires us to radically restore our relationship with the natural world around us . . . No one is better equipped to lead this vision than the Indigenous people who have maintained reciprocal relationships with their homelands for millennia."

It's possible, insists Cronon, to celebrate the beauty and power of wild places, to advocate for biological diversity and endangered species, and to worry about the threat humans pose to the natural world without upholding the myth of wilderness. To truly care well for the environment, we have to learn to see ourselves as part of nature, as well as part of history, and to see all places as worthy of care. Idealizing the pristine wilderness, as with idealizing the perfect mother, can prevent us from realizing our interconnectedness and the power of giving and receiving care.

While, of course, I want to foster a secure attachment to my children, these days I'm drawn to thinking more about care than attachment, because in it, I find language that is capacious enough to encompass our reciprocal relationships to each other as well as to the more-than-human world.

As a species, claims writer Elissa Strauss, we are "predisposed to care." In her book *When You Care*, Strauss puts forward care as a compelling alternative to our culture's overemphasis on attachment. "For much of modern science, the act of caregiving was overshadowed by research on attachment, or what it is like to be cared *for*," she writes. But in recent decades, the question of how caregiving changes us has become a focus of research.

To make her case for the power of caregiving, Strauss labors to correct a popular misconception about Darwin's revolutionary work. Darwin didn't just theorize about competition but also about cooperation and caregiving. Strauss stresses that he did not coin the phrase "survival of the fittest," though it later came to be associated with Darwin, especially by those seeking to uphold racial and social hierarchies. A phrase Darwin actually used was the "survival of the most sympathetic," which describes his observation that "communities which included the greatest number of the most sympathetic members, would flourish best, and rear the greatest number of offspring." He was a devoted father, as Strauss and various Darwin biographers have shown, and here, it seems there's a tension between Darwin's personal experiences of caregiving and the way he positions raising children as a gendered task in his writing. What is clear is that the experience of caring for his children shaped his thinking about the evolution of social instincts. He came to believe that care, or in his words, "sympathy," was crucial to survival. In other words, it is an evolutionary advantage to care.

One definition of care ethics commonly cited is that put forward by Berenice Fisher and Joan Tronto, who write: "On the most general level, we suggest that caring be viewed as a species activity that includes everything that we do to maintain, continue, and repair our 'world' so that we can live in it as well as possible. That world includes our bodies, ourselves, and our environment, all of which we seek to interweave in a complex, life-sustaining web." This way of defining care resonates with my experiences of early parenthood, how my circle of care expanded outward to include not only my children, but my community and bioregion, a reaching outward that extends further into time and space.

Unlike traditional ethics, argues philosopher Elena Pulcini, care ethics also encompasses concern for future generations, making it particularly salient for addressing the climate crisis. Emphasizing that care is a practice, Pulcini writes that it consists "not only of decisive public battles (such as the struggle for access to common goods or the political denunciation of environmental disasters) but also of small, everyday gestures such as not wasting water, recycling, or defending a green area in a neighborhood." These small acts of care, closer to home, can foster as deep an attachment to place as time spent chasing the sublime.

Wilderness educator Elan Shapiro has observed that when people return from extended wilderness journeys, they "are often left with a deep sense of powerlessness and depression upon returning to 'normal' life." But, by contrast, when people engage in acts of environmental service, they are likely to leave feeling motivated and engaged. Further, these acts of care can often lead people to a more reciprocal relationship in which they also recognize how they are cared for and supported by the Earth.

There's a pivotal moment near the end of *The Wild Robot*. While Brightbill is off on his long journey of migration, Roz remains on the island, facing a long and difficult winter. To survive an extreme winter storm, she gathers the other animals together in her shelter and urges them to form a truce and live cooperatively, at least until winter's end.

"Kindness," says the fox, who helped Roz raise Brightbill, "is a survival skill."

Watching this scene, I noticed the stark contrast between the film's example of cross-species cooperation and the isolation I'd observed while watching *Alone*, how the reality show contestants had suffered from the absence of care and connection.

Roz reunites with Brightbill in the moments just before reconnaissance robots arrive by airship to return her to TechLab Industries and reassign her to the work that she is programmed to do. Yet, the animals Roz has befriended come to her rescue. Though the RECO robot tells Roz that she doesn't belong in the wilderness, she resists. "I'm already home," shouts Roz, with Brightbill on her shoulder. "And I am a wild robot." She then howls alongside the bear and the fox and the moose.

My friend told me that when she took her daughter to see the film at the theater, her daughter and many of the other kids in the theater began howling.

The other day, my son asked to see a photo from the day he was born. Scrolling through my camera roll, I found one of the first photos I took with him. Both kids leaned over my shoulders to see. Though I can recall the bone-deep fatigue I felt after giving birth, in the picture, I look surprisingly content, lying in bed during the quiet moments after a feeding with my sleeping son swaddled and tucked comfortably against my side. Having a second child was no less astonishing than the first, but I was more able to take in the newborn stage, to wonder over the details of the tiny fingers which gripped my own so tightly, instead of feeling utterly overwhelmed by the responsibility of caring for someone so vulnerable. Our son was a different baby, and we were different parents, changed by our caregiving experiences.

As we continued looking over family photos together, I began to quiz my son—playing a game that my daughter and I had enjoyed when she was a toddler—prompting him to list his family members, reviewing the names and faces of those who live far away.

"Who loves you," I asked.

"Mama and dada," he said.

"Who else?" I asked, putting my arm around him and pulling him close, and without hesitation, he named his sister, followed by his grandparents and aunts, and a preschool teacher.

"Who else?" I asked.

"The birds," he said. This was an unexpected break from our typical litany of loved ones, and I was curious to hear what he'd say next.

"Who else?" I asked.

"The grass," he said. "And the trees."

I was glad to know he felt himself to be in relationship with our neighborhood birds and trees and hoped this sense of being cared for by the living world would sustain him into adulthood. As Shapiro puts it, "Once we have bonded with the Earth, we cannot escape growing up and learning to treat this primal parent as partner, friend, and ally as well . . . In such a relationship we naturally, ask, 'How can I give back as well as receive?'"

Once, at a reading I attended, a poet who writes about motherhood answered a question from a reader who sought her best parenting tip. Instead of giving prescriptive parenting advice, the poet shared what her aunt said during a baby shower: "Children are not a problem to be solved."

Upon hearing this, I felt my shoulders settle. Children weren't the problem, our culture's ideas about motherhood were the problem.

Likewise, I hadn't realized that I'd transferred my worries about climate change to the planet itself, turning the places I love into problems to be solved. There are many problems to be solved, to be sure—like patriarchy, colonialism, and capitalism—but the planet itself is not one of them.

Seated in the audience, I thought to myself: *The Earth is not a problem to be solved.* And, for a moment, I relaxed into the feeling of being nurtured by the place where I live, a reminder that I am already home.

When I think about place attachment now, what comes to mind isn't a solo wilderness hike but a recent day I spent with my family in a city park near our bustling downtown waterfront, at the place where Whatcom Creek rushes into the bay. We were there to participate in releasing chum salmon, which had been raised from eggs to fry in an aquarium in the children's department of our public library.

We gathered with other parents and children on the concrete steps of an outdoor amphitheater. At its center was a portable PA system and a gardening wagon with a large cooler, filled with salmon fry.

We were greeted by Shirley Williams, a local Indigenous activist and member of the Lummi Nation, and listened as she told the story of the place where we were gathered, which was the site of an ancestral village. "In 1852, right here, at this creek," she said, of her ancestors, "they welcomed the first settlers by canoe and shared this land's natural wealth, freshwater, salmon, and peace."

She spoke of the significance of the salmon to the Lummi people and called on all of us to contribute to the work of restoring the salmon and healing the land. "We need to face each other with truth, with history, and with hope . . . Supporting our presence and practice as Indigenous people means protecting the water, the salmon, and the sacred relationships that have sustained this place since time immemorial. We invite you to join us," she said.

Families like mine were participants in the very systems that had caused harm and were now being challenged to participate in repair. The invitation reminded me of the questions I'd read in Robin Wall Kimmerer's *Braiding Sweetgrass*: can the descendants of settlers and immigrants "learn to live here as if we were staying? With both feet on the shore?"

After the presentation, we were led by conservationists and educators to the creek bank, where several small chutes, each about the size of a yardstick, had been extended into the cool water. When it was our family's turn, we approached a chute and were handed a clear plastic cup, half-filled with water and containing one salmon fry, whom we were asked to name.

"Let's call him Salmon O. Salmon," said my son, bringing his face to the rim of the cup, peering into it, as if to take a sip.

"Don't drink from it!" whispered my husband, as my hand reached out to still the cup. My daughter held the cup next, bringing it up to eye level to study the fry more closely, before following instructions for carefully tipping its contents into the chute.

We watched the salmon fry squirm down the chute and out into the rushing creek, where it would grow and swim for several months before making its way from the estuary to the bay. From there, it would travel through the sea, maybe as far as California or Alaska, or even Japan.

In four to six years, we were told, it would begin the long journey back to this creek, this place where it imprinted as a young fry. I considered the odds it now faced and wished the salmon a safe journey and hoped for its return.

Watching my children skip away down the path ahead of me, I thought of their attachment to this place and all the ways that it is shaping them, and wondered if, like the young salmon, they were also imprinting on the creek. On a fall day, years from now, perhaps we would all find ourselves gathered once more, still with both feet on the shore, waiting for Salmon O. Salmon to swim home.

Mother of All Messes

A friend and I walked the shoreline together wearing baseball caps, work gloves, and boots and holding five-gallon buckets and trash grabbers. We were looking down at the pebbly beach, eyes peeled for cigarette butts, food wrappers, and bits of foam and plastic while chatting about the start of kindergarten. Periodically, we glanced up at our five-year-olds, who had run ahead with their grabbers and were now crouched down, searching for interesting rocks and shells.

It was the last day of summer, and the afternoon was warmer than I expected. I paused to take off my sweatshirt and tie it around my waist. Scanning the beach, there appeared to be dozens of people participating in our community's event for the International Coastal Cleanup Day. I tried to picture us among the hundreds of thousands of people, worldwide, who were working together to remove as much as 14 million pounds of trash from 16,000 miles of coastline.

We were cleaning up a stretch of beach near the Cherry Point Aquatic Reserve, an expanse of state-owned aquatic land set aside to conserve native species and restore habitat. Despite our best efforts to gather marine debris, there was little to be found, probably owing to the volunteers who'd arrived just before us and had already completed a first pass. Still each time we added a piece of litter to the paltry contents of our buckets, we gave a little cheer and speculated about its origins.

Finally, after picking our way over a mile or so of beach, we conceded to the kids' requests to stop and play. I unzipped my belt bag and handed out fruit snacks and granola bars. When my daughter was finished eating, I called her over to reapply sunscreen, gently taking hold of her chin and swiping it over her nose and cheeks and using my thumb to wipe some crumbs from the corner of her lips, before she ran off.

My friend and I sat on a log, sipping from our water bottles, while our children removed their rain boots and rolled up their pants so that they could step out into the cool saltwater. To the kids' delight, and to ours, what had begun as a cleanup effort had turned into just another afternoon at the beach.

I don't have a trash grabber at home, but I might as well for the many times a day that I walk around the house, stooping to pick up abandoned Playmobil pieces and Lego bricks, spare doll shoes and misplaced googly eyes before schlepping these items to their proper places.

Even though we are trying to teach our kids to clean up after themselves, if you were to step into our home, on any given day, you would know immediately that young children live here. By which I mean, there are scuffed walls and windows with sticky handprints, plus plenty of toys, mostly plastic, strewn about the living room rug. Many have come to us by way of hand-me-downs from friends and neighbors who are all too eager to be relieved of them, and I don't pretend to know the provenance of my children's myriad stuffies, except for a suspicion that my daughter has commanded them to *be fruitful and multiply*.

I am, now, mostly resigned to the mess, but still I try to, at least, corral it, sort it, conceal it in various crates and baskets.

Like a lot of my friends, I was determined, at first, to limit all this stuff.

"Babies don't need much," my husband and I reminded each other while compiling our gift registry, speaking with the unearned confidence of people who had never parented. While pregnant, I browsed gender neutral onesies in soothing earth tones at the consignment shop and dreamed of a tidy playroom filled with dappled sunlight and simple wooden toys.

The reality is that the aesthetics of our home aren't in keeping with what I think of when I envision a sustainable home, much less a minimalist one. Babies may not require nearly as much as registry checklists would have us believe, but as our children have grown, the amount of stuff in their possession has increased considerably. Their shared bedroom is littered with toy cars, beading kits and baby dolls, a marble run, princess-y dress-up clothes, markers and crayons, construction sets, and paper crafts—all the trinkets and treasures that they would certainly miss, with an alarming degree of specificity, if I were to attempt to declutter.

I'm drawn to the aesthetics of slow culture in all its iterations—slow fashion, slow food, slow parenting—which are alluring to me because of how *slow* has become synonymous with *sustainable*, but I find *slow*, like *simple*, like *clean*, like *natural*, to be frustratingly unattainable.

This hasn't stopped me from trying to reduce our family's environmental impact. Along the way, I've made plenty of sustainable swaps—from using cloth napkins and tea towels instead of paper products to making cleaning solutions from concentrate to washing our clothes on cold—behaviors which I adopted over time and are now as habitual as the ones they replaced, requiring little thought or effort. But, I've never sought to claim labels like *slow* or *clean* for my domestic labor, nor the related label, *crunchy*, for my mothering.

Perhaps it's because my sensibilities were so shaped by my midwestern upbringing that it never occurred to me, for example, that it might be feasible, financially or otherwise, to maintain a zero-waste, toxin-free home or to feed my children exclusively organic whole foods. The cleaning supplies stored in our laundry cupboard are mostly low-waste and low-toxin, but there's also a no-nonsense bleach spray leftover from our most recent bout with norovirus. Likewise, a peek inside our pantry reveals bulk beans and lentils alongside boxed mac-n-cheese—so much boxed mac-n-cheese. Though I serve many plant-based family dinners, my primary goals are introducing my children to a wide variety of foods and limiting their exposure to diet culture. I want my behaviors to reflect my values, yet I'm also cautious of overidentifying with them such that they become my identity.

It may be a result of the evangelical purity culture I encountered as a teenager that I now bristle at the thought of attempting to be a purist about anything. Or it could be, simply, a pragmatic acceptance of our limitations, that to be working parents necessarily means that my husband and I must sometimes choose fast and convenient over slow and homemade.

Evaluating the environmental impact of consumer goods and sourcing alternatives; altering cooking, cleaning, and shopping habits; attempting to reduce plastics, packaging, and food waste; and learning to mend and repair—I hadn't realized that this kind of environmental care work amounted to what some researchers have called a "third green shift." It's a term that builds on the idea of the "second shift," which describes the unpaid caregiving and household labor that many women perform after the workday and reflects how even in egalitarian marriages, women in heterosexual partnerships report spending more time cooking, cleaning, and caring for children than their male partners.

Research has shown that parenting today is more time-intensive, expensive, and hands-on than it was for previous generations, especially for moms, who are inundated with expert parenting content. Working mothers now report spending more time parenting than stay-at-home mothers did in the 1970s.

Further, millennials—a generation which has had notoriously bad economic luck, having weathered two major recessions, student loan debt, the housing crisis, and a pandemic—are now raising children at a time in American history when, for the first time, kids are as likely as not to be less prosperous than their parents.

The result is that parents are overwhelmed with information and putting in a lot of emotional labor, expense, and effort to get it right. And, in the United States, they are doing so without structural support—all while worrying about the state of democracy and the health of the social and planetary systems their children will inherit. When the pressure to live more slowly and sustainably in order to avert climate catastrophe is added to the intensive parenting milieu, it's no wonder that many parents don't know where to begin and question whether it's worth the effort.

Allison C. Davis, one of the researchers who coined the term "maternal ecodistress," considers green motherhood to be a form of intensive mothering. According to Davis, green motherhood "positions mothers as planetary saviors, urging them to protect the Earth through 'sustainable' parenting: cloth diapers, organic snacks, toxin-free homes."

The greening of motherhood puts an undue burden on mothers and often fails to adequately address the ecological issues they're most concerned about. Davis works to untangle this "double bind of green motherhood," writing that the pressure to perform environmental care work can reinforce limiting gender norms and lead to maternal exhaustion and burnout. It also privatizes the work of improving planetary health and restricts the site of environmental advocacy to the family.

In pregnancy and early motherhood, I'd tried to divest from unhelpful ideas about what it means to be a good mother, but I hadn't realized how much I was still being influenced by the ideal of green motherhood. It's not that I considered it possible to live up to such an exacting ideal—I knew I would not be able to perform green motherhood perfectly—but that didn't prevent me from scrutinizing our household purchases and shopping for secondhand and sustainable alternatives.

While pregnant with my daughter, I began to knit a pair of baby overalls. I didn't complete the project until well after her first birthday had come and gone, and by then, of course, they didn't fit. When I finally finished binding off and weaving in the loose ends, I gave the overalls to a friend who was expecting. For the briefest moment, though, when I first picked up my double-pointed needles and cast on in a deliciously soft, olive-green cashmerino wool, I imagined I might somehow become the kind of mother who dresses her children in coordinated handknits.

I am not now, nor have I ever been, that mother. My efforts to curb our family's overconsumption have been achieved more by dint of my skill at shopping secondhand than by my aptitude for handicrafts or budget for slow fashion. Still, the pressure to be an ethical consumer is hard to disentangle from my desire to live sustainably.

Surveying the packaging on many of the products around our home, much of it conspicuously announces our values. There's breakfast cereal that promises to save chimpanzees and baby wipes that are the world's purest, there's bamboo toilet paper and plastic-free laundry powder. I've even tried making the switch to solid shampoo and conditioner bars, though once we'd finished them up, I was all too glad to return to my usual shampoo. I pay more for many of these products, despite my skepticism toward lofty marketing claims, because with each purchase I feel like I am swiping my way toward something like progress.

"Ethical Consumers," writes Elizabeth L. Cline, "are people who believe that we are slowly and inexorably driving business and society to be more responsible *one purchase at a time*." In an essay called "The Twilight of the Ethical Consumer," Cline describes how, after years of buying organic vegetarian food and avoiding fast fashion, she began to rethink her efforts, writing, "I have started to wonder not only if Ethical Consumerism is ineffective but also . . . why we continue to throw our power away on ethical shopping."

She links the rise of the ethical consumer to the rise of neoliberalism, which emphasizes the marketplace's role in solving social problems, instead of the government or civil society. Cline describes the transformation that took place over the 1980s and 1990s: "Out went strong environmental regulations, social welfare programs, labor unions, and, most crucially, our generations-long history and culture of how to make change through public rather than private means."

As an alternative to the ethical consumer, Cline points to the figure of the consumer activist. The difference between an ethical consumer and a consumer activist, according to Cline, comes down to a matter of responsibility. Whereas ethical consumers blame themselves for supporting corporate bad actors, consumer activists place the blame squarely on corporations, which they seek to hold responsible through government regulations and policies. Examples of consumer activists, says Cline, are those who drove midcentury social movements, including the boycotts of the Civil Rights movement and the protests that led to the creation of the Environmental Protection Agency.

More recent examples of consumer activism that come to mind are the strategic boycotts that have sought to push back against billionaire-owned corporations as well as against businesses that have caved to political pressure to roll back diversity efforts.

"My argument is not a free pass to stop caring about the impact of consumer product companies on people and the planet," Cline writes, clarifying her intent. "Rather, it's the opposite: This is a call to action to take all that time and energy you would be putting toward curating that perfect ethical lifestyle and weaponizing it to transform the marketplace in ways that tackle root causes."

I'm motivated by Cline's call to action, but I admit that it's difficult to shift my focus entirely from private to public actions, in part because it's simpler to shop than to tackle root causes. More significantly, I'm hesitant to give up completely on ethical consumption because it troubles my conscience not to at least attempt, to the extent that I'm able, to live in ways that are aligned in with my values. I don't know how to change culture without also changing myself, and very often, taking action through both private and public means is what changes me.

Instead, what I am trying to give up on is the shame I feel when I fail to live according to my values. As Min Hyoung Song acknowledges in his book about climate writing, it is "counterproductive, not to mention exhausting, to feel shame (much less direct it at others) at the inability to lead a fully postcarbon life in a world still dominated by carbon."

It helps to remind myself that even for those with unlimited resources, it's impossible to consume perfectly. In *Against Purity*, philosopher Alexis Shotwell writes, "There is no food we can eat, clothing we can buy, or energy we can use without deepening our ties to complex webs of suffering. So, what happens if we start from there?"

Rather than focusing on individual purity when confronted with situations that feel outside our control, she argues, it might be better and more productive to acknowledge complexity, complicity, and compromise while working to build power for collective action. "Purism is a de-collectivizing, de-mobilizing, paradoxical politics of despair," concludes Shotwell. "This world deserves better."

If this world deserves better, I'd argue that parents and families also deserve better.

At the coastal cleanup event, when my daughter and I first arrived and walked over to the volunteer check-in tent to collect our supplies, I looked around for our friends and surveyed the stretch of coastline, which was unfamiliar to us.

Located about a half hour from home, it wasn't a beach we'd had reason to visit before. Though we'd camped at the state park nearby, all I knew of the aquatic reserve was that it was located in close proximity to two oil refineries as well as the site of a proposed coal terminal which, nearly a decade before, had been defeated.

If it had been built, it would have been the largest coal export terminal in North America. Every day, nine mile-and-a-half long trains carrying strip-mined coal would have traveled through our city, spreading coal dust in neighborhoods and waterways. Hundreds of bulk carriers each year would have shipped this coal overseas, crowding the region's waters with noisy marine traffic and risking accidents and collisions that could lead to oil or coal spills, as well as impacting water quality and harming nearshore habitats for vulnerable species. This annual export of 48 million metric tons of coal would have resulted in the release of 150 million tons of new greenhouse gases each year.

After an extensive environmental impact review, ultimately the project was denied permitting because of the violations it posed to the treaty rights of the Coast Salish peoples, including the protection of an ancestral burial site and the fishing rights of the Lummi Nation.

The defeat of the coal export terminal, how it prevented the release of so much excess carbon dioxide into the atmosphere, reminds me of the power of acting locally. Even in the absence of ambitious federal policies, meaningful climate action is still possible at the state and local level.

Standing on the beach with my trash grabber, I recalled the gratitude I felt for the tribal opposition that was central to the project's defeat and considered how vastly different our cleanup efforts would have been had the export terminal been built, how it would have altered the landscape and our view of the horizon.

The tension between working collectively to protect the environment and focusing instead on taking individual action to protect ourselves and our families from environmental harms is a phenomenon Andrew Szasz explores in his book *Shopping Our Way to Safety*. As an example, he looks to the threat that the hole in the ozone layer posed to human health and safety, namely the increased risk of skin cancer, and argues that the problem was solved not by shopping but by regulation.

When I was in elementary school, the hole in the ozone layer was a particularly gripping problem—it was easy, if not terrifying, to imagine a great cloud of hairspray drifting up, up, up until it burned a literal hole in the sky. That frightful imagery also captured the imagination of adults. As Nathaniel Rich suggests in his historical reporting on climate change, the metaphor helped people understand the threat posed by ozone-depleting emissions of chlorofluorocarbons, or CFCs. Rich writes, "An abstract, atmospheric problem had been reduced to the size of the human imagination. It had been made just small enough, and just large enough, to break through."

The collective response to the hole in the ozone layer was so swift and effective that the Montreal Protocol, an international agreement to phase out ozone-depleting chemicals, was signed in 1987. As a result, the ozone layer is steadily healing and on track to fully recover—without anyone having to give up hair spray or refrigerators—and, for a time, it seemed likely that policies to reduce carbon emissions would follow suit.

"What if society had chosen the personal protection, sunscreen, hats-and-long-sleeves response while allowing continued production, use, and release of CFCs and other ozone depleting substances?" Szasz asks. "It would have proven to be another classic case of . . . individuals *falsely* believing that they have managed to protect themselves, while collective, ecological conditions are allowed to continue to deteriorate, with uncertain, potentially quite dire consequences." Szasz's point is not that applying sunscreen to prevent skin cancer is bad, simply that these individual responses would not have sufficiently addressed the problem caused by ozone depleting substances.

Unfortunately, the scale of the threat posed by global warming challenges the human imagination. For many of us, it can feel too big and overwhelming to think productively about, which can lead to the individual attempts at purity and the politics of despair that Shotwell names.

Though I recognize that I cannot shop my way to protecting the people and places I care about, when faced with everyday consumer choices I've continued to purchase the secondhand and sustainable products that make sense for me and my family. I've come to think about shopping my values as akin to putting on sunscreen—still important to the extent that it's possible, but not enough on its own to solve the problem. At the same time, I'm doubling down on contributions to the civic and political processes that can actually move the needle on climate justice.

Eager for ideas of climate actions we could take as a family, I picked up Mary DeMocker's book *The Parents' Guide to Climate Revolution*.

Though I was looking for actionable advice, part of me was also worried I'd come away feeling even more time-pressed and strained by a growing to-do list.

While her book contains helpful suggestions for green family living, the framework DeMocker lays out in the book's introduction goes beyond ethical consumption and environmental care work to also urge parents toward political engagement. For example, she compares the impact of taking three minutes to clean and dry an empty peanut butter jar to phoning a representative about climate legislation, writing, that "it's more effective—and more important at this point in the climate crisis—to make the call and throw the dirty jar in the trash." She concludes, "If you have to make a choice, always choose system change over lightbulb change."

This perspective led to a subtle shift in how I think about sustainability; it was an opening to think more critically about my efforts as a citizen to contribute to system change. What I've realized is that, for those of us who do have three minutes to spare, often the challenge doesn't lie in making the choice between doing the recycling or making the phone call, but in overcoming the cynicism that says neither action matters.

In reality, both personal and political engagement matters to the climate movement and each depends on the other. It's difficult to recycle a peanut butter jar, for example, without a citywide recycling program.

Public infrastructure, especially at the local level, is what makes many of our family's most sustainable choices possible. Here, I'm thinking about our city's network of bike lanes that make it safer and more enjoyable to bike with our children; local ordinances that restrict plastic bags and single-use plastic, which means that when we opt for takeout or delivery our food arrives in compostable containers; and curbside compost bins that are picked up by our sanitation service. Wherever we go, whether to the park or the library, there are three waste bins and even young children know to sort for garbage, recycling, and compost.

Without these citywide efforts, which are the result of people acting collaboratively as citizens, it would be much more difficult for us, acting independently as a family, to reduce our environmental impact.

As homeowners, we are also participating in community-wide efforts to electrify. Our city estimates that 40 percent of local carbon emissions can be attributed to gas consumption in buildings, more than all the cars on all our roads, so we see this as doing our part. We live in an old home, which I love for its many charms, but, the fact is, it's sorely outdated. During a walk-through, our home inspector had to show me how to use a butane lighter to start the gas cooktop since its igniter was broken. Soon after moving in, we made the switch to an electric cooktop, which has improved both our experience of cooking and our indoor air quality. But instead of fully remodeling the kitchen, we chose to take out a loan to install solar panels and a heat pump. Not only did this reduce our carbon emissions and energy bills, it also meant that during heat waves, as well as wildfire smoke events, we could cool the house—since our home, like most in the region, was built without central air conditioning.

The fact that we can afford home ownership and have access to credit is itself a significant privilege, but since we are able to make these changes, we feel it's important to do so, while also recognizing that, for many, these measures are out of reach. This points to one of the most challenging aspects of the green motherhood ideal—it often assumes access to significant investments of time and money. It can lead climate-aware parents to feel shame over all the ways in which they cannot measure up.

When I spoke with Allison C. Davis about the double bind of green motherhood, she described her first reaction when she started her research. "I was looking at how mothers are targeted as consumers, and how they're sold this solution which ultimately harms the Earth," she recalls. "And it made me so mad." Allison links green motherhood to "a narrow ideal of motherhood defined by whiteness, heterosexuality, and middle-class privilege," what Audre Lorde described as the "mythical norm." In this, Allison suggests, there is some overlap between the green motherhood ideal and the tradwife movement, since both "shift the burden of care onto individual mothers" while "reinforcing a consumerist and patriarchal status quo."

The green motherhood myth doesn't work for anyone, as Allison points out, not even for those who try their hardest to get it right. Transformation, she says, comes from naming this dangerous ideal and letting go of the buried guilt we feel when we fail to achieve it. Part of what holds us back, she told me, is that "as mothers, we don't get angry, we get perfect."

Allison said that when the focus is on "prioritizing individual, task-based responsibilities" it can, in severe cases, lead to behavioral addiction and self-harm. *Ecofixia* is the clinical term she has proposed to describe the condition in which guilt-driven environmental care work becomes compulsive and disruptive to daily life, a condition that can arise in parents who experience maternal ecodistress. She writes, "As healthy eating can become a compulsion, called orthorexia nervosa . . . so too can the labor of taking care of the environment become an unhealthy obsession in matrescence."

Hearing this, I thought of the question Jacqueline Rose poses in *Mothers*: "What are we doing *to* mothers—when we expect them to carry the burden of everything that is hardest to contemplate about our society and ourselves?" She warns, "Unless we recognize what we are asking mothers to perform in the world—and for the world—we will continue to tear both the world and mothers to pieces."

If environmental care work is increasingly among the burdens that mothers are taking up on behalf of their children and the planet, what this suggests to me is that moving toward gender equity is climate action. Making family life more sustainable for women and mothers is part of making the planet more sustainable for all of us.

Allison urges the mothers she works with in her clinical practice and support groups to "root whatever care work they're doing in their values and who they are." She makes a distinction between environmental care work and ecological care work—the latter approach focuses on interdependence and reciprocity. It involves reconnecting with nature and recognizing that mothering takes place in a larger web of life, in which we are also cared for and nurtured by the planet.

I was still thinking about our conversation when I biked to pick up my children from kindergarten and preschool. Pedaling down streets beneath trees laden with cherry blossoms, listening to my children's laughter from behind me in the bike trailer, I realized that biking was a choice I was making based on who I am and what brings me joy.

I could have driven, and probably would have if it were pouring, but I wanted to be outside in the sunshine, moving my body. I wanted to wave at my neighbor walking her dog. I wanted to hear the squawking of the Steller's jay on the fence, pointing it out as I pedaled by. I wanted to be biking with my children.

"Mothers," says Allison, "are always asked to do motherhood rather than to be mothers." Biking, gardening, going to the beach—these are activities that allow me to just be with my kids instead of striving to perform goodness, and it feels deeply restorative to reclaim them as acts of ecological care work.

"Mama, mama," my daughter shouted, running up the stairs. "I need you to fix my heart!" Her charm necklace had broken, and she wanted my help restringing it. This was a request I was all too happy to oblige, especially since someday, I know, her heart will break in ways that are beyond my ability to mend.

Both our children regularly come to my husband and I with these requests, perhaps overconfident in our abilities to patch things up with a dab of super glue or a needle and thread. By this point, I have performed emergency surgery on countless stuffies, among the most memorable patients are a giraffe who suffered a gaping leg wound and a unicorn with a severed tail. Many times our children have also witnessed us tackle ambitious repairs around the house. My hope is that we're modeling for our children how to thoughtfully embrace the things that bring us comfort and pleasure while exercising the resourcefulness and creativity it takes to care for them and extend their usefulness.

Last fall, in the weeks after the beach cleanup, I found myself tangled up in a giant spider web made of thin, white rope. It's the one Halloween decoration I put up year after year, and it had become impossibly tangled in storage. I stretched it out across our front yard and set about the process of untangling the rope. I stepped into and out of the web, carrying rope ends up and over, twisting and turning it this way and that. Even though I worry about one-time-use costumes, and I'm never sure if the candy I'm buying is ethical, Halloween is one of my favorite holidays, because it's one we celebrate outdoors with our neighbors, traipsing up and down porch steps we wouldn't otherwise visit, and the giant spider web was part of the experience I wanted to give my children.

As dusk fell and the air took on a chill, I stood in our front yard utterly ensnared in rope, fighting back frustrated tears. At this point, my husband, who had joined me in the web, gently suggested we throw it away and consider buying a new one, but I was determined to sort out the mess. The next morning, my husband and I renewed our efforts, plodding along knot by knot, and eventually we found our way out. When I think about that spider web now, I realize how much I am still tangled up in my relationship to stuff, to consumerism and ethical consumption, and to the double bind of green motherhood.

Even though, like all of us, I'm caught in a complex web of suffering, it's important to me that my children learn to see that some knots can be untangled, that sometimes it's possible to clean up a mess, to repair what's broken—things, relationships, and even ecosystems.

Writing about the value of small-scale change and the importance of transforming ourselves in order to transform the world, activist adrienne maree brown explains, "This doesn't mean to get lost in the self, but rather to see our own lives and work and relationships as a front line, a first place we can practice justice, liberation, and alignment with each other and the planet."

The space between doing nothing and doing everything—at home, in my community, and at the beach—is where I practice living my values. The goal of these efforts is not to perfect our home, but to preserve the planet.

For me, I'd rather pick up the beach than my living room floor any day. And, at the aquatic reserve, there is still work to be done, work that inevitably will fall to our children's generation to continue.

For the past two years, the Cherry Point herring population has failed to spawn. After fifty years of steep decline, the herring have simply disappeared, a grave disturbance to the Salish Sea food web. It's possible that their habitat has been damaged by the ecological impact of nearby refineries or that rising temperatures have prompted them to spawn in cooler waters across the Canadian border.

The beach cleanup was just a small part of efforts to restore this vital habitat and a species that so many others depend upon—from the scoters, orcas, and seals that rely on herring as food source to the Lummi people who have practiced reef net fishing there for thousands of years.

It's a place that remains threatened by fossil fuels and climate change, a place that will continue to require collective action to protect and to restore.

But events like the International Coastal Cleanup Day bring people together around a shared ethic of care and can be as healing for participants as for the places being restored. As Elan Shapiro notes, environmental service projects can be especially impactful for "[a]ctivists who generally relate to the 'environment' with tension and worry." It feels good to work together, to step back and see the tangible evidence of progress.

As my daughter and I made our way back to the volunteer tent, I noticed a rusted, derelict conveyer, abandoned by industry, which spanned the beach and extended out over the waves until it reached its abrupt end, and beyond that, I saw much further down the shoreline, a gleaming conveyer still in use, and I tried to imagine a time when it has outlived its usefulness.

Because I Said So

In December 2018, I was in the final days of my first pregnancy and following news reports from the climate negotiations at COP24. Greta Thunberg, who was then 15 years old, delivered a speech about her Fridays for Future strike. "I've learned you are never too small to make a difference," she said. "And if a few children can get headlines all over the world just by not going to school, then imagine what we could all do together if we really wanted to."

From her living room in Seattle, climate scientist Heather Price was watching the proceedings on her laptop, when her 11-year-old son, Ian, overheard Thunberg's speech. Inspired to strike, he asked, "Can I do that?" Heather, who'd protested before, including at COP6, readily agreed and notified Ian's teacher that she would pick him up after lunch on Friday. Ian invited several friends who were supportive but couldn't join, so Heather brought Oreos and their family dog for encouragement. Striking alone at Seattle City Hall, Ian held a bright red poster with a drawing of the planet, colored with blue and green marker. His sign read, IT'S GETTING HOT...CLIMATE ACTION NOW."

Ian was among the first students in the United States to strike with Fridays for Future, and he continued to protest most Friday afternoons. He eventually became connected with Climate Action Families, a Seattle-based climate justice organization that offers training and support to youth activists. There, Heather and her children came to know young people, like Aji Piper, a plaintiff in the

2015 landmark climate change lawsuit *Juliana vs. United States of America*, in which 21 children and teens sued the federal government for violating their rights to a safe and stable climate. And Jamie Margolin, who, in July 2018, co-founded the youth-led organization Zero Hour and helped plan its Youth March on Washington—an event which inspired Thunberg's Fridays for Future.

On September 20, 2019, the student climate movement coalesced in the Global Climate Strike. Margolin penned a stirring op-ed about her decision to strike, writing, "I am striking for a decolonized future. A decolonized world is one where those most affected by the climate crisis—poor and indigenous communities and those in the global south—are heard and have a seat at the table . . . a decolonized world is the only one that will be able to turn the tide on the climate crisis." Here was a seventeen-year-old, who had committed her high school years to activism, boldly naming the root causes of the climate crisis and calling for an end to the exploitation of communities in the Global South. She put her hope in solutions that would not just transform our energy systems but also transform how we relate to each other and to the natural world.

Inspired by the example of student activists like Margolin and Thunberg, four million protesters, including my daughter and me, gathered in thousands of cities worldwide, making it what was likely the largest day of action for climate justice in world history.

Days later, speaking to the U.N. Climate Action Summit, Thunberg was indignant. She accused those in attendance of stealing her childhood, stating that she should be in school instead of engaged in climate activism, yet noting that among young people worldwide she was "one of the lucky ones." As a counterpoint to those who spoke of technological solutions and economic growth, she went on to speak instead of ecosystem collapse, mass extinction, and human suffering. She decried proposed emissions targets that failed to adequately reduce the risks of overshooting 1.5 degrees Celsius of warming, warning that the generations of people who would be forced to live with the consequences "are starting to understand your betrayal." She saved her strongest criticism for adults who look to children for inspiration. "Yet you all come to us young people for hope," she scolded. "How dare you!"

As a parent—phone in hand while holding my infant daughter—reading Margolin's op-ed and watching Thunberg's speech, I felt admiration for the youth activists who were taking on the fossil fuel industry, and also moved to act. I looked up at the ceiling, blinking back tears, as if searching for an answer to the question of what love asked of me in this moment, and the next. I was grateful for the young people, worldwide, who were advancing the movement for climate justice, and yet, I knew deep down, that children should not be forced by the inaction of adults, like me, to become activists.

I knew that, like Thunberg, my children were among those considered lucky, from a global perspective, and yet, even our many privileges would not be enough to protect them from the chaos of living in a changed climate, would not prevent them from someday looking to me and demanding to know if I'd done what I could, and if I could not answer them honestly, then, perhaps, they too would have every right to say, "how dare you."

In 2021, an international survey of 10,000 youth found that an overwhelming majority felt betrayed by their governments' inadequate responses to climate change and that this sense of institutional betrayal exacerbated their feelings of climate anxiety and distress. "They feel abandoned by adults," said one of the study's authors, psychotherapist Caroline Hickman, in a magazine interview. "They are confused by adults, who are basically lying to them." For Heather, showing up for her children is part of what motivates her ongoing participation in

Climate Action Families, where she now serves on the board. Heather told me about a pivotal conversation she once had with her teenaged daughter, who mentioned that a friend was losing sleep over climate change.

"I was like, 'Oh, honey, that's really sad,'" Heather recalls, "How are you feeling about it? Do you feel like you lose sleep?'"

To Heather's surprise, her daughter replied, "No, I told my friend that I don't lose sleep because my mom's working on it." For Heather, the conversation underscores how impactful it is for children to witness their parents' involvement in activism. She says, "When parents and leaders take climate action, it's protective of our children's mental health." Here, her thinking resonates with the survey findings. When it comes to addressing the impacts of climate change on youth mental health, Hickman and her co-authors write that protective factors include "having one's feelings and views heard, validated, respected, and acted upon, particularly by those in positions of power and upon whom we are dependent, accompanied by collective pro-environmental actions."

An understanding of these protective factors is now shaping Climate Action Families programming. While the organization was initially created to help youth activists connect with each other and prepare for protests, lawsuits, and lobby days, increasingly its activities are intended for the whole family. "We're moving toward a model where it's not just the kids supporting each other in their activism, but it's also parents who are supporting their kids," says Heather. "We feel like it helps protect kids from climate anxiety and it strengthens family ties and builds community."

Heather, who has hosted an "ask a climate scientist" booth at protests, offers reassurance to fellow parents who want to speak up but aren't scientists. "Fossil fuels are one of the deadliest products on our planet. The particulate matter from burning coal, oil, and methane is responsible for one in five deaths worldwide, and in the United States, more than 950 premature deaths a day," she told me. "I always say that you don't have to be a doctor to tell somebody to stop smoking around your baby, and you don't have to be a climate scientist to do something about climate justice."

Maternal rhetoric is a tool that many mothers reach for in their advocacy for climate action. Every time I email or phone my representatives about an environmental issue, I begin by stating that I'm the mother of two young children, deliberately framing my demands in terms of my maternal role. But this approach can make for "slippery rhetorical terrain for women," writes Lindal Buchanan in her book *Rhetorics of Motherhood*, "on the one hand, affording them authority and credibility, but on the other, positioning them disadvantageously within the gendered status quo." Invoking motherhood also risks "ignoring critical differences among women and their mothering practices," writes Buchanan, including how our social locations shape our performances of motherhood.

These differences can be shaped by geography, as in the Global South, for example, where the worsening effects of the climate crisis make parent-led advocacy more crucial as well as more challenging than ever. "Parenting toward climate justice means something very different to us here in the Global South than it does to you in the North," is how Nigerian activist Amuche Nnabueze put it, describing the difficulties that political corruption, poverty, hunger, and lack of access to clean water pose to movement-building.

And in the United States, racial identity is one of the critical differences that influence mothering practices. For many Black mothers, engaging in political activism and challenging racism, including environmental racism, on behalf of their children is one of the central demands of motherhood. In her book, *We Live for the We*, journalist

Dani McClain describes the political project of Black motherhood as one that extends beyond care for one's family to include advocacy and activism that leads to collective liberation. She draws on scholar Patricia Hill Collins's term "motherwork" to name the reproductive and domestic labor that Black mothers perform in addition to their efforts to reform oppressive systems. McClain writes, "Black mothers advocate for our children everywhere . . . Activism is woven into the fabric of our daily lives."

The climate justice movement is rooted in the activism of women of color, like Hazel M. Johnson, who led the fight in the 1970s against environmental racism on Chicago's South Side and is considered the mother of environmental justice, as well as organizations like the Mothers of East Los Angeles, a group which formed in the 1980s and protested the development of a toxic waste incinerator and oil pipeline near Latino and Black neighborhoods.

Throughout the United States, mothers are working to form diverse coalitions and build political power to protest climate change. I wanted to know more about how parents, especially mothers, are organizing in response to the climate crisis, so I reached out to representatives from parent-led environmental groups. The mothers I spoke to—scientists, activists, and politicians—shared how they meaningfully draw on their maternal identities in order to advocate for a livable planet. They are tapping into the fear, grief, and anger that parents feel on behalf of their children, and also, crucially their love, as a catalyst for climate action.

"As moms, we go to the halls of Congress and we use our voices to make change," says Liz Hurtado, a Connecticut mother of four whose children range in age from eight to 16. "Who can deny that we need to protect children? That's not a partisan issue. We like to say it's a 'mom partisan' issue."

Liz works as the national field manager for EcoMadres, a Moms Clean Air Force program that empowers Latinos to fight air pollution and other climate justice issues that disproportionately impact them. Liz is not a climate scientist but was drawn to environmental advocacy after working in public health to address the needs of underrepresented communities.

She cites research showing that Latinos are more likely than the non-Hispanic white population to live in urban heat islands that lack trees and neighborhood green spaces, as well as near sources of air pollution, like highways and polluting facilities. All of which adversely impacts Latina maternal health. "There's no doubt that Latino communities know climate change is real. We see it happening in our neighborhoods," says Liz. "Poll after poll shows that the majority of Latinos are concerned, so our founder, Gabriela Rivera, was inspired to empower moms to take action."

A major focus for EcoMadres is civic engagement education with programming that aims to equip parents for political participation. Organizers help parents prepare for town halls and public hearings. They also plan national lobbying days and special events, like the annual Play-In for Climate Action held each year in Washington, D.C.

One of the organization's signature issues, the transition to electric school buses, is a personal one for Liz, whose daughter began complaining that she felt light-headed and woozy after sitting on an idling bus for fifteen to twenty minutes each morning before the start of the school day. Liz recalls bringing her daughter the first time she went lobbying. Her daughter was able to explain to congressional staffers how pollution affects her and why environmental protections are so important.

Transitioning away from toxic diesel pollution is important for children's health, but also for the bus drivers and teacher aides who are similarly exposed to fumes. In the United States, there are now 5,000 electric school buses serving students across nearly every state and territory, including seven tribal schools, with more than 12,000 additional electric school bus commitments at various stages of the purchasing and manufacturing process. Whenever a new electric bus arrives, group members hold celebratory events with key decision makers. Liz says these events are motivating, because it gives activists the opportunity see the tangible results of their efforts.

"More important than our talking points are our stories," says Liz, "Elected officials need to hear from constituents about how they're being impacted by air pollution, plastics pollution, and extreme heat. We have to urge them to put our children's health at the top of their priority list and demand stronger protections, because unless we're right in front of them, they're going to prioritize something else. But unless we have a livable future, there is nothing else."

Since the Trump administration took office in 2025 and began its rollback of environmental protections, Liz says she's been feeling a million and one worries, but that it's motivating to show up for work with other moms who are united in the mission to fight pollution. "We all need this work and feel that moral obligation to protect our children and leave them as bright a future as we can," Liz says, "We have to harness the most renewable source of energy, which is love."

For Marlena Fontes, a mother of two and co-founder of Climate Families NYC, becoming a parent was the catalyst in her journey to climate activism. Like me, Marlena was pregnant with her first child when the IPCC released its 2018 report calling for decisive action by 2030. The day after her son was born was the hottest day of the year, and as she held him in their sweltering apartment, her thoughts kept turning to the next twelve years. "I'd put up thick walls around my climate anxiety. Thinking about it was too big, too scary," Marlena says, describing how her postpartum anxiety centered on climate change. "But giving birth to my son just broke down those walls. It was a reckoning. I realized that I have to face this."

When her son was eight weeks old, she pumped enough breast milk for a bottle, put it in the fridge, and left for an hour to attend a local meeting hosted by the Sunrise Movement. Taking this first step helped ease her anxiety, but she felt that the organization was mostly geared toward younger activists. Through the group, however, she was introduced to several other moms who together formed Climate Families NYC.

"I can't say that the climate anxiety went away," says Marlena, "but it became an engine that moved me forward to create change."

Climate Families NYC makes activism accessible to families, including by holding play dates at parks to recruit parents. "Recruitment isn't hard," Marlena says. "Parents are freaked out about climate and when you give them the opportunity to take action, so many of them get involved, especially moms." During online meetings, they welcome interruptions, like children playing in the background or parents who participate while also cooking dinner. And when they show up at protests and marches, they pack plenty of snacks and toys, even bubbles.

One of the group's more memorable actions took place at Governor Kathleen Hochul's office. Parents and children went together to deliver a letter, and when the governor was unavailable to meet with them, they staged a play-in, like a sit-in but with kids. "We put a bunch of toys down on a blanket, pulled out the snacks, and started singing," says Marlena. "And we stayed for hours with our kids running around and playing." When she told me this, I laughed, imagining the familiar chaos of young children put to use to apply political pressure.

Another time the group brought their toddlers to ring the doorbell at the home of BlackRock CEO Larry Fink. "Because we're parents with kids, and especially because we're women, and many of us are white women, we can take aggressive action without appearing threatening," Marlena says.

Fink called the police, but came outside to speak with them, though he seemed to believe he was powerless to stop his firm from investing in fossil fuels. "We heard arguably one of the most powerful men in the world say that he couldn't do anything and his hands were tied," says Marlena. "I was disgusted to see someone with so much power refuse to wield it."

After their conversation, however, Fink agreed to set up a meeting between the activists and his representatives. Marlena says that whenever the group gains that kind of access, they make sure to invite partner organizations and other parents to the table who can represent working class communities and communities of color.

Marlena now works as the organizing director for the Brooklyn-based Climate Organizing Hub, a job she applied for during the summer of 2023, when New York's skies turned orange with wildfire smoke. "I was out at a rally," she remembers. "And it felt like a small taste of the end of the world. I thought about my kids living in a world of orange skies, and it was horrifying."

Marlena's message for moms is simple: "If you've organized a birthday party or a holiday dinner, you can be an organizer." She adds, "This is not something you can do alone. Find your people—even just three other parents—and connect with a local climate organization to support their campaigns."

Kia Smith, who is a co-executive director for Mothers Out Front and based in Atlanta, Georgia, agrees that meeting moms where they're at is key. "If you want collective action, you have to build an organization where people have the space and capacity to act collectively," she told me.

The organization builds teams through hosting small, in-home gatherings that welcome babies and children. "We want people to know you don't have to find a babysitter in order to come, and that it's okay if your baby cries or needs to breastfeed during our meetings," Kia says.

When moms first join Mothers Out Front, many feel powerless as individuals, but the organization emphasizes that climate activism is not a super-mom story. "Our superpower is in coming together," Kia says, adding, "We won't ask you to take on work for our campaigns that would disrupt your ability to parent."

Mothers Out Front was founded in 2013 and is now focused on three main initiatives: making schools healthier for kids by investing in electric school buses and HVAC systems; pushing back against the construction of new pipelines through Black and Brown communities while advocating to replace existing gas infrastructure with clean energy sources; and making polluters pay through climate superfund bills. "Moms teach people to clean up their own mess," quips Kia, of this last initiative. "Which is why we want polluters to pay for their own mess."

Before joining Mothers Out Front, Kia worked in nonprofit communications for faith-based and reproductive justice organizations. For her, participating in climate advocacy began to take on greater urgency in the mid-2010s. When the 2018 IPCC report came out, it was at a time when Kia was already concerned about the state of democracy and having conversations with her daughter about being Black in the justice system. "I'm holding all of this as the parent of a Black trans kid, and really seeing how this world is not safe for my child," Kia says, "So I made the decision, rooted in reproductive justice, not to have more kids but to instead do the work of making our communities safer for my kid and all kids."

One of the challenges of building community-based teams, Kia says, is that most of us live segregated lives. Mothers Out Front trains its team leaders using curriculum that centers climate justice and racial justice, and they are intentional about asking them to build coalitions that are racially and economically diverse. "We are building an organization where frontline communities feel that they belong," says Kia, "We are doing this work for all our kids—there are no sacrifice zones."

Kia, who has a background in English literature, thinks a lot about the impact of storytelling in climate activism. "We talk about how important it is to identify the protagonists and antagonists," she says. "The protagonists are the moms who are working together to fight for their kids and the antagonists are the big oil and gas companies—the wealthy, powerful few who are making decisions to prioritize their profits over our well-being."

When I asked Kia why she believes mothers can be a powerful force in the fight for climate justice, she told me, "We are in very polarizing times, so we need to lean into our shared values and experiences to talk across differences. There are no better messengers for that than moms. Moms have a moral authority in their communities. When moms speak, people listen."

The fight for their children's futures has led some mothers to run for office. In 2022, first-time candidate Katie Darling launched a long-shot campaign for Congress, challenging Steve Scalise, who at the time, was the Republican House minority whip. Katie, who had never held public office, was seven months pregnant when she decided to run to represent Louisiana's first congressional district. Her pregnancy was high risk, and after *Roe v. Wade* was overturned, she worried about what the state's strict abortion ban would mean for her care.

Her campaign ad went viral within hours of its release. I remember texting crying-face emojis back and forth with my mom friends after watching; we had never seen anything like it. In the ad, Katie, who is filmed in the final weeks of her pregnancy, introduces us to her husband and five-year-old daughter and shows us around their farm. In a voice over, Katie tells us, "Our family composts, collects rainwater, and grows our own food." She continues, "But these days I worry about storms that are stronger and more frequent because of climate change, about our kids' underperforming public schools, and about Louisiana's new abortion ban, one of the strictest and most severe in the country."

Then, we watch as Katie's husband drives her to the hospital, as she is wheeled into a hospital room, as she breathes through contractions, and, finally, as she holds her son after giving birth. "I'm running because I want that better path for you, for her," she says as the video cuts to an image of her daughter playing on the farm, then to an image of Katie, still in a hospital gown, holding her newborn son to her chest, "and for him."

It was one of the first times I've ever felt my concerns, as a mother, so viscerally represented in a campaign ad. Katie, who has since had a third child and now serves as the first vice chair for the Louisiana Democratic Party, spoke to me by Zoom from her family farm. "The reason the ad was different is because I was a candidate who was different. I didn't have political ambitions, and I was never going to beat Steve Scalise," says Katie. "But I ran because there was no one else running to fight for me in that moment. I'd already had three miscarriages and I needed people to understand why abortion bans are so dangerous—human to human, neighbor to neighbor, friend to friend, mom to mom." The ad skillfully deployed maternal rhetoric to argue for reproductive self-determination, leaning into the persuasive force of mother-child imagery to show that abortion care is for everyone, including mothers.

It was also important to Katie that the ad address the climate crisis, since her family has been forced to evacuate many times during severe storms, like when Hurricane Ida struck in 2021 and power was out for a month. "Climate change is a crisis that's occurring all around us every day," she says. "When I had my daughter, I began to think about her future quality of life. Becoming a mother opened my eyes to how society isn't structured to support families and future generations."

Katie sees potential for bipartisan collaboration to address climate change, despite what people may see in the media. "In real life, there are plenty of Democrats and Republications working to solve climate and environmental issues," she insists.

"Our generation didn't start the problem, we didn't create the plastics industry, we didn't create the oil and gas industry, but so much damage has been done in our lifetime, and we are continuing the problem," says Katie. "We need a couple of adults in the room to say, here's what we're going to do about it."

I first heard of the Science Moms when I saw their commercial, which aired in the Los Angeles region during the 2025 Super Bowl in the weeks following the Eaton and Palisades fires that killed at least 29 people, including a disabled father and son who could not evacuate, and displaced thousands of families. The timing of the commercial was significant, given that the Super Bowl was being held in New Orleans at the rebuilt Superdome months before the twentieth anniversary of Hurricane Katrina, and that damages from the L.A. wildfires were expected to surpass that storm as the costliest climate disaster in U.S. history.

The 60-second commercial, called "By the Time," follows a young girl's life from birth through college. It opens with an ultrasound image, like the printed ones stored in my desk drawer for safekeeping. Then, the narration begins: "As a scientist, I know by the time she takes her first breath, 9 billion more tons of carbon pollution will be in the air." Scenes of mothers and daughters at different life stages fill the screen, juxtaposing developmental milestones with progressively worse evidence of environmental degradation—wildfires that burn millions of acres, thousands of newly extinct species. Finally, as a mother and daughter hug in a dorm room: "By the time a child born today goes to college, it may be too late to leave them the world we promised."

Watching it from the vantage point of early motherhood, I felt the push and pull of the future. I longed for my children to experience those same milestones, but also, not for the first time, did I wish that I could hit pause—both to stop the climate clock and also to linger for a little longer in the sweetness of these years of sticky faces and skinned knees.

Science Moms, a non-partisan group of climate scientists who are also mothers, was founded in 2021 with the goal of boosting climate change awareness among parents. When I spoke with Melissa Burt, an atmospheric scientist at Colorado State University and one of the Science Moms, she said, "We want to be trusted messengers to other moms and parents."

Melissa says it's important to talk about climate change in terms of shared values and to include it in everyday conversations, like the time she was waiting with her daughter at the bus stop and found herself answering another mom's questions about how climate change was impacting wildfire season. "As a mom, you always reach out to other moms to get advice—about strollers, breast pumps, those types of things," she says, "So why not reach out to other moms about how climate change is impacting our children's future."

Another time, after she represented Science Moms on a panel at a parenting event, an attendee contacted her. Melissa recalls, "She emailed to say, 'I'm a Black mom who lives in Brooklyn, and I didn't realize climate change was something that mattered to me and my community, because I'd never seen anyone who looked like me talk about the importance of it.'" For Melissa, the experience underscores the significance of representation and increasing the visibility of Black women and women of color in climate science.

Whenever she speaks about the climate crisis, Melissa says she gets asked about hope. "I have hope, first, because of my daughter—I'm going to keep fighting because of her," she says. "But I also have hope because we have the tools to make the changes we need. Whether you're on the right or the left, the important thing is that we need policies. History shows us that with policy changes, like the Clean Air Act, we can make a difference."

State and local policies matter, too, says Melissa. For example, she says, "I'm on the parent-teacher association at my daughter's school, so I ask questions like, 'What is the school district doing to address pollution?'" She encourages fellow moms to advocate for climate action by drawing on shared values wherever they have the power to make change, including by influencing the decision making of city councils and school boards.

"Grandparents, uncles, coaches, pediatricians, and neighbors share an interest in our children's well-being, one that can transcend political differences and divides," writes activist Mary DeMocker. "Parents have unique access to people's heartstrings, and it's time to pull them—hard—for our kids' future."

Rachel Rivera, a mother of six children and grandmother to three who lives in East Brooklyn, is an activist who pulls hard on the heartstrings of policymakers, even if it means getting arrested for civil disobedience. The night that Hurricane Sandy hit, Rachel's five-year-old daughter was asleep in bed when Rachel heard a cracking noise coming from the bedroom ceiling. Rachel grabbed her daughter just before it caved in. Her other children were staying with relatives, but Rachel and her daughter spent that night in an emergency shelter. While Rachel translated for other Spanish speakers and advocated for people who were undocumented and afraid to speak up, her daughter kept the younger kids entertained, playing games with them.

But the ordeal was traumatic for her daughter, who has since suffered from intense anxiety and fear. For Rachel, the storm that forced her and her children from their apartment and into the shelter system also propelled her to take action. Rachel is now a community organizer for New York Communities for Change and has participated in campaigns that secured key climate victories, like shutting down the proposed Williams pipeline between New York and New Jersey and convincing New York City to divest its pension funds from fossil fuel industries.

Rachel, who is from Puerto Rico, lost a childhood friend to Hurricane Maria and had several family members lose their homes. "People need to know how difficult it is to lose somebody because of the one-percenters who want to keep fracking and lining their pockets with cash," she says. Rachel draws on her parenting experience in her political work. Some politicians, she tells me, you have to treat with patience, you have to gentle parent them. With others, you have to take a stricter approach, which she demonstrates by locking eyes with me over Zoom in a powerful stare that can only be described as an "angry mom face"—and I love her for it. It's a look I recognize from childhood, one I'm sure my own children are familiar with as well.

When I ask Rachel how she copes with burnout, she told me that she refuses to quit fighting for her children and grandchildren. "If I lose hope," says Rachel, "My children lose their future."

Working together to take climate action on behalf of our children and future generations has never been more urgent. The most recent

World Meteorological Organization's annual "State of the Global Climate" report indicates that not only was 2024 the hottest year on record, but it was also the first to reach an average global temperature that was 1.55 degrees Celsius above pre-industrial levels. This means that the long-term temperature goals of the Paris Agreement are still within reach, but we are closer than ever to breaching the barrier of 1.5 degrees Celsius and may do so within the next 20 years.

Other key indicators of planetary health are similarly alarming. According to the report, levels of atmospheric carbon dioxide are now at their highest point in 800,000 years. The ocean has warmed twice as fast, in the last twenty years, as it had between 1960 and 2005, and it's the hottest it's ever been in 65 years of recordkeeping. The world's glaciers are losing mass at the fastest rates recorded and sea levels are at their highest and rising at double the rate of previous decades. From record rains in Italy and flash floods in Pakistan to heatwaves in Iran and Mali to Hurricane Helene in the United States, the report documents 151 unprecedented extreme weather events in 2024 that displaced more than 800,000 people.

Reading through a report like this one, while watching out the window as my children pour out sand in our backyard sandbox, letting the grains run through their grubby fingers, I hear echoes of the voiceover from the Science Moms' commercial, its final line a powerful warning: "Our window to act on climate change is like watching them grow up. We blink, and we miss it."

Saving Seeds

"I wouldn't want to be a sea turtle," my daughter said, when I asked her what costume she'd like to make for the Procession of the Species parade.

"Why not?" I replied.

"Because sea turtles never get to meet their moms."

This wasn't something I had considered before.

"They just lay their eggs on the beach and swim away," she explained.

"Well I'm glad we're not sea turtles," I said, putting my arm around her and giving her a quick squeeze, before asking once more about her costume.

"Guess!" she said.

"A penguin?" I asked, playing along.

"No!" she said, with a sly grin, before offering me a hint: "I'm not chilly!"

"Okay, what about a cheetah?"

"Nope!" she said again, even more triumphantly, before twitching her nose and hopping around the kitchen floor.

"A bunny," I guessed.

"Yes!"

Together, we browsed tutorials for simple bunny costumes and made a list: a headband with floppy felt ears, a white circle of a belly sewn onto a gray sweatshirt, and a cotton-ball tail.

Later, when I asked my son what he'd like to be, he replied without hesitation: "an excavator." After some creative brainstorming, we settled on a crab costume with felt claws sewn onto a red long-sleeve tee.

"Pinch, pinch," he shouted, darting around the kitchen table, opening and closing his hands.

I remember watching the parade the spring that I was pregnant with my daughter. I had marveled at the creativity on display as a cyclist pedaled by, animating a 12-foot-wide raven that flapped overhead, and as a couple dressed as dung beetles pushed a giant ball of dung, made from a brown tarp and duct tape, down the street. The circus guild and area musicians added to the festive atmosphere, walking on stilts and playing percussive instruments. And I was charmed as parents pushed face-painted toddlers in decorated strollers and small children in fuzzy bumblebee and green crocodile costumes waved to the crowds.

The first Procession of the Species event was held thirty years ago in our state capital to celebrate Earth Day and support the Endangered Species Act. Since then, it has become a well-known regional event, drawing tens of thousands of spectators and inspiring similar parades in cities around the world. Our local procession is a beloved, albeit much smaller, more relaxed event. I have always felt that it is an embodied celebration of what E. B. White called "the glory of everything."

When the parks and recreation department announced, in 2025, that it was partnering with a children's arts organization to bring back the parade after a pandemic-induced pause, it generated lots of excitement among our friends with kids. But I was wrong in thinking of the procession as an event primarily for children and families, since founder Eli Sterling initially conceived of it as a public art event for adults, with kids welcome. "When kids see all these adults dancing, playing music, and doing art in a public setting," he told a local newspaper, "They think, 'Oh! That's what adults do. I don't have to be embarrassed by that!'"

Dancing, playing music, making art, celebrating nature—these are activities I want my children to enjoy now and into adulthood, so I added the procession to our calendar. When I looked up the details for a free costume-making workshop, I saw that the procession has just three rules: no motorized vehicles, no live animals, and no written words. In all the years I'd witnessed the parade, I hadn't noticed the absence of writing.

According to Sterling, "there are no written words in nature." The prohibition is intended to prevent corporate sponsorships and level the playing field among participants. While I supported these aims, and was happy to follow the rules, I wasn't sure what to make of his claim about the absence of written words in nature. For one thing, humans make writing, and are we not part of nature? Still, by denying humans the written word, I thought, it's possible that it also levels the playing field among species.

It called to mind several lines from poet Etel Adnan I'd copied into my notebook after her passing: "Our words don't suit prophecies anymore. That power is left to other species: to oak trees, for example, to the tides, which through their restlessness carry a phosphorescence we're not equipped to hear." What would change, I wondered, if only we could learn to listen to the more-than-human world, to read the writing of other species?

In addition to the three ground rules, Sterling is particular about calling the event a procession instead of a parade because "[w]hen people conquer they parade; when people are liberated they process." And, he's quoted as saying that the procession recognizes that "there is something beyond us, that which is infinity, which means that somewhere along the line we have to recognize the miracle that we're part of and we should be a kinder people."

To walk forward not in conquest but in liberation, to celebrate the abundance and diversity of the planet, to be part of something beyond us, something delightful and miraculous, even—these are more than just lofty ideas, these are still yet possible.

My children and I began cutting and sewing their bunny and crab costumes in earnest the same spring weekend that we began to plant our garden, the same weekend that the fall bulbs my daughter calls "surprise bulbs" burst into bloom, frilly daffodils and ruffled tulips that lived up to the name, since I'd forgotten where exactly I'd planted them.

Like we do every year, we sowed heirloom sweet peas along a trellis in the backyard. My children squatted in the dirt beside me, and I carefully tipped the jam jar of seeds we'd saved into their open hands.

The previous fall, my daughter had sat cross-legged in the grass in the late afternoon sunshine, wearing an iridescent rainbow cape, removing seeds from spent pods. Holding one up to the light, she looked through the pod's papery skin, to the dark, round shadows of seeds held within, and cracked it open, letting the seeds fall into a bowl that had belonged to my grandmother.

While she worked, I stood harvesting the seed pods, taking care not to crush the chamomile and love-in-a-mist underfoot. The pods shuddered and rattled in the wind, attached to tendrils that had once wandered, green and in search of support, but were now dry and twined around the trellis in a tangle of spirals. Sometimes, when I went to pull a pod from the vine, it would crack under the force, scattering seeds to the ground, seeds which, come spring, would surely sprout alongside those we planted.

After I finished harvesting the seed pods, I joined my daughter and we worked together, two pairs of hands set to the task. When we were done, she ran her fingers through the bowl of seeds and scooped up a handful, cradling in her palm so many little worlds.

Now, my children were bent to the ground, gently shooing seeds from their hands into the furrow I'd drawn with my finger in the soil.

Whenever I am planting seeds, a few lines from Emily Dickinson return to me:

Seed—summer—tomb—
Who's Doom to whom?

What else is a furrow, I thought, patting the soil firmly over the seeds with my palms, but an em-dash, that long line of punctuation that resists closure, a way of writing something new into being.

In "Sowing Worlds," Donna Haraway writes that "planting seeds requires medium, soil, matter, mutter, mother." Here, her playful work with etymology draws our attention to the connections between humus and human, between words and the making of worlds.

"It matters," writes Haraway, "what stories we tell to tell other stories with; it matters what concepts we think to think other concepts with."

She takes up Ursula Le Guin's "carrier bag theory of fiction" to advance her own theory of the "seed bag" from which we might sow "stories of becoming-with" the more-than-human world, of restoring the planet by working alongside other species, of reseeding a livable future.

Le Guin wrote that for much of our history, humans preferred the hero's story, which emerged from tales that hunters told of their kills. By drawing on the work of anthropologist Elizabeth Fisher—

who argued that the earliest tools humans invented were containers, not weapons—Le Guin proposed that our first stories were perhaps those told by foragers, not hunters, who told tales of what they discovered and gathered, who boasted not of what they speared but of what they carried in their bags and baskets. The former she called "the killer story," the latter "the life story."

Fiction, in Le Guin's view, can be a forager's story, "a way of trying to describe what is in fact going on, what people actually do and feel, how people relate to everything else in this vast sack, this belly of the universe, this womb of things to be and tomb of things that were, this unending story."

As an example of her "seed bag theory" Haraway, turns to a short story in which Le Guin imagines research findings from what she called the "Journal of the Association of Therolinguistics." In it, animal communication scholars report on their attempts to translate the languages of Ant, Penguin, Dolphin, among others. They puzzle over a manuscript composed by an ant. They theorize about the kinetic literature of penguins. Finally, they move from animal communication to speculating about plant communication. They consider the possibility that in the near future phytolinguists may be able to read plant languages, like Eggplant and Lichen. And further off, as the study of nonhuman communication advances, there may be geolinguists who can read the poetry of rocks. "We do not know. All we can guess is that the putative Art of the Plant is entirely different from the Art of the Animal," concludes the association president. "What it is, we cannot say; we have not yet discovered it."

When I re-read this short story, now, I wonder if perhaps one way to recognize a "life story" is by noticing who has the power to speak. In Le Guin's story, literacy is not limited to humans, but is accorded to a procession of animals, plants, and rocks, who compose not just mere utterances, but art. The ending resists closure but rather holds open the possibility of advancements in scholarship, the possibility of new fields of study, the possibility of future revelations.

Haraway writes, "With Le Guin, I am committed to the finicky, disruptive details of good stories that don't know how to finish. Good stories reach into rich pasts to sustain thick presents to keep the story going for those who come after."

In addition to Le Guin's short stories, Haraway also draws on Octavia Butler's novel *Parable of the Sower*, which is set in a climate-ravaged, post-apocalyptic northern California. In it, Lauren Oya Olamina, a visionary Black teenager and theologian, leads a group of refugees north in search of a place to settle. When they finally arrive at a plot of land owned by one of the group members, they must decide whether to stay or keep traveling.

Lauren speaks persuasively of the seeds she has saved and carried with her—summer crops like corn, beans, and squash; winter crops like cabbage, broccoli, and onions; as well as tree seeds, like oak, pear, and almond—saying, "It will be hard to live here, but if we work together, and if we're careful, it should be possible. We can build a community here."

It's a novel I often assigned in my undergraduate courses, and whenever I discussed it with my students, inevitably someone would ask about the title. So, I would explain that Lauren, who was raised by a Baptist minister, would have been familiar with the parables of Jesus, like the one about the sower, in which a person sets out to sow seeds. Some fall along the path, some fall on rocky ground, some fall among thorns, and some fall in good soil. Later, Jesus interprets this parable for his disciples, saying that the seed is the word and the soil is those who hear it.

Growing up, I used to worry that my heart was like the rocky ground, where faith could not grow. Now, I think that sometimes it takes a while for the right stories to find you and to take root, and that my job as a parent is to become a trustworthy storyteller, to do the work of saving seeds and nurturing the soil, to wait and see what grows.

In the end, Lauren and her companions decide to stay and garden. But first, they honor those they've lost by planting a grove of oak trees in their memory, naming their new home, Acorn. Butler's novel is not a hopeful book—it warns of the dire consequences of continuing down our present path of ecological and political ruin—yet it remains committed to the belief that it is possible to begin again, to coax new growth from the soil.

It makes sense to turn to those who write futures—futures rooted in the problems of the past and the possibilities of the present—to imagine what life might be like in the decades to come. In her introduction to an anthology of science fiction inspired by the works of Octavia Butler, scholar and writer Walidah Imarisha writes, "[T]he decolonization of the imagination is the most dangerous and subversive form there is: for it is where all other forms of decolonization are born. Once the imagination is unshackled, liberation is limitless." She argues for the importance of narratives that envision "new, freer worlds" and of recognizing the imagination as a site of resistance and change-making.

Both Haraway and Le Guin call for stories that unfold into the future, stories that help us imagine the flourishing of humans alongside all other beings. "The slight curve of the shell that holds just a little water, just a few seeds to give away and to receive," writes Haraway, of her seed bag theory, "suggests stories of becoming-with, of reciprocal induction, of companion species whose job in living and dying is not to end the storying, the worlding."

I like to think that before there were stories of things carried in bags and baskets, there were the stories we held with our own cupped hands, and these were the hands that brought cool water to our lips, that caught and cradled newborns, that scooped soil into mounds, that first sowed the unending story. And still, writes Le Guin, "the story isn't over. Still there are seeds to be gathered, and room in the bag of stars."

"Will Earth ever burst," my daughter asked me on a recent Saturday morning after watching a *Magic School Bus* rerun.

"What do you mean?" I asked.

"You know, because planets explode," she said.

"Someday the Earth will end, but not for billions of years," I said, because I know that the Sun, like all other stars, was born and will someday die.

"But where will humans go," she asked.

"Maybe by then we'll have figured out space travel," I offered, before another show began, capturing her attention. I could hear the theme music for *Ada Twist, Scientist*, as I went to the kitchen to pour another cup of coffee.

That far-off catastrophe feels unimaginable to me. Scrolling through headlines while the coffee brewed, I had the thought, that some days it's difficult for me to imagine five years from now, let alone fifty.

In his book *Falter*, Bill McKibben sketches out possible scenarios which could spell the end game of humanity, scenarios which could take place within just a few generations. Maybe the oceans will warm to such an extent that the phytoplankton responsible for producing much of Earth's oxygen will become unable to photosynthesize, leaving humans to suffocate. Or maybe the weight of seawater from melting ice sheets will put so much pressure on the Earth's crust that it will usher in an era of extreme volcanic activity and catastrophic tsunamis. Or maybe the thawing permafrost will unleash a long-frozen deadly contagion. Or maybe the food supply will breakdown entirely or maybe excess carbon dioxide will utterly damage our brains.

Even for me, someone who likes to know what we're up against, it feels like five maybes too many. Stirring my coffee, I recalled how some scientists, like geologist Jan Zalasiewicz, have speculated that after humans, giant rats may take over the Earth. I could ruminate on such a future in which hordes of giant rats prowl ruins, but what if, instead, I tried imagining a future where we cooperate to solve our present ecological and political crises? Sometimes I think it's easier to imagine the rats.

I heard the words "climate change" coming from the TV, so I took my coffee into the living room, joining my daughter on the sofa to check in on what she was watching. As it turns out, she'd selected an Earth Day playlist, and a climate-themed episode, "Ada and the Green Team," was now playing. Ada and her friends are discussing climate change in the park when they flash forward to the future they will inhabit when they are old enough to be grandparents. In that world, they find that the park is now a barren wasteland of parched soil and tumbleweeds. Wearing masks to protect against the dust, they tour the park in a Mad Max-style rig, complete with a speaker stack and an electric guitar. A heartbroken child asks if it's too late. "No, it's not," Ada insists, "We can save it."

They flash forward to an alternate future. The park is covered in lush, green grass and flowering trees and the people look happy. Butterflies and bees flutter through the air. "Good thing there's another version of the future, a better one," says one of the Ada's friends, driving an electric vehicle through a neighborhood of community gardens and homes with solar panels. If they want this version of the future, the children conclude, they have to take care of the planet. So they return to the present, ready to get to work.

At the end of the episode, I turned to my daughter and gently asked, "What did you think of the Green Team?"

"I want to live in that future," she said. "The green one."

I want that future for my children, too.

In Sheila Heti's novel *Pure Colour*, she describes the horrors of contemporary life—the melting icebergs, the dying species, the burning fossil fuels. "It was like being in a plane that was slowly twirling to the ground," she writes. Even now there is a group of artists working in Tasmania to build what they're calling "Earth's Black Box," like the black boxes that tell the story of plane crashes. They're creating a solar-powered, virtually indestructible vault that will store data about climate change for perpetuity in order to preserve a record of human activity capable of outlasting humans.

But I want to believe that such a black box won't be necessary, that we can land the plane, that perhaps it's not even an airplane we're riding, at all, that perhaps it's more like a maple seed, what my sister and I grew up calling whirligigs as they careened to the ground in late spring, spinning and twirling.

Perhaps we can try, at the very least, to imagine a landing that is not so much explosive as it is generative, like a seed gently drifting to the ground, where it will someday take root.

Saving seeds is a practice that insists that the end of the growing season is not the end of the story, nor the end of the world.

When planning our garden, this year, I searched for heirloom seeds through an online exchange that connects seed savers with growers. I browsed the offerings located within Washington state and mailed off a request for jack-o-lantern pumpkin seeds. I'd promised my children we'd plant a small pumpkin patch to grow fruit for carving and sharing with neighbor friends. Plus, I figured it would be reasonably straightforward to clean, dry, and store the heirloom pumpkin seeds after my own harvest—a responsibility I did not take lightly.

It's estimated that within the last century, owing in part to the rise of hybrid and genetically-modified seeds, as much as 75 percent of the world's edible plant varieties have been lost. To safeguard humanity's food supply, there are 1,700 gene banks worldwide, as well as a global seed vault buried deep within a mountain on a remote, icy island in the arctic circle, known as the Doomsday Vault.

Fresh deposits of seeds are sometimes brought there for safekeeping from places threatened by natural disasters and armed conflicts. "There are big and small doomsdays going on around the world every day," the executive director of Crop Trust told *Time* magazine, and all of these threaten genetic material.

But even the Doomsday Vault is not invulnerable to the effects of a changing climate. A few years ago, it required reinforcements against flooding from the melting permafrost, caused by rising temperatures. Small-scale efforts to save seeds have also been threatened by climate disaster.

After Hurricane Helene struck western North Carolina in September 2024, there was widespread reporting on the storm's impact on the region's seed savers, people who had devoted their lives to gathering and preserving heirloom seeds. In the aftermath of the storm, volunteers worked to salvage seeds that were stored in freezers in collapsed barns and flooded basements or drying in climate-controlled trailers that had lost power. These were regionally adapted seeds, many of them culturally significant plants, sometimes collected alongside oral histories, which made them an invaluable record of the entanglements of plants and people. As one naturalist and seed saver remarked, "The loss of stories of seeds makes us a more vulnerable people."

Unlike the Doomsday Vault, the aim of these grassroots seed saving projects is to conserve biodiversity not by stashing away genetic material for the future but by keeping the seeds in circulation in the present, working with local growers who cultivate these plants year after year. And, unlike the corporate plant breeders who patent the seeds they produce, these seed savers participate in exchanges and lending libraries, freely giving away their stories and their seeds—like the pumpkin seeds I sent off for.

The other day, my children and I worked together to prepare the soil for our pumpkin patch, pulling bindweed and horsetail from a wide sunny slope in our front yard, readying it for the heirloom seeds I'd been given for the price of postage. When the seeds arrived, our mail carrier had handed the shipping envelope directly to me, noting the scrawling cursive that marked it as "seeds fragile!!!!" Inside, was a note with detailed instructions for germinating the seeds, penned in handwriting that called to mind my own grandmother's, how her letters had become labored as her hands became stiff and arthritic.

Reading it, I wondered how it must feel to let go of seeds you'd saved and cared for, to offer them up to a stranger who could only promise to tend them well, to know there are never guarantees when it comes to gardening. I wondered if perhaps this was something like the experience of letting go of your children's hands and watching them make their own way into the world, knowing that anything can happen and that you can control exactly none of it.

Good luck with these seeds, the note read. *Please do write me back, if possible, to let me know how they did for you.* And I knew I would.

While we weeded and turned the soil, my children chatted about what designs they'd carve into their pumpkins come fall and their favorite way to eat the seeds—toasted with cinnamon and sugar. And, I looked forward to those seeds that I'd save next year, and the next, and the next.

"A gardener is always a futurist," writes Deborah Levy, "with a vision of how a small, humble plant will spring up and blaze in time."

I can imagine, months from now, the garden I'm planting,

which will soon be crowded with green leaves, ripe tomatoes and summer squash, and heavy, fragrant blooms, but I struggle, in this era of rising authoritarianism and the obliteration of rights and the dismantling of the common good, to imagine a future of global flourishing.

Part of living on this planet is knowing that while my children and I gardened, planting sweet peas and chamomile, lettuce and radishes, other children, living here and abroad, were starving, were dying of preventable, curable diseases, were breathing polluted air and drinking poisoned water, were laboring in mines and factories, other children's homes were burning, were flooding, were being reduced to rubble, and knowing, too, that all this could be otherwise, that we could create a world in which all children can thrive, a world of abundance that, in many ways, is already within reach.

Scarcity is a choice, argue Ezra Klein and Derek Thompson in their book *Abundance*. It is important, they write, to "imagine a just—even a delightful—future and work backward to the technological advances that would hasten its arrival." Instead of scarcity, we could choose abundance, we could build a different future powered by clean energy technology that's already invented, that's already affordable and scalable, that doesn't require imagination but the installation of solar panels and wind turbines—nothing short of the electrification of everything. They write, "Two decades ago, it was not possible to imagine that modernity was compatible with renewable energy. Now we need not imagine it."

In this view, decarbonization is not an ending but a beginning, one that promises to usher in an era of "energy overabundance." Klein and Thompson urge us into the future, writing, "We are early in the story of humanity's relationship with energy."

For models of how we can accomplish the urgent, necessary transition to a decarbonized economy, Robin Wall Kimmerer looks to the wisdom of plants. In *The Serviceberry*, her book about abundance, she suggests that we could imitate how forests change over time. Ecological succession, the process by which plant communities replace species that once dominated landscapes, relies on two mechanisms: incremental change and creative disruption. We can and should, she says, deploy both in order to make our communities more just. She cites Charles Einstein's work in *Sacred Economics*, quoting him to describe how as ecosystems mature, they move away from colonizing, fast-growing species marked by extraction and competition and toward the direction of "complex interdependency, symbiosis, cooperation, and the cycling of resources."

Kimmerer envisions a regenerative economy bounded by ecological limits and a commitment to social justice. She writes, "I want to be part of a system in which wealth means having enough to share, and where the gratification of meeting your family's needs is not poisoned by destroying the possibility for someone else." I want this, too. This alternative economy, she says, could grow in the gaps of the present market economy, could succeed in replacing extraction and competition, writing, "Regenerative economies that reciprocate the gift are the only path forward. To replenish the possibility of mutual flourishing, for birds and berries and people, we need an economy that shares the gifts of the Earth, following the lead of our oldest teachers, the plants."

Kimmerer's definition of abundance is rooted in a commitment to mutual flourishing that includes humans as well as all other beings. I read this, and think, this is a vision of what it means to become-with other species, to liberate rather than to conquer, to recognize the miracle that we're part of.

Helping my children try on their costumes, adjusting my daughter's bunny ears and pulling the crab shirt over my son's head, I longed to give them a hundred more springs exactly like this one, a spring that was anything but silent.

It was a day when the air was fragrant with blooms. They stood on the deck, in sunshine that was gentle and warm, smiling back at me. But I can't promise my children the future, I can only give them the present, these fleeting moments together.

I stepped back, taking in their costumes, which as per the event guidelines, contained no written words, and wondered what rabbits and crabs might have to say for themselves, a question that is becoming increasingly less speculative. In her book *The Sounds of Life*, researcher Karen Bakker demonstrates how advances in audio recording and artificial intelligence are bringing us closer to understanding animal and plant communication and, incidentally, making Le Guin's science fiction closer to reality. Western science is beginning to "discover" what many Indigenous peoples have always held to be true.

"Our physiologies—and perhaps our psyches—limit our capacity to listen to our nonhuman kin. But humanity is beginning to expand its hearing ability," writes Bakker. "Digital technologies, so often associated with our alienation with nature, are offering us an opportunity to listen to nonhumans in powerful ways, reviving our connection to the natural world."

We now know, for example, that sea turtle hatchlings call to each other from within their shells, communicating with clicks, meows, and grunts, so that they can coordinate the timing of their births and therefore depart from their nests within the safety of a group. We know that baby bats can babble, much like human infants, and that mother bats speak to their young in baby talk, or motherese. And that humpback whale calves are noisiest in the mornings, making snorts, burps, and grunts to ask their mothers for milk.

Taken together, the sizeable evidence for complex communication among animals is beginning to challenge the notion that language is a gift unique to humans. Writes Katarina Zimmer for *Atmos*, "Scientists are now coming to see language as a constellation of different capabilities that each evolved on the evolutionary tree before our time, granting many other animals unique ways of conversing about their world." Writing of the potential for digital technologies to unlock interspecies communication, asks Bakker, "How might we choose to live on this planet when the voices of creation are (once again) both audible and meaningful to us?"

It's an important question, especially as digital technologies are also beginning to help us to understand the threat that climate change poses to sound-sensitive plants and animals, even as these same technologies, as in the case of artificial intelligence, are currently driving up carbon emissions and water consumption. The world's leading acoustic scientists, writes Bakker, tell us that climate change is literally "breaking the Earth's beat" by "rupturing the sonic rhythms of life." Climate change is affecting the songs of cicadas and crickets, frogs and fish and altering the vocalizations of migratory birds and the music of whales. If we learn to listen, deeply, the more-than-human world could possibly guide us away from our present path of destruction toward one that is more connected, that honors all voices, and that ensures these stories continue.

Late last summer, my husband was working in the yard with our kids, when he noticed my daughter snipping tomato leaves with her children's safety scissors. He went to stop her, worried that she might be damaging the plants. But she was confident in her skills, telling him, "This is how mom does it."

When I first moved here, I wanted to learn how to grow tomatoes in a maritime climate, where even in June the weather can be rainy and chilly. One of my neighbors, an avid gardener who often surprised us by hanging grocery sacks full of surplus produce on the handle of our back gate, told me that to prevent disease and ensure air flow I needed to trim the plants carefully, removing most of the lower leaves except for those on fruit-bearing stems. I have followed this advice successfully for over a decade now.

I wasn't even conscious of the fact that my children had been watching and imitating me, just as I'd grown up watching and imitating my grandmother in her garden, and still to this day sometimes find myself standing just like her, hands clasped behind my back, bending forward to greet my plants.

There will come a day when my children won't be able to visit my garden, just like I cannot return to my grandmother's, though I have stood holding them across the street from the house where she once lived, but I hope by then they'll know how to fill their own gardens with plants that offer nourishment and beauty, to share their produce with neighbors, and to leave their plants to overwinter so that insects and pollinators can seek shelter and birds can forage among the seedheads.

Something I love about Charles Darwin's *On the Origin of the Species*, a book that helped me to see more clearly the tree of life and our place in it, is that his children scrawled doodles and fanciful drawings all over the backs of his manuscripts. There are drawings of a windmill, tropical birds, a fruit-and-vegetable calvary, a sad-faced hound dog, and, my favorite, a frog holding an umbrella.

My children, too, have made their marks on my writing, drawing on printed manuscript pages, leaving messages for me to decipher. A scribbled heart, my daughter's name, the words MOM I LOVE.

Darwin published his book in the wake of his ten-year-old daughter Annie's death. Some suggest that this tragedy, also, left traces on his manuscript. Even as he grieved, Darwin affirmed what biographer Lyanda Lynn Haupt describes as "the endless unfolding of life." She writes, "In Darwin's thinking, both the past and the future converge in the living beings before us, all of which have grown out of a sustaining history and will participate, all of them, by the uniqueness of their deaths and their lives, in the creation of the future."

Sometimes, at the park, I look around at all the other parents, and think, do you feel this, too? This love that could shatter you, the sense that it could all splinter in an instant into so many ungraspable shards of grief, and the desire to hold on forever to these little ones, these living beings before us, who are even now creating the future.

Biographer Adam Gopnik says that while Darwin was writing, he grappled with the existential dilemma that everything dies, and yet, this produces life. After her mother died, Emily Dickinson wrote that that her mother had become "part of the drift called 'the infinite.'" This reminder that we are part of something larger than ourselves is one of the only ways in which I am willing to imagine death—somehow, to me, it makes the incomprehensible legible.

In the closing lines of his revolutionary book, Darwin concludes, "There is grandeur in this view of life." He writes, finally, that "from so simple a beginning endless forms most beautiful and most wonderful have been, and are being, evolved."

"Why do you want to be a jellyfish," my daughter asked me, once I'd decided on my costume for the Procession of the Species.

"Because immortal jellyfish can live forever," I said.

My children and I knew this from watching an *Octonauts* episode about the immortal jellyfish, which can shift from medusa back into polyp form when damaged or threatened, and regenerate endlessly. We'd also recently listened to a science podcast for kids, in which my children learned the endlessly repeatable fact that jellyfish "have mouths that are also their butts." On the podcast, a biologist described the challenge of studying immortal jellyfish, "In order to really know if something can go on forever, you kind of have to watch it forever," she said. "And no one's been watching them that long, so we've got a little ways to go before we know if it's really immortal."

It's not that I actually desire immortality, it's just that I don't want this story to end—we've still got a little ways to go before we know if it can go on forever, we have to keep watching.

In the meantime, we can gather seeds, songs and stories, we can gather each other, we can gather momentum, we can gather ourselves into a force for change. And this, too, is part of the life story, the miracle of our becoming-with other species, our mutual, endless unfolding.

So, for now, I would turn my umbrella into a jellyfish costume, attaching ribbon and kitchen twine to its rim so that my tentacles would flow and flutter as I walked, an umbrella, so that I could keep my children close beside me, warm and dry, if it rained.

This was not a race or a march, nor was it a funerary procession or a military parade, no, though it was a procession, perhaps one that flowed out of grief and into collective effervescence, a drift toward the infinite and a celebration of the glory of everything.

We would proceed together, all of us, human, animal and tree, circus clown and acrobat, friends and neighbors, on foot and in strollers and on stilts, so many beautiful, wonderful forms moving together from the public library to the waterfront park where migrating salmon return each fall, down city streets that someday may crack and crumble and turn to dust, we would bike and walk beside one another, holding the hands of our children, and waving at the onlookers, dancing and singing and clapping, until we reached the end, and that's when the party would begin.

Acknowledgments

I owe this book to the generosity of many writers, editors, and friends. Most especially, to Nicole Cunningham, my literary agent—I'm endlessly grateful to you for seeing the possibilities in this project and lending your expertise and enthusiasm to its development. Special thanks to my brilliant editor Kirby Sandmeyer for your belief in this book and for asking exactly the right questions to guide each essay forward, as well as to the entire Harper Perennial team.

To the researchers, journalists, writers and activists I reference and quote in this book—thank you for your beautiful, life-giving work on behalf of the world. Yours are the stories with which I've told my own stories. For Melissa Burt, Katie Darling, Leslie Davenport, Allison C. Davis, Marlena Fontes, Liz Hurtado, Jane Merewether, Annitra Peck, Heather Price, Rena Priest, Rachel Rivera, and Kia Smith, thank you for the insights and expertise you shared in our interviews.

To Kristan Childs and the Good Grief Network participants, thank you for listening with an abundance of care. Your work and your stories give me hope. To Ann Marie Read and the BTC "Baby and Me" class, thank you for all you taught me in matrescence.

I'm deeply grateful to Tajja Isen for her hand in shaping the *Catapult* column that launched this book, as well as to the editors of publications in which several essays first appeared, including *Redivider* and *Orion*. To Priscilla Long, Levi Fuller, and the 2023 Jack

Straw Writers, it was an honor to spend a year reading and writing alongside you. To the students and faculty at Western Washington University, for all the ways you've influenced my teaching, learning, and writing. I'm especially grateful to Ryler Dustin, Lauren Peterson, and Ellen Rogers for the gifts of your friendship and your feedback as early readers. To the Bellingham Public Library, for generous borrowing limits and grace periods.

Thank you to my writing partners, Brenda Miller, Kristiana Kahakauwila, and Courtney Putnam. Without the constancy of your support, especially when I was in the earliest years of motherhood, I might never have found my way to this project. Brenda, thank you for all you've taught me. For Chelsea Bieker, Cassie Mannes Murray, and Sara Petersen, whose early support gave me the confidence to bring this book into the world.

To Joanna Goddard and the Cup of Jo team, I'm grateful for your heart-forward embrace of stories that honor the beauty and complexity of women's lives.

To the Nooksack Salmon Enhancement Association and RE Sources, for all the ways you nurture and protect our local waterways, and, most especially, to the Coast Salish peoples for ongoing stewardship of their ancestral homelands.

To Sarah, for catching my babies and reading my first drafts. To Liz, for the cloth diapers and camaraderie. To Cortney, for all the Friday afternoons and to the mom friends who have taught me as much about friendship as they have about motherhood. To Allison, Addie, Annika, and all the neighbors who make our community a joy. To Shannon and Annika, for the surprises and delights of our group chat and the companionship that keeps me going.

To my parents and sister, thank you for the goodness of your love and for knowing just when to send a care package. To Mimi and Pop, thank you for caring for us as your own. To Auntie Amber, for the irreplaceable role you play in our family. To my in-laws and extended family, for cheering me on. To Eddy, Kade, Jenny, Kobi, Keeley, and the other babysitters and early childhood educators who, through the years, have cared so well for our children.

To my husband, it would have been impossible to write this book without you.

To my children, all these words are for you. I love you to the Mariana Trench and back.

Notes

Epigraph

ix *"It could happen any time:* William Stafford, "Yes," *The Way It Is: New and Selected Poems* (Graywolf Press, 1999), 247.

Preface

xiv *"the practice of creating, nurturing:* Alexis Pauline Gumbs, "Introduction," in *Revolutionary Mothering: Love on the Front Lines*, eds. Alexis Pauline Gumbs, China Martens, and Mai'a Williams, (PM Press, 2016), 9.

xiv *"We find strength and safety:* Robert Furrow and Donna Jo Napoli, *We Are Starlings: Inside the Mesmerizing Magic of a Murmuration* (Random House, 2023), 13-16.

xv *"We will expand:* Ayana Elizabeth Johnson with Oana Stănescu, *What If We Get It Right?: Visions of Climate Futures* (Penguin Random House, 2024), 421–422.

Drawing a Disappearing World

3 *the highly infectious and deadly chytrid fungus*: Erik Stokstad, "This Fungus Has Wiped Out More Species Than Any Other Disease," Science, March 28, 2019.

3 *"Naked skin makes frogs:* Vancouver Aquarium, *Frogs Forever?*, Vancouver, British Columbia, Canada.

4 *"canaries in the coal mine"*: Kevin Zippel, "Our Planet's Canaries in the Coal Mines," Amphibian Ark, YouTube, July 26, 2011, https://www.youtube.com/watch?v=xz0A7mTbz20.

4 *Even fashion houses*: Max Berlinger, "Shop the Apocalypse," *New York Times*, December 15, 2018.

4 *Seattle-area scientists warned*: Kara Kostanich, "Smoky Summers the New Normal Around Pacific Northwest, Scientists Say," KOMO News, August 21, 2018.

4 *Doomsday Report*: David Wallace-Wells, "Why Is the World Ignoring the Latest U.N. Climate Report?" *Intelligencer*, March 14, 2022.

4 *"rapid, far-reaching and unprecedented changes*: United Nations Environment Programme, "Rapid and Unprecedented Action Required to Stay Within 1.5°C Says UN's Intergovernmental Panel on Climate Change," news release, October 8, 2018, https://www.unep.org/news-and-stories/press-release/rapid-and-unprecedented-action-required-stay-within-15oc-says-uns.

5 *"planet has only until 2030*: Brandon Miller and Jay Croft, "Planet Has Only Until 2030 to Stem Catastrophic Climate Change, Experts Warn," CNN, October 8, 2018, https://www.cnn.com/2018/10/07/world/climate-change-new-ipcc-report-wxc/index.html.

6 *"The world had changed*: Italo Calvino, "The Dinosaurs," *The Complete Cosmicomics* (Mariner Books, 2015), 94.

8 *"F is for Frog*: Eric Carle, *The Very Hungry Caterpillar's ABC* (New York: Grosset & Dunlap, 2016).

9 *Herpetologists first reported*: Brian Resnick, "What We Lose When We Lose the World's Frogs," *Vox*, December 16, 2016.

9 *Estimates suggest that since the 1970s*: Chelsea Harvey, "We're Risking a Mass Extinction of Frogs—and They're The 'Canary in the Coal Mine,'" *The Washington Post*, October 5, 2015.

9 *On average, one amphibian species*: Elizabeth Kolbert, *The Sixth Extinction* (Henry Holt, 2014), 15–19.

9 *the extinction rate is one thousand times higher*: Jurriaan M. De Vos, et al., "Estimating the Normal Background Rate of Species Extinction," *Conservation Biology* 29, no. 2 (April 2015): 452–462, https://doi.org/10.1111/cobi.12380.

9 *"It is estimated that one-third*: Kolbert, *The Sixth Extinction*, 17–18.

9 *"destroying the conditions that make human life*: Gerardo Ceballos and Paul R. Ehrlich, "Mutilation of the Tree of Life Via Mass Extinction of Animal Genera," Proceedings of the National Academy of Sciences, 120, no. 39 (September 18, 2023), https://doi.org/10.1073/pnas.2306987120.

10 *"[T]hose of us alive today*: Kolbert, *The Sixth Extinction*, 7–8.

10 *"hopping drugstores"*: Vancouver Aquarium, *Frogs Forever?*

11 *"If we fear that the mess*: Joanna Macy and Chris Johnstone, *Active Hope* (New World Library, 2022), 36.

11 *"catalytic hope"*: Ayana Elizabeth Johnson, *What If We Get It Right?: Visions of Climate Futures* (Penguin Random House, 2024), 399.

11 *"muscular hope"*: Krista Tippett quoted in David Marchese, "Krista Tippett Wants You to See All the Hope That's Being Hidden," *The New York Times Magazine*, July 7, 2022.

11 *"hope in the dark"*: Rebecca Solnit, *Hope in the Dark: Untold Histories, Wild Possibilities* (Haymarket Books, 2016).

11 *"Hope, like love*: Rebecca Solnit, "Difficult Is Not the Same as Impossible," *Not Too Late*, eds. Rebecca Solnit and Thelma Young Lutunatabua (Haymarket Books, 2023), 5.

- 11 *Activist Greta Thunberg argues*: Greta Thunberg, "You're Acting Like Spoiled Children." Transcript of speech delivered at "Civil Society for rEUnaissance," February 21, 2019, https://www.eesc.europa.eu/en/news-media/videos/youre-acting-spoiled-irresponsible-children-speech-greta-thunberg-climate-activist.
- 11 "*To earn hope*: Elizabeth Cripps, *Parenting on Earth: A Philosopher's Guide to Doing Right by Your Kids—and Everyone Else* (The MIT Press, 2023), 5.
- 12 "*I have often noticed*: Lama Rod Owens, *The New Saints: From Broken Hearts to Spiritual Warriors* (Sounds True, 2023), 10.
- 12 "*unveil opportunities for hope*: Paulo Freire, *Pedagogy of Hope: Reliving Pedagogy of the Oppressed* (The Continuum Publishing Company, 2004), 3.
- 12 "*ontological need*": Freire, *Pedagogy of Hope*, 2.
- 13 "*When it becomes a program*: Freire, *Pedagogy of Hope*, 2.
- 13 "*critical hope*": Freire, *Pedagogy of Hope*, 2.
- 13 "*People save what they love.*": Michael Soulé quoted in Deborah Bird Rose, *Wild Dog Dreaming: Love and Extinction* (University of Virginia Press, 2011), 5.
- 13 "*Within Amphibian Ark facilities*: Eben Kirksey, "The Utopia for the Golden Frog of Panama," *Cryopolitics: Frozen Life in a Melting World*, eds. Joanna Radin and Emma Kowal, (The MIT Press, 2017), 307–334.
- 14 "*To care is wet, emotional*: Donna Haraway, "Speculative Fabulations for Technoculture's Generations: Taking Care of Unexpected Country," *Australian Humanities Review*, 50 (May 2011): 95–118.
- 15 "*To ask to whom*: Deborah Bird Rose, *Wild Dog Dreaming: Love and Extinction* (University of Virginia Press, 2011), 13.
- 15 *When I ticked my way through*: Save the Frogs, "How to Help," accessed January 6, 2025, https://savethefrogs.com/help/.

If Birds Can't Survive

- 24 *bird populations have decreased by nearly 30 percent*: Carl Zimmer, "Birds Are Vanishing From North America," *New York Times*, September 19, 2019.
- 24 "*Declines in your common sparrow*: Hillary Young quoted in Zimmer, "Birds Are Vanishing From North America."
- 24 "*the very fabric of North America's ecosystem*: John W. Fitzpatrick and Peter P. Marra, "The Crisis for Birds Is a Crisis for Us All," *New York Times*, September 19, 2019.
- 24 "*What will we do with our fear?*": Eula Biss, *On Immunity: An Inoculation* (Graywolf Press, 2014), 152.
- 25 "*salient contemporary emotion*: Sarah Menkedick, *Ordinary Insanity: Fear and the Silent Crisis of Motherhood in America* (Pantheon Books, 2020), xiii.
- 25 "*care and love and intelligence*": Menkedick, *Ordinary Insanity*, x.
- 25 "*Anxiety is a handy device*: Menkedick, *Ordinary Insanity*, 10.

25 *When I read that a survey found*: Nehal Aggarwal, "Parents Make 1,750 Tough Decisions in Baby's First Year, Survey Says," *The Bump*, July 9, 2020.

26 *it takes 500 years for single-use diapers*: Cansu Tokat, et. al, "The History of Diapers and Their Environmental Impact," *Pediatric Research* 97 (July 2024), 854–857, https://doi.org/10.1038/s41390-024-03347-5.

26 *"Keeping a baby alive*: Lucy Jones, *Matrescence* (Pantheon Books, 2023), 228.

26 *"awaken to ecological concerns*: Allison C. Davis and Aurélie Athan, "Ecopsychological Development and Maternal Ecodistress During Matrescence," *The Journal of Ecopsychology* 15 (September 2023), 281–293, https://doi.org/10.1089/eco.2022.0084.

27 *Though the term matrescence*: Grace Bastidas and Audrey Nguyen, "The Emotional Rollercoaster of Being a New Mom," NPR, August 8, 2021.

27 *"It's a holistic change*: Aurélie Athan quoted in Bastidas and Nguyen, "The Emotional Rollercoaster of Being a New Mom."

27 *"[U]ntil the late twentieth century*: Joanna Macy, "Working through Environmental Despair," *Ecopsychology: Restoring the Earth, Healing the Mind*, eds. Roszak, Gomes, and Kanner (Counterpoint, 1995), 241.

27 *Athan, along with ecopsychologist Allison C. Davis*: Davis and Athan, "Ecopsychological Development and Maternal Ecodistress During Matrescence," 287.

28 *"[M]aternal ecodistress*: Allison C. Davis, "Understanding Maternal Ecodistress: A Pathway to Resilience and Ecological Awareness," dralliedavis.com (blog), https://www.dralliedavis.com/blog/understanding-maternal-ecodistress-a-pathway-to-resilience-and-ecological-awareness.

28 *Athan and Davis identify three primary conflicts*: Davis and Athan, "Ecopsychological Development and Maternal Ecodistress During Matrescence," 287.

28 *"greenwashing of motherhood,"*: Davis and Athan, "Ecopsychological Development and Maternal Ecodistress During Matrescence," 287.

28 *"deeper and warmer"*: Davis and Athan, "Ecopsychological Development and Maternal Ecodistress During Matrescence," 287.

29 *"our house is on fire."*: Greta Thunberg, "Our House Is On Fire," Transcript of speech delivered at World Economic Forum at Davos, Switzerland, January 25, 2019, https://awpc.cattcenter.iastate.edu/2019/12/02/address-at-davos-our-house-is-on-fire-jan-25-2019.

29 *"The future doesn't look promising*: Rylan Neem quoted in Robert Mittendorf, "About 2,500 People March in Downtown Bellingham as Part of Worldwide Climate Strike," *Bellingham Herald*, September 20, 2019.

30 *"Climate justice tells us that*: Tori Tsui, *It's Not Just You: How to Navigate Eco-Anxiety and the Climate Crisis* (Simon & Schuster UK, 2023), 97.

31 *"The principal emotion*: Britt Wray, *Generation Dread: Finding Purpose in an Age of Climate Crisis* (Alfred A. Knopf Canada, 2022), 136.

NOTES 259

32 "*Listening is an act of solidarity*: Ai-jen Poo quoted in Rebecca Ruiz, "The Best Way to Support Every Mother on the Planet, Starting Now," Mashable, May 8, 2016.

32 "*We can teach younger generations*: LaUra Schmidt et. al, *How to Live in a Chaotic Climate* (Publications, 2023), 261.

32 "*inner activism*,": Wray, *Generation Dread*, 110-131.

33 "*If our goal for kids is to be resilient*: Kristan Childs (Good Grief Network facilitator) in discussion with the author, February 10, 2025.

33 "*For kids to thrive*: Park Guthrie quoted in Schmidt, et al., *How to Live in a Chaotic Climate*, 262.

World Without End

38 "*[w]hen the apocalypse comes*: Krista Tippett, host, "Ocean Vuong: A Life Worthy of Our Breath," On Being (podcast), April 30, 2020, accessed, September 2, 2024, https://onbeing.org/programs/ocean-vuong-a-life-worthy-of-our-breath-2022.

38 "*It isn't their fault*: Bill McKibben, "Foreword" in Mary DeMocker, *The Parents' Guide to Climate Revolution* (New World Library, 2018), xvii.

38 *more harmful to children's respiratory health*: Alexander Rabin and Lisa Patel, "Our Children's Lungs Are Uniquely Vulnerable to All This Wildfire Smoke," *New York Times*, July 2, 2023.

39 "*If grandma is sick*: Heather Price (atmospheric chemist) in discussion with the author, February 24, 2025.

40 "*truth without trauma*.": Jo McAndrews, *Truth Without Trauma: Talking with Children About Climate Change* (self-pub, PDF), accessed, February 20, 2025, https://www.jomcandrews.com.

40 "*The urgency, the absolute morals, the passion*: Matthew Avery Sutton, *American Apocalypse: A History of Modern Evangelicalism* (Belknap Press, 2017), 372.

41 "*the biblical mandate for stewardship*: Katherine Hayhoe, *Saving Us: A Climate Scientist's Case for Hope and Healing in a Divided World* (Atria, 2021), 23.

41 "*The spread of Green Theology*: Heather McTeer Toney, *Before the Streetlights Come On: Black America's Urgent Call for Climate Solutions* (Broadleaf Books, 2023), 155.

41 *Nonetheless, research indicates that even for highly religious people*: Becka A. Alper, "How Religion Intersects With Americans' Views on the Environment," Pew Research Center, November 17, 2022, https://www.pewresearch.org/religion/2022/11/17/how-religion-intersects-with-americans-views-on-the-environment.

41 "*[w]ithin each of the major Christian traditions*,: Alper, "How Religion Intersects With Americans' Views on the Environment."

42 "*[T]he dangerous hope*: Catherine Keller, *Facing Apocalypse: Climate, Democracy, and Other Last Chances* (Orbis Books, 2021), ix.

43 *A 2023 survey of 16,000 people*: R. Eric Lewandowski, et al., "Climate Emotions,

Thoughts, and Plans Among US Adolescents and Young Adults: A Cross-Sectional Descriptive Survey and Analysis by Political Party Identification and Self-Reported Exposure to Severe Weather Events," *The Lancet Planetary Health*, 8, (November 2024), e879–93.

43 *Nearly 60 percent indicated that climate change*: Lewandowski, et al., "Climate Emotions, Thoughts, and Plans Among US Adolescents and Young Adults."

43 *And an international poll conducted in 2021*: Caroline Hickman, et al., "Climate Anxiety in Children and Young People and Their Beliefs About Government Responses to Climate Change: A Global Survey," *The Lancet Planetary Health* 5, no. 12 (December 2021): e863-e873.

43 *"child rights crisis."*: UNICEF, "The Climate-Changed Child: A Children's Climate Risk Index Supplement," November 2023, https://www.unicef.org/reports/climate-changed-child#download-the-report.

43 *In recent years, for example, there have been an average*: UNICEF, "The Climate-Changed Child."

44 *in 2024, at least 242 million students*: UNICEF, "Nearly a Quarter of a Billion Children's Schooling was Disrupted by Climate Crises in 2024," January 24, 2025, https://www.unicef.org/eca/press-releases/nearly-quarter-billion-childrens-schooling-was-disrupted-climate-crises-2024-unicef.

44 *nearly every child on earth*: UNICEF, "The Climate Crisis Is a Child Rights Crisis," August 2021, https://www.unicef.org/media/105376/file/UNICEF-climate-crisis-child-rights-crisis.pdf.

44 *One billion, or nearly half*: UNICEF, "The Climate Crisis Is a Child Rights Crisis."

44 *global inequality means that the 10 countries*: UNICEF, "The Climate Crisis Is a Child Rights Crisis."

44 *Children have not caused the climate crisis*: UNICEF, "The Climate-Changed Child."

44 *Yet, for the most part, according to UNICEF, climate discourse ignores*: UNICEF, "The Climate-Changed Child."

44 *"Children and young people themselves have consistently made urgent calls*: Catherine Russell in UNICEF, "The Climate-Changed Child."

45 *Scientists estimate that children born in 2020*: Wim Thiery, et al., "Intergenerational Inequities in Exposure to Climate Extremes," *Science* 374 (September 2021): 158–60.

45 *"I try to have it be very child-led:* Leslie Davenport (therapist), in discussion with the author, February 27, 2025.

46 *"every student has the right*: Washington Office of Superintendent of Public Instruction, "Climate Education," https://ospi.k12.wa.us/student-success/resources-subject-area/science/climate-education, accessed March 5, 2025.

49 *"an epitome, a miniature*: Phillip Mauro quoted in Matthew Avery Sutton, *American Apocalypse: A History of Modern Evangelicalism* (Belknap Press, 2017), 372.

NOTES 261

50 "*Arkism is bailing out the self*: Sally Weintrobe, *Psychological Roots of the Climate Crisis* (Bloomsbury Academic, 2021), 252.

50 "*None of them said*: Rebecca Solnit, *Hope in the Dark: Untold Histories, Wild Possibilities* (Haymarket Books, 2016), xxiii.

51 "*[W]e are confronting truth*: Lama Rod Owens, *The New Saints: From Broken Hearts to Spiritual Warriors* (Sounds True, 2023), 8.

51 "*[t]he apocalypse has been happening for a long time*": Owens, *The New Saints*, 9.

51 "*Worlds, in that sense*: Keller, *Facing Apocalypse*, xvi.

52 "*save the planet.*": Marc Brown, *Arthur Turns Green* (Little, Brown, 2014).

52 "*make the planet a better place to live,*": Brown, *Arthur Turns Green*.

52 "*Less than a mile?*: Jane O'Connor, *Fancy Nancy: Every Day Is Earth Day* (HarperCollins, 2010).

52 "*at a certain point*: Bill McKibben in Mary DeMocker, *The Parents' Guide to Climate Revolution* (New World Library, 2018), xvii.

52 "*What will solve it*: Bill McKibben in DeMocker, *The Parents' Guide to Climate Revolution*, xvii.

53 "*The vast, complex planetary crisis*: Naomi Klein, *Doppelganger: A Trip into the Mirror World* (Farrar, Straus and Giroux, 2023), 66.

Watching the Clock

57 "*Earth has a deadline,*": Colin Moynihan, "A New York Clock That Told Time Now Tells the Time Remaining," *New York Times*, September 20, 2020.

58 "*polytemporal worldview,*": Marcia Bjornerud, *Timefulness: How Thinking Like A Geologist Can Help Save the World* (Princeton University Press, 2020), 179.

58 *While it's true that geologic changes*: Bjornerud, *Timefulness*, 16–17.

58 *Take, for example, the mindbogglingly fast*: Bjornerud, *Timefulness*, 90.

61 *The Doomsday Clock was the work of Martyl Langsdorf*: William Yardley, "Martyl Langsdorf, Doomsday Clock Designer, Dies at 96," *The New York Times*, April 10, 2013.

61 "*[T]he Clock remains the closest*": Bulletin of the Atomic Scientists, "At Doom's Doorstep: It Is 100 Seconds to Midnight," news release, January 20, 2022, https://thebulletin.org/2022/01/press-release-at-dooms-doorstep-it-is-100-seconds-to-midnight.

61 "*Which is the greater threat*: Bulletin of the Atomic Scientists, "Doomsday Clock: FAQ," https://thebulletin.org/doomsday-clock/faq, accessed September 2, 2024.

62 "*recurring feeling of déjà vu*: Britt Wray, *Generation Dread: Finding Purpose in an Age of Climate Crisis* (Toronto: Alfred A. Knopf Canada, 2022), 2.

63 "*The work of caregiving*: Julie Phillips, *The Baby on the Fire Escape: Creativity, Motherhood, and The Mind-Baby Problem* (W.W. Norton & Company, 2022), 271.

64 "*Making my pond swimmable*: Robin Wall Kimmerer, *Braiding Sweetgrass* (Milkweed Editions, 2013), 86.

64 "*Time is not a river,*": Kimmerer, *Braiding Sweetgrass*, 206–207.

66 "*[I]f the 4.5 billion-year story*: Bjornerud, *Timefulness*, 16.

66 "*[W]hat happens after midnight?*": Bjornerud, *Timefulness*, 17.

66 "*It takes my breath away*: Mary Anne Hitt, "A Love Letter from the Clean Energy Future," *Not Too Late*, eds. Rebecca Solnit and Thelma Young Lutunatabua (Haymarket Books, 2023), 170–176.

Little Things

69 *A beetle native to Europe*: Carnegie Museum of Natural History, "The Devil's Coach Horse Beetle," YouTube, October 28, 2022, https://www.youtube.com/watch?v=X2s0Od8m9kA.

70 "*Vertebrates look big*: Jess French, *The Book of Brilliant Bugs* (DK, 2020), 7.

71 *About two-thirds of all known animal species*: Julia Janicki, et al., "The Collapse of Insects," *Reuters*, December 6, 2022.

71 *four million insect species yet to be documented*: Maggie Koerth, "The Bugs of the World Could Squish Us All," *Five Thirty-Eight*, May 2, 2017.

71 *40 percent of insect species*: Francisco Sánchez-Bayo and Kris A.G. Wyckhuys, "Worldwide Decline of the Entomofauna: A Review of Its Drivers," *Biological Conservation*, Volume 232, 2019, 8–27, https://doi.org/10.1016/j.biocon.2019.01.020.

71 "*I doubt that the human species*: Edward O. Wilson, "The Little Things That Run the World (The Importance and Conservation of Invertebrates)," *Conservation Biology* 1, no. 4, (December 1987): 344–346, http://www.jstor.org/stable/2386020.

71 *Thirty years later, a landmark study sparked headlines*: Brooke Jarvis, "The Insect Apocalypse Is Here," *The New York Times Magazine*, November 27, 2018.

71 "*Humans seem innately better*: Kevin Gaston quoted in Jarvis, "The Insect Apocalypse Is Here."

72 "*Once upon a time*: Robert MacFarlane and Jackie Morris, *The Lost Words: A Spell Book* (House of Anansi Press, 2018), 1.

72 "*We do not care*: Robert MacFarlane quoted in Alison Flood, "Oxford Junior Dictionary's Replacement of 'Natural' Words With 21st-Century Terms Sparks Outcry," *The Guardian*, January 13, 2015.

72 *Though the changes to the dictionary were first made in 2007*: Stefan Fatsis, "Panic at the Dictionary," *The New Yorker*, January 30, 2015.

73 *The resulting open letter*: Andrew Walsh, "Authors' Letter to the Oxford University Press," Caught by the River (blog). January 15, 2015, https://www.caughtbytheriver.net/2015/01/letter-oxford-university-press-atwood-macfarlane.

73 "*You hold in your hands*: MacFarlane and Morris, *The Lost Words*, 1.

74 *In 2022, a late season cold snap*: Cheryl Schweizer, "'Mother Nature Was Not Kind':

Bad Weather Reduces 2022 Washington Apple Harvest," *Basin Business Journal*, January 8, 2023.

75 *as much as one third of U.S. diets*: U.S. Food & Drug Administration, "Helping Agriculture's Helpful Honey Bees," July 30, 2018.

75 *about a million colonies*: Hannah Nordhaus, *The Beekeeper's Lament* (Harper Perennial, 2011), 5–10.

76 *plummeted by 87 percent*: Jarvis, "The Insect Apocalypse Is Here."

76 *a pair of rusty-patched bumblebees*: Benji Jones, "The Surprising Value of a Small Patch of Grass," Vox, November 3, 2022.

77 *In the end, the airport bulldozed much of it*: Illinois Environmental Council, "Priceless Bell Bowl Prairie Demolished in Rockford, IL," news release, March 9, 2023, https://ilenviro.org/priceless-bell-bowl-prairie-demolished-in-rockford-il.

77 *"Sprawl, monocrops,*: Nordhaus, *The Beekeeper's Lament*, 248–249.

77 *"Make meadows, not lawns."*: Nordhaus, *The Beekeeper's Lament*, 248–249.

77 *"What if half of every lawn*: Douglas W. Tallamy and Sarah L. Thomson, *Nature's Best Hope: How You Can Save the World in Your Own Yard* (Timber Press, 2023), 72.

77 *"The crisis is everywhere, massive*: adrienne maree brown, *Emergent Strategy* (AK Press, 2017), 3.

78 *"Where, after all, do universal human rights begin?"*: Eleanor Roosevelt quoted in Eloise Rickman, *It's Not Fair: Why It's Time for a Grown-up Conversation About How Adults Treat Children* (Scribe, 2024).

78 *adultism is "the structural discrimination"*: Rickman, *It's Not Fair*, 37–58.

78 *"The roots of much of the violence*: Rickman, *It's Not Fair*, 6.

79 *"Adultism is the first injustice*: Rickman, *It's Not Fair*, 6.

79 *"Gentle parenting can be really hard*: Annie Pezalla, "Gentle Parenting Can Be Really Hard on New Parents, Research Suggests," *The Conversation*, November 29, 2023.

80 *"The broadest agreement among experts*: Jessica Grose, "I'll Say It Again: There's More Than One Way to Raise Kids Who Thrive," *The New York Times*, March 9, 2022.

80 *"In England, that land of gardeners*: Alison Gopnik, *The Gardener and The Carpenter* (Farrar, Straus and Giroux, 2016), 19.

81 *"man's war against nature."*: Rachel Carson, *Silent Spring* (Mariner Books, 2002), 7.

81 *"Some evil spell had settled*: Carson, *Silent Spring*, 2.

81 *"No witchcraft, no enemy action*: Carson, *Silent Spring*, 3.

82 *"crude weapon"*: Carson, *Silent Spring*, 297.

82 *"Silent Spring proved that*: Linda Lear in Carson, *Silent Spring*, xvi-xvii.

82 *"Help Your Child to Wonder."*: Rachel Carson, "Help Your Child to Wonder," *Women's Home Companion*, July 1956, 25–48, https://rachelcarsoncouncil.org/wp-content/uploads/2019/08/whc_rc_sow_web.pdf, accessed March 1, 2025.

83 *One study on language acquisition and biophilia*: Jean Burko Gleason, "Parent-Child Interaction and Lexical Acquisition in Two Domains: Color Words and Animal Names," *Psychology of Language and Communication* 18 (2014), 204–210.

83 *"The point is that we have an enormous connection*: Krista Tippett, "Jean Burko Gleason: Unfolding Language, Unfolding Life," On Being (podcast), November 3, 2011. accessed, September 5, 2024. https://onbeing.org/programs/jean-berko-gleason-unfolding-language-unfolding-life.

84 *"It seems reasonable*: Rachel Carson, *Lost Woods: The Discovered Writing of Rachel Carson*, ed. Linda Lear (Beacon Press, 1999), 94.

84 *"The insect world*: C. J. Briejèr quoted in Carson, *Silent Spring*, 245.

84 *"Where's papa going*: E. B. White, *Charlotte's Web* (HarperCollins, 2012), 1.

84 *"It's because that's how we treat kids"*: Krista Tippett, "Kate DiCamillo: On Nurturing Capacious Hearts," On Being (podcast), March 17, 2022, https://onbeing.org/programs/kate-dicamillo-on-nurturing-capacious-hearts, accessed, September 2, 2024.

85 *"always be on the watch*: E. B. White, *Charlotte's Web* (HarperCollins, 2012), 85.

85 *the "sacred task of telling stories*: Krista Tippett, "Kate DiCamillo: On Nurturing Capacious Hearts."

86 *"How do we tell the truth*: Krista Tippett, "Kate DiCamillo: On Nurturing Capacious Hearts."

On Mother Trees

88 *"Once there was a tree*: Shel Silverstein, *The Giving Tree* (HarperCollins, 2014).

88 *"And the tree was happy."*: Silverstein, *The Giving Tree* (HarperCollins, 2014).

90 *Firmageddon*: Nathan Gilles, "Climate Change Is Hastening the Demise of Pacific Northwest Forests," Associated Press, November 16, 2023.

90 *"resisting in place,"*: Jenny Odell, *How to Do Nothing* (Melville House, 2019), xvi.

91 *"capitalist perception of time*: Jenny Odell, *How to Do Nothing* (Melville House, 2019), xii.

91 *"restore individuals who can then help*: Jenny Odell, *How to Do Nothing* (Melville House, 2019), xxii.

94 *"A simple refusal*: Jenny Odell, *How to Do Nothing* (Melville House, 2019), xvi.

95 *"I propose that rerouting*: Jenny Odell, *How to Do Nothing* (Melville House, 2019), xii.

96 *Simard calls the oldest trees in a forest "mother trees,"*: Suzanne Simard, *Finding the Mother Tree* (New York, Alfred A. Knopf, 2021).

96 *Mothers barely holding it together*: Jessica Grose, "This Is a Primal Scream," *New York Times*, February 4, 2021.

97 *"When we manage ecosystems*: Krista Tippett, host, "Suzanne Simard: How Forests

Are Wired for Wisdom," On Being (podcast), September 9, 2021, https://onbeing.org/programs/suzanne-simard-forests-are-wired-for-wisdom/, accessed December 15, 2024.

97 *"Other countries have social safety nets.*: Jessica Calarco, interviewed by Anne Helen Petersen, "Other Countries Have Social Safety Nets. The U.S. Has Women," *Culture Study*, November 11, 2020.

97 *"live with dignity*: Jessica Calarco, *Holding It Together: How Women Became America's Safety Net* (Portfolio/Penguin, 2024), 189–202.

98 *"care for the people who care"*: Jessica Calarco, *Holding It Together: How Women Became America's Safety Net* (Portfolio/Penguin, 2024), 189–202.

98 *"This is the world we ought to be imagining,"*: Jessica Calarco, *Holding It Together: How Women Became America's Safety Net* (Portfolio/Penguin, 2024), 189–202.

99 *"We are living in a contradiction*: Mia Birdsong, *How We Show Up* (Hachette Go, 2020), 226.

101 *But at the dripline*: Suzanne Simard, *Finding the Mother Tree* (Alfred A. Knopf, 2021), 226–227.

102 *"The currency of this economy*: Robin Wall Kimmerer, *The Serviceberry* (Simon & Schuster, 2024), 18–19.

Predictive Text

105 *"everything west of Interstate 5*: Kathryn Schulz, "The Really Big One," *The New Yorker*, July 13, 2015.

107 *"It could be ten minutes from now*: Sandi Doughton, *Full-Rip 9.0: The Next Big Earthquake in the Pacific Northwest* (Sasquatch Books, 2013), 237.

108 *"operate on a time scale*: Sandi Doughton, *Full-Rip 9.0*, 237.

108 *Taking into account 10,000 years*: Eric Scigliano, "It's Only a Matter of Time Before a Tsunami Hits the Northwest. Why Is It Missing from FEMA's Risk Analysis?" Politico.com, December 14, 2023.

108 *Scientists put the risk of a big quake*: Kathryn Schulz, "The Really Big One."

108 *The chances of a full rip*: David Guterson, "A Deadly Earthquake Absolutely, Positively Will Ravage Seattle at Some Point. Here's How to Survive It," *Seattle Times*, April 1, 2022.

108 *"The Cascadia situation*: Kathryn Schulz, "The Really Big One."

109 *"[W]e humans are bad at*: Amanda Cox and Josh Katz, "The Upshot: Presidential Forecast Post-mortem," *New York Times*, November 15, 2016.

109 *"All models are wrong*: George Box quoted in Amanda Cox and Josh Katz, "The Upshot: Presidential Forecast Post-mortem."

109 *In an update for COP29:* "As the Climate Crisis Worsens, the Warming Outlook Stagnates," Climate Action Tracker, https://climateactiontracker.org/publications/the-climate-crisis-worsens-the-warming-outlook-stagnates, accessed March 2, 2025.

110 *A hindcasting study*: "Study Confirms Climate Models are Getting Future Warming Projections Right," NASA, January 9, 2020, https://science.nasa.gov/earth/climate-change/study-confirms-climate-models-are-getting-future-warming-projections-right/, accessed December 15, 2024.

110 *We know that the Earth is the hottest*: Ayana Elizabeth Johnson, *What If We Get It Right?: Visions of Climate Futures* (Penguin Random House, 2024), 11–15.

110 *forces like climate change hyperobjects*: Laura Hudson, "At the End of the World, It's Hyperobjects All the Way Down," *Wired*, November 16, 2021.

110 *one-fifth of the planet's land area*: Sean Fleming, "3 Billion People Could Live in Places as Hot as the Sahara by 2070 Unless We Tackle Climate Change," World Economic Forum, May 13, 2020.

110 *one million species are driven to extinction*: Jeff Tollefson, "Humans Are Driving One Million Species to Extinction," *Nature*, May 6, 2019.

110 *hundreds of millions of climate migrants*: David Wallace-Wells, "The New World: Envisioning Life After Climate Change," *New York Times*, October 26, 2022.

111 *"Although climate change is far from*: Jade S. Sasser, *Climate Anxiety and the Kid Question: Deciding Whether to Have Children in an Uncertain Future* (University of California Press, 2024), xii-xii.

111 *A 2021 survey of 10,000 people aged 16–25 in ten nations*: Caroline Hickman, et al., "Climate Anxiety in Children and Young People and Their Beliefs about Government Responses to Climate Change: A Global Survey," *The Lancet Planetary Health* 5, (December 2021), e863–e873.

111 *In the United States, a 2024 survey by the Pew Research Center*: Rachel Minkin, et. al., "The Experiences of U.S. Adults Who Don't Have Children," Pew Research Center, July 25, 2024, https://www.pewresearch.org/social-trends/2024/07/25/the-experiences-of-u-s-adults-who-dont-have-children/, accessed December 15, 2024.

112 *research that suggests raising a child*: Paul Murtaugh, et al., "Reproduction and the Carbon Legacies of Individuals," *Global Environmental Change* 19, February 2009, 14–20, https://doi.org/10.1016/j.gloenvcha.2008.10.007.

112 *For one, the study doesn't account for changes*: Sigal Samuel, "Having Fewer Kids Will Not Save the Climate," Vox, February 13, 2020.

112 *assumes that future generations*: Martin Sticker, et al., "Why Parents Shouldn't Be Saddled With Environmental Guilt for Having Children," *The Conversation*, September 22, 2022.

112 *But in the United States, for example, per-capita emissions*: Martin Sticker, et al., "Why Parents Shouldn't Be Saddled With Environmental Guilt for Having Children."

112 *"is a more hopeful outcome*: David Wallace-Wells, "The New World."

112 *Some scientists also take issue with the concept of a carbon legacy*: Shannon Osaka, "Should You Not Have Kids Because of Climate Change? It's Complicated," *Washington Post*, December 2, 2022.

NOTES 267

113 *An alternative model*: Sigal Samuel, "Having Fewer Kids Will Not Save the Climate."

113 *Global child mortality rates*: Hannah Ritchie, *Not the End of the World: How We Can Be the First Generation to Build a Sustainable Planet* (Little Brown, Spark, 2024), 21.

113 *There have also been substantial improvements*: Hannah Ritchie, *Not the End of the World*, 1–36.

114 *"an active way of fighting back*: Jade S. Sasser, *Climate Anxiety and the Kid Question*, 26.

114 *"This kind of reproductive resilience*: Jade S. Sasser, *Climate Anxiety and the Kid Question* 36.

114 *"Reproductive justice comprehensively supports*: Jade S. Sasser, *Climate Anxiety and the Kid Question*, 10.

115 *"The choice young people face*: Elizabeth Cripps, *Parenting on Earth: A Philosopher's Guide to Doing Right By Your Kids—And Everyone Else* (The MIT Press, 2023), 89.

115 *"when people feel like they cannot have children*: Roxane Gay, "When the World Is on Fire, What Does Reproductive Choice Really Mean?" Atmos, May 21, 2025.

115 *In the mid-2050s*: David Wallace-Wells, "The New World."

116 *"The kids coming now*: Britt Wray, *Generation Dread: Finding Purpose in an Age of Climate Crisis* (Alfred A. Knopf Canada, 2022), 236.

116 *"On many days*: Rivka Galchen, *Little Labors* (New Directions, 2016), 18.

117 *"'I want you to be'*: Hannah Arendt quoted in Jennifer Banks, *Natality: Toward a Philosophy of Birth* (W.W. Norton & Co., 2023), 28.

118 *"'Will there be any warning'*: "How bad is the Cascadia earthquake gonna be?" Reddit (post). October 2024, https://www.reddit.com/r/geology/comments/1g5iujy/how_bad_is_the_cascadia_earthquake_gonna_be.

118 *"puts into narrative form*: Min Hyoung Song, *Climate Lyricism* (Duke University Press, 2022), 102.

118 *"The human mind has a tendency to wander*: Sandi Doughton, *Full-Rip 9.0*, 237.

119 *"We remain ourselves for the most part*: Rebecca Solnit, *A Paradise Built in Hell: The Extraordinary Communities That Arise in Disaster* (Penguin Books, 2009), 70.

120 *"In a disaster, your most immediate*: Washington State Emergency Management Division, "Neighbors Helping Neighbors," https://mil.wa.gov/neighborhoods, accessed March 1, 2025.

121 *As a first step, disaster justice expert*: Ayana Elizabeth Johnson, "Disasterology: Interview with Samantha Montano," *What If We Get It Right?: Visions of Climate Futures* (Penguin Random House, 2024), 347–362.

121 *"being effective and equitable in how we do preparedness*: Samantha Montano quoted in Ayana Elizabeth Johnson, "Disasterology," 351.

121 *disaster is a lot like revolution*: Rebecca Solnit, *Hope in the Dark: Untold Histories, Wild Possibilities* (Haymarket Books, 2016), xviii.

121 *social, cultural, or political change*: Rebecca Solnit, *Hope in the Dark: Untold Histories, Wild Possibilities* (Haymarket Books, 2016), xxii-xxiii.

121 *"care can become the revolutionary value*: Elena Pulcini, "Global Vulnerability: Why Take Care of Future Generations," *Care Ethics in the Age of Precarity*, eds. Maurice Hamington and Michael Flower, (University of Minnesota Press, 2021), 120–143.

123 *"For those of us who aren't lucky*: Cheryl Strayed, "The Ghost Ship That Didn't Carry Us," *The Rumpus*, April 21, 2011, https://therumpus.net/2011/04/21/dear-sugar-the-rumpus-advice-column-71-the-ghost-ship-that-didnt-carry-us, accessed March 7, 2025.

123 *"I'll never know and neither will you*: Cheryl Strayed, "The Ghost Ship That Didn't Carry Us."

What to Expect

125 *On the way to our hike, we'd sung along*: Raffi and Yo-Yo Ma, "Baby Beluga (40th Anniversary Version)," Craft Recordings, 2020.

126 *a Southern Resident orca named Tahlequah*: Lori Cuthbert, et al., "Orca Mother Drops Calf, After Unprecedented 17 Days of Mourning," *National Geographic*, August 13, 2018.

126 *"Before planning an outing*: Bayard H. McConnaughey and Evelyn McConnaughey, *Pacific Coast* (A. A. Knopf: 1998), 8.

127 *"If the world's environment*: Sandra Steingraber, *Having Faith* (Perseus Publishing, 2001), x.

128 *"I drink water*: Sandra Steingraber, *Having Faith* (Perseus Publishing, 2001), 66–68.

129 *"When we figure our addresses*: Scott Russell Sanders, *Staying Put: Making a Home in a Restless World* (Beacon Press, 1993), 62.

129 *"both to geographical terrain*: Peter Berg and Raymond Dasmann quoted in Tristan Bove, "Bioregionalism: A Model for a Self-Sufficient and Democratic Economy," *Earth*, March 16, 2021, https://earth.org/bioregionalism.

130 *It described a place-based writing assignment*: Paul Lynch, "Composition's New Thing: Bruno Latour and the Apocalyptic Turn," *College English* 74, no. 5 (May 2012), 458–476.

130 *"Only by understanding where I live*: Sanders, *Staying Put*, xiv.

131 *"The lack of salmon*: Rena Priest (poet) in discussion with the author, October 29, 2025.

131 *"increase everyone's sense of place*: Annitra Peck (executive director of Nooksack Salmon Enhancement Association) in discussion with the author, March 24, 2025.

132 *Our watershed bears the scars*: Derek Moscato, "The Lessons of Bellingham's Olympic Pipeline Explosion," *The Seattle Times*, June 4, 2019.

132 *"I no longer have children to protect*: Marlene Robinson quoted in Pipeline Safety

Trust, "The Tragedy As Described by the Parents," https://pstrust.org/olympic-pipe line-disaster/the-tragedy-as-described-by-the-parents.

133 *There is increasing evidence for the threat that fossil fuels:* Alexandra Herr, "The Climate Reality of *Roe v. Wade*," *Atmos*, May 9, 2022.

133 *But in the pregnancy book's revised fifth edition:* Heidi Eisenberg Murkoff and Sharon Mazel, *What to Expect When You're Expecting* (Workman Publishing, 2016), Nook edition, 364.

133 *another in the section on extreme heat:* Murkoff and Mazel, *What to Expect When You're Expecting*, 77–78.

134 *I learned that air pollutants:* Emilia Basilio, et al., "Wildfire Smoke Exposure during Pregnancy: A Review of Potential Mechanisms of Placental Toxicity, Impact on Obstetric Outcomes, and Strategies to Reduce Exposure," *International Journal of Environmental Research and Public Health* 19, October 2022, doi:10.3390/ijerph192113727.

134 *Studies also suggest that exposure to extreme heat:* Ramirez, Jazmin D et al. "Evaluating the Impact of Heat Stress on Placental Function: A Systematic Review," *International Journal of Environmental Research and Public Health* 21, August 2024, doi:10.3390/ijerph21081111.

134 *"chronicle of intrauterine life.":* Denise Grady, "The Mysterious Tree of a Newborn's Life," The New York Times, July 14, 2014, https://www.nytimes.com/2014/07/15/health/the-push-to-understand-the-placenta.html.

135 *It was 1988:* Nathaniel Rich, *Losing Earth: A Recent History* (Farrar, Straus and Giroux, 2019), 125–127.

135 *"the greenhouse effect has been detected:* James Hansen quoted in Rich, *Losing Earth*, 130.

135 *"Global Warming Has Begun.":* Rich, *Losing Earth*, 132.

135 *The next year, the United States:* Nathaniel Rich, "Losing Earth: The Decade We Almost Stopped Climate Change," *The New York Times Magazine*, August 1, 2018.

135 *"Somehow they must manage.":* McConnaughey and McConnaughey, *Pacific Coast*, 19.

136 *Follow the coastline north:* Ashley Strickland, "Ice Age Throwback: 13,000-year-old Footprints Found Off Canadian Coast," CNN, March 28, 2018.

137 *A temporary organ:* Apoorva Mandavilli, "The Placenta, an Afterthought No Longer," *New York Times*, December 3, 2018.

137 *But some environmental contaminants:* Moms Clean Air Force, "Pregnancy, the Placenta, and Pollution," February 2024, https://www.momscleanairforce.org/resources/pregnancy-the-placenta-and-pollution/, accessed May 1, 2025.

138 *more than one trillion pieces of plastic:* Amina Khan, "The Great Pacific Garbage Patch Counts 1.8 Trillion Pieces of Trash, Mostly Plastic," *Los Angeles Times*, March 22, 2018.

138 *I know that there are likely microplastics*: Stephanie Dutchen, "Microplastics Everywhere," *Harvard Medicine*, Spring 2023.

139 *"An albatross chick*: Susan Middleton and David Littschwager, "Contents of Laysan Albatross Stomach and Laysan Albatross Necropsy (moli Phoebastria Immutabilis)," 2004, archival pigment print, 30 x 60 inches, Marine Live Center, Bellingham, Washington.

139 *As it turns out, before our planet was formed*: Nicholas St. Fleur, "The Water in Your Glass Might Be Older Than the Sun," *New York Times*, April 15, 2016.

The Looking Glass

142 *Thus, sanitized of questionable humor*: Maria Tatar, *The Classic Fairy Tales*, (W.W. Norton & Co., 1999), ix–xviii.

142 *"Where else could I have gotten the idea*: Margaret Atwood quoted in Tatar, *The Classic Fairy Tales*, ix-xviii.

143 *"ghosts and monsters unsettle **anthropos***: Anna Tsing, et al., "Introduction: Bodies Tumbled Into Bodies," *Arts of Living on a Damaged Planet* (University of Minnesota Press, 2017), M2-M3.

145 *"a cultural agenda tied to*: Anna Lowenhaupt Tsing, *The Mushroom at the End of the World* (Princeton University Press, 2015), 156–157.

145 *"[W]e imagine well-being without them.*: Tsing, *The Mushroom at the End of the World*, 156–157.

145 *"normalized magic"*: Kate Bernheimer, "Fairy Tale Is Form, Form Is Fairy Tale," *The Writer's Notebook: Craft Essays from Tin House* (Tin House Books, 2009), 69.

146 *"primitive."*: Jean Piaget quoted in Jane Merewether, "Enchanted Animism: A Matter of Care," *Contemporary Issues in Early Childhood* 24, 2023, 21.

146 *"create conditions for curiosity*: Merewether, "Enchanted Animism."

147 *"privileges the well-being of the human*: Min Hyoung Song, *Climate Lyricism* (Duke University Press, 2022), 3.

147 *"speculative and playful animism*: Merewether, "Enchanted Animism."

147 *"Rocks, trees, wind, insects,"*: Jane Merewether (researcher) in discussion with the author, April 10, 2025.

148 *"The tupelo trees are greeting you*: Elizabeth Rush, *The Quickening: Creation and Community at the Ends of the Earth* (Milkweed, 2023), 357.

148 *When we objectify nature*: Robin Wall Kimmerer, interviewed by Helen Whybrow, "Robin Wall Kimmerer on the Language of Animacy," *Orion*, March/April 2017, July 17, 2017.

148 *"To become native to this place*: Robin Wall Kimmerer, *Braiding Sweetgrass* (Milkweed Editions, 2013), 58.

149 *some researchers are calling for managed retreat*: Kristen Walters, "New Study Identifies the Cost of Restoring the Sumas Xhotsa (Lake) as a Tool for Reconciliation, Climate

Adaptation, and Ecosystem Restoration," Raincoast Conservation Foundation, July 18, 2024.

150 *"Some people find it*: Chief Dalton Silver quoted in Steph Kwetásel'wet Wood, "After Disaster Strikes, How Much Is It Worth It to Rebuild?" *The Narwhal*, June 4, 2024.

150 *"'Floods' is the word they use"*: Toni Morrison, "The Site of Memory," in *Inventing the Truth: The Art and Craft of Memoir*, second edition, ed. William Zinsser (Houghton Mifflin, 1995), 83–102.

151 *"In Bangladesh, the river*: Mohammad Abdul Matin quoted in Ashley Westerman, "Should Rivers Have Same Legal Rights As Humans? A Growing Number Of Voices Say Yes," NPR, August 3, 2019.

151 *the "rights of nature" movement is growing*: Sigal Samuel, "Lake Erie Now Has Legal Rights, Just Like You," Vox, February 26, 2019.

151 *"[I]t gives the right to the river*: Amy Cordalis, interviewed by Lulu Garcia-Navarro, "Tribe Gives Personhood to Klamath River," NPR, September 29, 2019.

151 *"Women have been monsters*: Jess Zimmerman, *Women and Other Monsters*, (Beacon Press, 2021), 8–9.

153 *"[T]he stories we're given*: Zimmerman, *Women and Other Monsters*, 197–198.

Little Apocalypses

156 *"holding so tightly to your beliefs*: Rachel Held Evans, *Faith Unraveled: How a Girl Who Knew All the Answers Learned to Ask the Questions* (Zondervan, 2010), 17–18.

157 *"Plants and animals don't fight the winter*: Katherine May, *Wintering: The Power of Rest and Retreat in Difficult Times* (Riverhead Books, 2020), 14.

158 *"Mothers require protection*: Jacqueline Rose, *Mothers: An Essay on Love and Cruelty* (Farrar, Straus and Giroux, 2018), 25.

160 *It's a call for justice so radical*: D. L. Mayfield, "Mary's 'Magnificat' in the Bible Is Revolutionary. Some Evangelicals Silence Her," *Washington Post*, December 20, 2018.

160 *"God is a feast*: M Jade Kaiser, "Magnifcat," enfleshed.com. https://enfleshed.com/project/magnificat.

162 *"To give birth*: Kate Weiner, *Waking the Ground* (Loam, 2021), 2.

162 *"Childbirth is beautiful*: Angela Garbes, *Like a Mother: A Feminist Journey Through the Science and Culture of Pregnancy* (HarperCollins, 2018), 101.

162 *"We put our bodies on the line*: Weiner, *Waking the Ground*, 2

163 *"At the end of the Christian Bible*: Brian McLaren, *Life After Doom: Wisdom and Courage for a World Falling Apart* (St. Martin's, 2024), 123.

164 *"Before it became a synonym*: Dorian Lynskey, *Everything Must Go: The Stories We Tell About the End of the World* (Pantheon, 2025), 20.

164 *"If apocalypticism cannot be erased*: Catherine Keller, *Facing Apocalypse: Climate, Democracy, and Other Last Chances* (Orbis Books, 2021), xii.

165 "*keep us from acting it out*: Keller, *Facing Apocalypse*, xii.

165 "*It means to confront*: Keller, *Facing Apocalypse*, xiii.

165 "*To meet the apocalypse*: Lama Rod Owens, *The New Saints: From Broken Hearts to Spiritual Warriors* (Sounds True, 2023), 10.

165 "*It may be impossible*: Jia Tolentino, "What to Do With Climate Emotions," *The New Yorker*, July 10, 2023.

167 "*There is a wonderful and terrible*: Kate Bowler, *No Cure for Being Human (And Other Truths I Need to Hear)* (Random House, 2021), 126.

168 "*limited agency.*": Kate Bowler, "Living With the End in Mind With Kathryn Mannix," Everything Happens (podcast), October 15, 2024, https://katebowler.com/podcasts/living-with-the-end-in-mind, accessed March 4, 2025.

168 "*Do everything is a hope*: Bowler, "Living with the End in Mind with Kathryn Mannix."

169 *I know there's something miraculous coming*: adrienne maree brown, "Closing the Loop: adrienne maree brown on Harm and Accountability," *YES!*, February 10, 2021.

169 *The feeling that they have agency*: Jessica Grose, "Welcome to NYT Parenting. Here's Why We Won't Say 'Natural Birth,'" *New York Times*, May 7, 2019.

169 "*Birth is a beginning*: Sara Ruddick, *Maternal Thinking: Toward a Politics of Peace* (Beacon Press, 1995), 209.

170 "*Death has been humanity's central*: Jennifer Banks, *Natality: Toward a Philosophy of Birth* (W. W. Norton & Co., 2023), 3.

170 "*Because we were all born*: Banks, *Natality*, 8.

170 "*every new birth is the supreme*: Hannah Arendt quoted in Jacqueline Rose, *Mothers: An Essay on Love and Cruelty* (Farrar, Straus and Giroux, 2018), 79.

170 "*As a mother*: Thelma Young Lutunatabua, "Not Only Danger But a Promise," *Not Too Late*, eds. Rebecca Solnit and Thelma Young Lutunatabua (Haymarket Books, 2023), 197.

170 "*But again and again*: Rebecca Solnit, *Hope in the Dark: Untold Histories, Wild Possibilities* (Haymarket Books, 2016), 1.

171 "*The future is dark*: Rebecca Solnit, *Hope in the Dark: Untold Histories, Wild Possibilities* (Haymarket Books, 2016), 1.

171 "*the dark is not an end*: Gayle Boss, *All Creation Waits: The Advent Mystery of New Beginnings* (Paraclete Press, 2016).

Mother Nature

173 "*That gosling stalks me*: DreamWorks Animation *The Wild Robot*, 2004.

173 "*I do not have the programming*: DreamWorks, *The Wild Robot*.

174 "*No one does*: DreamWorks, *The Wild Robot*.

174 *"Anyone who commits her:* Sara Ruddick, *Maternal Thinking: Toward a Politics of Peace* (Beacon Press, 1995), xii.

174 *"Birthing a baby:* Chelsea Conaboy, *Mother Brain: How Neuroscience is Rewriting the Story of Parenthood* (Henry Holt, 2022), 6.

176 *place attachment—the idea that humans form:* Jennifer Case, "Place Studies: Theory and Practice in Environmental Nonfiction," *Assay: A Journal of Nonfiction Studies* 4, Fall 2017, https://www.assayjournal.com/jennifer-case-place-studies-theory-and-practice-in-environmental-nonfiction.html.

177 *"While we can question how much:* Case, "Place Studies."

178 *"All of attachment styles research:* Nancy Reddy, *The Good Mother Myth: Unlearning Our Bad Ideas About How to Be A Good Mom* (St. Martin's Press, 2025), 117.

179 *"The 'good mother ideal' never:* Conaboy, *Mother Brain* 40.

179 *John Bowlby, the founder of attachment theory:* Reddy, *The Good Mother Myth*, 127.

180 *While many have disparaged Thoreau for this:* Rebecca Solnit, "Mysteries of Thoreau, Unsolved," *Pushcart Prize XXXIX* (New York: Pushcart Prize Fellowships, 2015), 360–371.

183 *"popular thinking about parenthood:* Conaboy, *Mother Brain*, 118.

183 *Working in the 1950s, Lorenz's research on how birds imprint:* Conaboy, *Mother Brain*, 11–14.

183 *Despite having joined the Nazi Party:* Associated Press, "Austrian University Strips Nobel Prize Winner of Honors," *Washington Post*, December 21, 2015.

183 *As Conaboy reports, though Lorenz:* Conaboy, *Mother*, 11–14.

184 *"wasn't really trying to dispel:* Conaboy, *Mother Brain* 25.

184 *"Those caged mothers:* Reddy, *The Good Mother Myth*, 54.

184 *"[T]he use of **natural** as a synonym:* Eula Biss, *On Immunity: An Inoculation* (Graywolf Press, 2014), 40.

184 *"the more artificial:* Wendell Berry quoted in Biss, *On Immunity*, 40–41.

184 *"The wild and the domestic:* Wendell Berry quoted in Biss, *On Immunity*, 40–41.

185 *"Nature is a construct made:* Ursula K. Le Guin, "Woman / Wilderness," *Dancing at the Edge of the World: Thoughts on Words, Women, Places* (Grove Press, 1989), 161–164.

185 *"Only people whose relation to the land:* William Cronon, "The Trouble with Wilderness; or, Getting Back to the Wrong Nature," *Uncommon Ground: Rethinking the Human Place in Nature*, ed. William Cronon, (W. W. Norton & Co., 1995), 69–90.

186 *it wasn't until the nineteenth century:* Cronon, "The Trouble with Wilderness," 69–90.

186 *"grew out of an effort:* Erin Sharkey, "More to be Shaped By," *A Darker Wilderness: Black Nature Writing from Soil to Stars*, ed. Erin Sharkey, (Milkweed Editions, 2023), 16–17.

187 *These religious decrees were then cited:* Bill Chappell, "The Vatican Repudiates

'Doctrine of Discovery,' Which Was Used to Justify Colonialism," NPR, March 30, 2023.

187 *the wilderness became a place for elites*: Cronon, "The Trouble with Wilderness," 69–90.

187 *"Idealizing a distant wilderness*: Cronon, "The Trouble with Wilderness," 69–90.

188 *"Climate justice requires us to radically*: Kaniela Ing, "The Only Moral Path," *Required Reading: Climate Justice, Adaptation, and Investing in Indigenous Power*, ed. Kailea Frederick, (NDN Collective Climate Justice Campaign, 2021), 12.

188 *"predisposed to care."*: Elissa Strauss, *When You Care: The Unexpected Magic of Caring for Others* (Gallery Books, 2004), 157.

188 *"For much of modern science,"*: Strauss, *When You Care*, 156.

189 *"survival of the most sympathetic,"*: Charles Darwin quoted in Strauss, *When You Care*, 149.

189 *"On the most general level,*: Berenice Fisher and Joan C. Tronto, "Toward a Feminist Theory of Care," *Circles of Care: Work and Identity in Women's Lives*, eds. Emily Abel and Margaret Nelson, (State University of New York Press, 1991), 35–62.

190 *"not only of decisive public battles"*: Elena Pulcini, "Global Vulnerability: Why Take Care of Future Generations?" *Care Ethics in the Age of Precarity*, eds. Maurice Hamington and Michael Flower (University of Minnesota Press, 2021), 120–143.

190 *"are often left with a deep sense"*: Elan Shapiro, "Restoring Habitats, Communities, and Souls," *Ecopsychology: restoring the Earth, Healing the Mind Restoring the Earth, Healing the Mind*, eds. Roszak, Gomes, and Kanner (Counterpoint, 1995), 224–239.

190 raise Brightbill, *"is a survival skill."*: DreamWorks Animation, *The Wild Robot*.

191 *"I'm already home"*: DreamWorks, *The Wild Robot*.

192 *"In such a relationship"*: Shapiro, "Restoring Habitats, Communities, and Souls,", 224–239.

193 *"learn to live here*: Robin Wall Kimmerer, *The Serviceberry: Abundance and Reciprocity in the Natural World* (Scribner, 2024).

Mother of All Messes

195 *hundreds of thousands of people, worldwide*: Ocean Conservancy, "International Coastal Cleanup: 2024 Annual Report," September 2024, https://oceanconservancy.org/wp-content/uploads/2024/09/ICCAnnualReport2024_Digital.pdf.

195 *We were cleaning up a stretch of beach*: Cherry Point Aquatic Reserve, Washington State Department of Natural Resources, https://www.dnr.wa.gov/managed-lands/aquatic-reserves/cherry-point-aquatic-reserve, accessed April 25, 2024.

198 *"third green shift"*: Sarah Jaquette Ray quoted in Allison C. Davis, "Untangling the Double Bind of Carework in Green Motherhood: An Ecofeminist Developmental Path Forward," *Women's Studies International Forum* 98, April 2023, 6.

198 *even in egalitarian marriages*: Richard Fry, et al., "In a Growing Share of U.S. Mar-

riages, Husbands and Wives Earn About the Same," *Pew Research Center*, April 13, 2023, https://www.pewresearch.org/social-trends/2023/04/13/in-a-growing-share-of-u-s-marriages-husbands-and-wives-earn-about-the-same, accessed March 12, 2025.

199 *Research has shown that parenting today is more time-intensive*: Claire Cain Miller, "How Parenting Today Is Different, and Harder," *New York Times*, January 29, 2023.

199 *Working mothers now report*: Claire Cain Miller, "The Relentlessness of Modern Parenting," *New York Times*, December 25, 2018.

199 *green motherhood to be a form of intensive mothering*: Davis, "Untangling the Double Bind of Carework in Green Motherhood," 2.

199 *"positions mothers as planetary saviors*: Allison C. Davis, "Green Motherhood, Tradwives, and the Psychoecological Crisis: Reclaiming the Sacred in Maternal and Planetary Care," The Mother Tree (website), https://www.themothertreemethod.com/p/green-motherhood-tradwives-and-the, accessed March 12, 2025.

199 *"double bind of green motherhood"*: Davis, "Untangling the Double Bind of Carework in Green Motherhood," 1–9.

199 *It also privatizes*: Davis, "Untangling the Double Bind of Carework in Green Motherhood," 1–9.

201 *writes Elizabeth L. Cline, "are people who believe*: Elizabeth L. Cline, "The Twilight of the Ethical Consumer," *Atmos*, October 19, 2020.

201 *"I have started to wonder*: Cline, "The Twilight of the Ethical Consumer."

201 *"Out went strong environmental regulations*: Cline, "The Twilight of the Ethical Consumer."

202 *"My argument is not a free pass*: Cline, "The Twilight of the Ethical Consumer."

202 *"counterproductive, not to mention exhausting"*: Min Hyoung Song, *Climate Lyricism* (Duke University Press, 2022), 115.

202 *"There is no food we can eat*: Alexis Shotwell, *Against Purity: Living Ethically in Compromised in Times* (University of Minnesota Press, 2016), 5.

203 *"Purism is a de-collectivizing*: Shotwell, *Against Purity*, 8–9.

203 *This annual export of 48 million metric tons*: RE Sources, "What is the Gateway Pacific Terminal at Cherry Point?" January 9, 2016, https://www.re-sources.org/2016/01/what-is-the-gateway-pacific-terminal-at-cherry-point-xwechiexen, accessed May 1, 2025.

203 *After an extensive environmental impact*: Lynda V. Mapes, "Tribes Prevail, Kill Proposed Coal Terminal at Cherry Point," *Seattle Times*, May 9, 2016.

204 *"An abstract, atmospheric problem*: Nathaniel Rich, "Losing Earth: The Decade We Almost Stopped Climate Change," *The New York Times Magazine*, August 1, 2018.

205 *"What if society had chosen*: Andrew Szasz, *Shopping Our Way to Safety: How We Changed from Protecting the Environment to Protecting Ourselves* (University of Minnesota Press, 2007), 223–230.

206 *it's more effective—and more important*: Mary DeMocker, *The Parents' Guide to Climate Revolution: 100 Ways to Build a Fossil-Free Future, Raise Empowered Kids, and Still Get a Good Night's Sleep* (New World Library, 2018), xxvii.

207 *Our city estimates that 40 percent*: "Bellingham Sets Strong Standards for Climate- and Health-friendly Electric Buildings," RE Sources, February 7, 2022, https://www.re-sources.org/2022/02/bellingham-sets-strong-standards-for-climate-and-health-friendly-electric-buildings, accessed March 13, 2025.

208 "*I was looking at how mothers*: Allison C. Davis (researcher) in discussion with the author, March 31, 2025.

208 "*a narrow ideal of motherhood*: Davis, "Green Motherhood, Tradwives, and the Psychoecological Crisis."

208 "*shift the burden of care*: Davis, "Green Motherhood, Tradwives, and the Psychoecological Crisis."

208 "*As healthy eating can become a compulsion*: Davis, "Untangling the Double Bind of Carework in Green Motherhood," 1–9.

208 "*What are we doing to mothers*: Jacqueline Rose, *Mothers: An Essay on Love and Cruelty* (Farrar, Straus and Giroux, 2018), 1–2.

211 "*This doesn't mean to get lost in the self*: adrienne maree brown, *Emergent Strategy* (AK Press, 2017), 53.

211 *After fifty years of steep decline*: Julia Lerner, "'A Definite Alarm Bell': Cherry Point's Herring Population Didn't Spawn This Year," *Cascadia Daily*, July 19, 2023.

212 "*[a]ctivists who generally relate to the 'environment' with tension*: Elan Shapiro, "Restoring Habitats, Communities, and Souls," *Ecopsychology: restoring the Earth, Healing the Mind Restoring the Earth, Healing the Mind*, eds. Roszak, Gomes, and Kanner (Counterpoint, 1995), 224–239.

Because I Said So

213 "*I've learned you are never too small*: Greta Thunberg quoted in John Sutter and Lawrence Davidson, "Teen Tells Climate Negotiators They Aren't Mature Enough," CNN, December 17, 2018, https://www.cnn.com/2018/12/16/world/greta-thunberg-cop24/index.html.

213 "*It's getting hot*: Ian Price quoted in Kashmira Gander, "'Our Futures Are at Risk': Meet the Kids Skipping School to Join the Global Climate Strike," *Newsweek*, September 17, 2019.

213 *Ian was among the first students in the United States.*: Nick Engelfried, "How Generation Z is Leading the Climate Movement," Waging Nonviolence, January 14, 2020, https://wagingnonviolence.org/2020/01/youth-climate-movement-zero-hour-jamie-margolin-greta-thunberg.

214 "*I am striking for a decolonized future*: Jamie Margolin, "I'm Not Only Striking for the Climate," *New York Times*, September 20, 2019.

NOTES 277

214 *four million protesters*: Somini Sengupta, "Protesting Climate Change, Young People Take to Streets in a Global Strike," *New York Times*, September 20, 2019.

214 *"one of the lucky ones"*: Greta Thunberg, "Transcript: Greta Thunberg's Speech at the U.N. Climate Action Summit," NPR, September 23, 2019, https://www.npr.org/2019/09/23/763452863/transcript-greta-thunbergs-speech-at-the-u-n-climate-action-summit, accessed March 18, 2025.

215 *"are starting to understand your betrayal"*: Greta Thunberg, "Transcript: Greta Thunberg's Speech At The U.N. Climate Action Summit."

215 *"Yet you all come to us young people*: Greta Thunberg, "Transcript: Greta Thunberg's Speech at the U.N. Climate Action Summit."

215 *In 2021, an international survey*: Caroline Hickman, et. al., "Climate Anxiety in Children and Young People and Their Beliefs About Government Responses to Climate Change: A Global Survey," *The Lancet Planetary Health*, 5, December 2021, e863-e873.

215 *"They feel abandoned by adults"*: Caroline Hickman quoted in Sara Kiley Watson, "Kids Are Suffering from Climate Anxiety. It's Time for Adults to Do Something," *Popular Science*, July 8, 2021.

216 *"I was like, 'Oh, honey, that's really sad,'"*: Heather Price (atmospheric chemist) in discussion with the author, February 24, 2025.

216 *"having one's feelings and views heard*: Caroline Hickman, et. al., "Climate Anxiety in Children and Young People and Their Beliefs About Government Responses to Climate Change: A Global Survey," *The Lancet Planetary Health* 5, December 2021, e863-e873.

217 *"slippery rhetorical terrain"*: Lindal Buchanan, *Rhetorics of Motherhood* (Southern Illinois University Press, 2013), xvii.

217 *"ignoring critical differences*: Buchanan, *Rhetorics of Motherhood*, xvii.

217 *"Parenting toward climate justice*: Amuche Nnabueze quoted in Mary DeMocker, "Parent Participation in Climate Justice Efforts Is on the Rise," *Truthout*, September 4, 2022.

218 *"Black mothers advocate for our children*: Dani McClain, *We Live for the We: The Political Power of Black Motherhood* (Bold Type Books, 2019), 199–224.

218 *"As moms, we go to the halls of Congress*: Liz Hurtado (national field manager) in discussion with the author, March 17, 2025.

219 *She cites research showing that*: Moms Clean Air Force, "Extreme Heat and Latino Communities," July 2022, https://www.momscleanairforce.org/resources/extreme-heat-and-latino-communities, accessed March 1, 2025.

219 *All of which adversely impacts*: Moms Clean Air Force, "Air Pollution, Extreme Heat, and Latina Maternal Health: Fact Sheet," August 2024, https://www.momscleanairforce.org/resources/air-pollution-extreme-heat-and-latina-maternal-health, accessed March 1, 2025.

221 *"I'd put up thick walls around my climate anxiety:* Marlena Fontes (climate activist) in discussion with the author, March 27, 2025.

222 *"If you want collective action:* Kia Smith (co-executive director) in discussion with the author, March 27, 2025.

225 *"The reason the ad was different:* Katie Darling (political candidate) in discussion with the author, February 21, 2025.

226 *damages from the L.A. wildfires:* Umair Irfan, "The LA Fires Have a Shocking Price Tag—And We'll All Have to Pick Up the Tab," *Vox*, February 12, 2025.

226 *The 60-second commercial, called "By the Time":* Science Moms, "By the Time," https://www.youtube.com/watch?v=8rnfywUFFSU, accessed March 1, 2025.

227 *"We want to be trusted messengers:* Melissa Burt (atmospheric scientist) in discussion with the author, April 3, 2025.

228 *"Grandparents, uncles, coaches:* Mary DeMocker, *The Parents' Guide to Climate Revolution* (New World Library, 2018), xxii.

229 *"People need to know how difficult it is:* Rachel Rivera (organizer) in discussion with the author, March 31, 2025.

229 *The most recent World Meteorological Organization's annual:* World Meteorological Organization, "State of the Global Climate Report 2024," March 19, 2025, https://library.wmo.int/idurl/4/69455, accessed March 30, 2025.

230 *within the next 20 years:* Emanuele Bevacqua, et. al., "A Year Above 1.5 °C Signals that Earth is Most Probably Within the 20-year Period that Will Reach the Paris Agreement Limit," *Nature Climate Change* 5, February 10, 2025, 262–265.

230 *From record rains in Italy:* Damian Carrington, "More than 150 'Unprecedented' Climate Disasters Struck World in 2024, Says UN," *The Guardian*, March 18, 2025.

230 *"Our window to act:* Science Moms, "By the Time."

Saving Seeds

232 *drawing tens of thousands of spectators:* Esther Kronenberg, "Return of the "Procession of the Species," *Works in Progress*, March 9, 2024.

232 *"the glory of everything":* E. B. White, *Charlotte's Web* (HarperCollins, 2012), 183.

233 *"When kids see all these adults dancing:* Eli Sterling quoted in Desdra Dawning, "What's at Stake for Procession of the Species," *Works in Progress*, 23, March 2013.

233 *"there are no written words in nature":* Eli Sterling quoted in Dawning, "What's at Stake for Procession of the Species."

233 *"Our words don't suit prophecies anymore:* Etel Adnan, *Shifting the Silence* (Nightboat Books, 2020), 12.

233 *"[w]hen people conquer they parade:* Eli Sterling quoted in Dawning, "What's at Stake for Procession of the Species."

233 *"there is something beyond us:* Eli Sterling quoted in Rebecca Sanchez, "Olympia History: The Origins of the Procession of the Species," Thurston Talk, March 29, 2024,

https://www.thurstontalk.com/2024/03/29/olympia-history-the-origins-of-the-procession-of-the-species, accessed March 13, 2025.

235 *Seed—summer—tomb*: Emily Dickinson, "1712," *The Complete Poems of Emily Dickinson*, ed. Thomas H. Johnson (Little, Brown and Company, 1960), 696.

235 *"It matters," writes Haraway, "what stories we tell*: Donna J. Haraway, *Staying With the Trouble* (Duke University Press, 2016), 117–125.

235 *"stories of becoming-with"*: Haraway, *Staying With the Trouble* (, 117–125.

236 *"the life story"*: Ursula K. Le Guin, *Dancing at the Edge of the World: Thoughts on Words, Women, Places* (Grove, 1989), 165–170.

236 *"a way of trying to describe what is in fact going on*: Ursula K. Le Guin, *Dancing at the Edge of the World*, 165–170.

236 *"We do not know*: Ursula K. Le Guin, "The Author of the Acacia Seeds" *The Unreal and the Real* (Simon & Schuster, 2017), 624.

237 *"With Le Guin, I am committed*: Haraway, *Staying With the Trouble*, 117–125.

237 *"It will be hard to live here*: Octavia Butler, *Parable of the Sower* (Grand Central Publishing, 200), 319.

238 *"[T]he decolonization of the imagination*: Walidah Imarisha, "Introduction," *Octavia's Brood*, eds. Walidah Imarisha and adrienne maree brown (AK Press, 2015), 3–5.

238 *"The slight curve of the shell*: Haraway, *Staying With the Trouble*, 117–125.

239 *"the story isn't over*: Le Guin, *Dancing at the Edge of the World*, 165–170.

239 *In his book* Falter: Bill McKibben, *Falter* (Henry Holt, 2019), 34–45.

240 *some scientists, like geologist Jan Zalasiewicz,*: Elizabeth Kolbert, *The Sixth Extinction* (Henry Holt, 2014), 104–107.

241 *"It was like being in a plane*: Sheila Heti, *Pure Colour* (Farrar, Straus and Giroux, 2022), 157.

241 *Even now there is a group of artists*: Livia Albeck-Ripka, "Earth Is Getting a 'Black Box' to Hold Humans Accountable for Climate Change," *New York Times*, December 9, 2021.

242 *1,700 gene banks worldwide*: Jennifer Duggan, "Inside the 'Doomsday Vault,'" *TIME*, April 8, 2017.

242 *"There are big and small doomsdays*: Marie Haga quoted in Jennifer Duggan, "Inside the 'Doomsday Vault,'" *TIME*, April 8, 2017.

242 *reinforcements against flooding from the melting permafrost*: Amelia Nierenberg, "The World's Doomsday Plant Vault Gets Thousands of New Seeds," *New York Times*, October 29, 2024.

242 *"The loss of stories of seeds*: Jannisse Ray quoted in Helen Bradshaw, "In the Hurricane-Ravaged South, Old-School Seed Saving Becomes More Important than Ever," *Garden & Gun*, October 28, 2024.

243 "A gardener is always a futurist": Deborah Levy, *The Cost of Living* (Bloomsbury, 2018), 76.

244 "*imagine a just—even a delightful*: Ezra Klein and Derek Thompson, *Abundance* (Avid Reader Press, 2025), 13.

244 "*Two decades ago, it was not possible*: Klein and Thompson, *Abundance*, 64.

244 "*We are early in the story*: Klein and Thompson, *Abundance*, 67.

245 "*complex interdependency, symbiosis, cooperation*": Charles Einstein quoted in Robin Wall Kimmerer, *The Serviceberry: Abundance and Reciprocity in the Natural World* (Scribner, 2024), 93.

245 "*I want to be part of a system*: Kimmerer, *The Serviceberry*, 91.

245 "*Regenerative economies that reciprocate*: Kimmerer, *The Serviceberry*, 91.

246 "*Our physiologies—and perhaps our psyches*: Karen Bakker, *The Sounds of Life: How Digital Technology is Bringing Us Closer to the Worlds of Animals and Plants* (Princeton University Press, 2022), 2.

246 *We know that baby bats can babble*: Karen Bakker, *The Sounds of Life*, 3.

246 *And that humpback whale calves*: Jack Tamisiea, "Hear How Baby Humpback Whales Burp and Bark to Beg for Food," *Scientific American*, December 17, 2024.

247 "*Scientists are now coming to see*: Katarina Zimmer, "Decoding the Astonishing Secret Languages of Animals," *Atmos*, March 25, 2025.

247 "*How might we choose to live*: Bakker, *The Sounds of Life*, 202.

247 "*breaking the Earth's beat*: Jérôme Sueur, et al., quoted in Bakker, *The Sounds of Life*, 198.

247 "*rupturing the sonic rhythms*: Bakker, *The Sounds of Life*, 198.

248 *Something I love about Charles Darwin's* **On the Origin**: Maria Popova, "The Charming Doodles Charles Darwin's Children Left All Over the Manuscript of 'On the Origin of Species,'" The Marginalian, April 6, 2016, https://www.themarginalian.org/2016/04/06/charles-darwin-children-doodles-origin-of-species.

249 "*the endless unfolding of life*": Lyanda Lynn Haupt quoted in Robert Krulwich, "Death of Child May Have Influenced Darwin's Work," NPR, February 12, 2009.

249 "*In Darwin's thinking*: Lyanda Lynn Haupt, *Pilgrim on the Great Bird Continent* (Little, Brown, 2006), 233–253.

249 *Biographer Adam Gopnik*: Robert Krulwich, "Death of Child May Have Influenced Darwin's Work," NPR, February 12, 2009.

249 "*part of the drift called*: Emily Dickinson quoted in Maria Popova, "The Drift Called the Infinite: Emily Dickinson on Making Sense of Loss," The Marginalian, July 20, 2017, https://www.themarginalian.org/2017/07/20/emily-dickinson-mother-death.

249 "*There is grandeur*: Charles Darwin, *On the Origin of Species* (Penguin Books, 2009), 427.

NOTES 281

249 *"have mouths that are also their butts"*: Ruby Guthrie, "What's inside a jellyfish?" Brains On (podcast). July 25, 2023, https://www.brainson.org/episode/2023/07/25/whats-inside-a-jellyfish, accessed March 15, 2025.

250 *"And no one's been watching them:* Rebecca Helm interviewed by Molly Bloom, host, "What's inside a jellyfish?" *Brains On*. July 25, 2023, https://www.brainson.org/episode/2023/07/25/whats-inside-a-jellyfish, accessed March 15, 2025.

About the Author

Kaitlyn Teer is a senior editor at *Cup of Jo*. Her essays have appeared in *Orion, Catapult, Electric Lit, Prairie Schooner,* and elsewhere, and she has taught writing at Western Washington University. She lives in Bellingham, Washington, with her husband and two children.

www.ingramcontent.com/pod-product-compliance
Lightning Source LLC
LaVergne TN
LVHW031537060526
838200LV00056B/4531